Mediating the MESSAGE MESSAGE MESSAGE MESSAGE MESSAGE

Mediating the MESSAGE

Theories of Influences on Mass Media Content

Pamela J. Shoemaker
University of Texas, Austin
Stephen D. Reese
University of Texas, Austin

Mediating the Message: Theories of Influences on Mass Media Content

Longman, 95 Church Street, White Plains, N.Y. 10601

Associated companies:
Longman Group Ltd., London
Longman Cheshire Pty., Melbourne
Longman Paul Pty., Auckland
Copp Clark Pitman, Toronto

Executive editor: Gordon T. R. Anderson
Development editor: Virginia L. Blanford
Production editor: Linda W. Witzling
Cover design: Susan J. Moore
Production supervisor: Kathleen Ryan

Library of Congress Cataloging-in-Publication Data

Shoemaker, Pamela J.
Mediating the message: theories of influences on mass media content / Pamela Shoemaker, Stephen Reese.
p. cm.
Includes index.
ISBN 0-8013-0307-9
1. Mass media. 2. Content analysis (Communication) I. Reese, Stephen D. II. Title.
P91.S46 1991
302.23--dc20 90-6304
CIP

ABCDEFGHIJ-MU-99 98 97 96 95 94 93 92 91 90

Contents

Preface

On the morning of April 13, 1990, the president of the University of Texas at Austin scheduled a morning press conference outside the administration building to deliver an address to the news media—the topic was racism on campus. Like many campuses around the country, Texas has experienced an upsurge in activism among minority students who have been advocating a more mulicultural curriculum and the hiring of more minority faculty. In the weeks before the speech, two racial incidents at campus fraternities had been widely publicized. Stepping to the lectern, the president began to read a lengthy prepared text about his administration's steps to address minority issues. The large crowd of students that had gathered began to periodically heckle the president, causing him to stop momentarily each time, then resume his reading. Finally, toward the end of his address, the crowd became more vocal, leading the president to quit his speech and return to his office.

An analysis of subsequent news media—particularly television—coverage of the event, full-length raw videotape footage, and interviews with some of the black students present (and also enrolled in the authors' classes) revealed some important features of the media portrayals. The crowd members (of which many were Anglo) had apparently hoped to hear the president address them "from the heart," denouncing in more forceful terms the earlier racial incidents. The contrast between the emotion-charged setting and the president's formally recited speech directed to the press appeared to contribute to the crowd's frustration.

The footage that made the local television news focused on the final part of the speech when the crowd became its most vocal. Reporters trailed the president back to his office and, through their questions, allowed him to frame the event as a free speech issue: The students had unduly prevented him from speaking. Reacting to media coverage, black students felt that the television reports in particular had not given sufficient attention to their specific proposals for change. The televised version of the event suggested to viewers that the president had been disrupted from the start and throughout his speech, that the heckling was an unruly and irrational outburst—an unfortunate response to a legitimate university official's exercise of free speech. Had those viewers been present at the speech, they might have drawn a different conclusion—that the president was given ample opportunity to speak and could have finished had he wished. They might have felt, as did the black students, that his speech was not appropriate to the setting. Those same viewers might have seen the disruption of the speech as the culmination of the students' frustration that had built not only throughout the speech, but also over the previous months and years.

This gap between firsthand experience and the mediated version becomes particularly clear for events like this—when people are present at an event and compare their experience with media coverage, and when the issues involved are controversial—meaning that the stakes are high as to how the event is to be framed. Going back a quarter of a century, similar events gave rise to increasing scholarly attention to how the media frame reality. During the mid- to late 1960s, large crowds regularly took to the streets to protest for civil rights and against the Vietnam War. The inadequacy of the media in reflecting these social tensions became more apparent than ever before, particularly to the participants. The "credibility gap" became a problem for the news media as well as for the president.

Today, these questions relating to the media and social change are more important than ever, but we hope that our understanding of the media has improved. When students experience an event like the one on our campus, they question the role of the media, they want to discuss it in class and talk about it afterwards. We hope that this book will provide a framework within which issues like this can be understood, both for students and for researchers hoping to extend that understanding. We have tried to synthesize the growing body of research addressing these issues and propose how future research can be structured. As such, we hope faculty researchers and other media scholars—in addition to students—will find this book useful.

Although we cover a wide breadth of material, some choices had to be made. One of the issues we struggled with was how to treat news and entertainment content. By background we are primarily oriented toward news, although we wanted to produce a book that would address media content in general. As we found, much more research has been directed toward the production of news than entertainment (although many content analyses have examined the latter). More scholars, however, are beginning to explore this area of content and the influences behind the scenes, but a better treatment of this research will have to wait for another volume. Where possible, we do speak of media workers or media content, noting the commonalities across news and entertainment, and we include examples other than news as well.

We have directed this book to upper-level undergraduates and graduate students. Because of the diverse number of courses taught in university departments, it is hard to identify one specific class for which this book is best suited. Our emphasis on the news media makes this book most at home in a journalism and mass communication course—it could serve as the primary text for a media sociology course or seminar. But it could also serve as a framework text to be complemented by other sources for more general media courses. Whether departments of journalism, radio-television-film, telecommunications, mass communication, or communication, many have a course about how media content gets made, often under a "mass media and society" title. For introductory communication courses, the book could be paired with one of the many "introduction to mass communication" texts to give a greater conceptual thrust. It could also be used in a mass communication theory course to add "influences on media" theories to those about "media influences." This would, in effect, cover the complete range of mass communication theory from production to reception of media messages. Other courses about the mass media that might usefully include this book can also be found in departments of political science and sociology.

We have found textbook writing a challenge and a different task altogether from writing about our research projects for conference papers and journals. We have tried to write in a readable manner and to find organizing schemes and examples that convey our points as clearly as possible. Of course, we haven't successfully communicated until others read and understand those points. We hope that readers will come up with their own examples and alternative ways to organize this research. And, we would appreciate hearing from those who have suggestions for improvement.

Every book has a history behind it. To understand why this book takes the form it does, it may be helpful to recount how we came to write it. Both of us were trained in the media effects tradition at the University of Wisconsin, one of the major centers for research of that type, receiving our Ph.D.s in mass communication in 1982. While there and since then both of us have conducted many audience-centered studies of mass communication. Thus, when we critique the preoccupation of research with audiences and effects (as in Chapter 2), it is from firsthand experience. As it happened, however, our graduate school years represented a transition period in communication research. Critical scholars began asking serious questions about the prevailing research paradigm, its assumptions, methodologies, and theories. A growing number of scholars became interested in what "sets the media's agenda." As a result, our approaches to research have evolved considerably just within the past decade.

Since coming to the University of Texas we have taken different routes, yet have arrived at quite similar intellectual interests. In the case of Shoemaker, an interest in political communication led her to study media coverage of deviant political groups. Her finding that these groups are covered less legitimately than centrist groups led naturally to general questions of how such media content was formed and to several studies showing that the more deviant an event is, the more prominently it is covered by the media. Reese has had a long interest in the exercise of political power, and came to view the power-oriented study of news production as a way to combine those interests with media studies. His studies of audience use of news media, particularly broadcast, had been based on the assumption that news is a good thing for society and that people should read and watch as much of it as possible. Closer study of news content, however, shows its limitations, leading us both to question what factors prevent it from doing a better job. This book allowed us both to explore these interests more completely.

We consider ourselves true coauthors, sharing equally in the conceptualization and writing of the present volume. Based on our respective interests, Shoemaker took primary responsibility for Chapters 1, 5, 8, 10, and 11, and Reese did so for Chapters 2, 3, 6, 7, and 9; Chapter 4 was a joint effort. Beyond the simple division of labor, this book is a synergistic result of a close friendship that began in graduate school. Our academic training is similar enough to give us a common ground, but our approaches are different, such that we do not simply echo each other's ideas.

Intellectual work is more enjoyable when it can be shared, particularly with a supportive friend. A work's quality is improved by continual discussion, which leads to checking, clarification, and revision. In addition, wheedling and cajoling each other helped keep us not too far behind schedule. We are fortunate to be members of an active community of scholars at the University of Texas. Of our many colleagues here, specific discussions have included Al Anderson, Barbara Brown, Wayne Danielson, Dominic Lasorsa, Max McCombs, Joan Schleuder, Griff Singer, Jim Tankard, and Gale Wiley. We especially thank Wayne Danielson, who, when we were stumped for a good title, provided one. The Department of Journalism at the University of Texas has provided a comfortable and friendly academic home, ever since former chairman Dwight Teeter brought us here together eight years ago. Here we have had the opportunity to both study and teach the theories we examine in this book. Our present chairman, colleague, and friend, Maxwell McCombs, has helped provide a supportive intellectual atmosphere where both are possible.

In some way or another we owe a debt to all of the instructors we have had and the academic friends and colleagues with whom we have worked over the years. Although the list would be too voluminous to include here, we particularly recognize our teachers from the University of Wisconsin: Steve Chaffee, Dan Drew, Robert Hawkins, Jim Hoyt, Jack McLeod, Mark Miller, and Byron Reeves.

Finally, but most importantly, we gratefully acknowledge the love, patience, and support of our spouses, Carol Reese and John Parrish, and our children, Jack Parrish, Aaron Reese, and (most recently) Daniel Reese. They have tolerated our sometimes excessive and often ill-timed work schedules. To them we dedicate this book.

Stephen D. Reese
Pamela J. Shoemaker

CHAPTER 1

Studying Influences on Media Content

This is a book about media content and the influences that shape it. Our perspective is different from that commonly taken in books about mass communication research, which tend to use media content as a starting point. Such studies typically ask: By what *process* is the message received and understood by the audience? What *effects* do the media have on the audience?

Instead of taking media content as a given, we ask: *What factors inside and outside media organizations affect media content?*

Figure 1.1 suggests how this book's theme fits in with the more traditional "process and effects" books. The studies we discuss address questions about the nature of media content, the ways in which such content is manufactured (how it is itself a result or an effect), and what interests it serves.

The impact of both the entertainment and the news and information aspects of media content has been widely studied. Research has looked, for example, at whether televised portrayals of violence make children more aggressive, and at whether the projection of presidential election results by television network news shows makes West Coast citizens less likely to vote. These are interesting areas for study, but we suggest that more important questions exist: *Why* do television networks produce shows that may make children more aggressive? *Why* do network news shows risk lowering voter turnout in California? The answers, we believe, lie in such factors as the personal attitudes and orientations of media workers; professionalism; corporate policies; corporate ownership patterns; the economic environment; advertisers; and ideological influences.

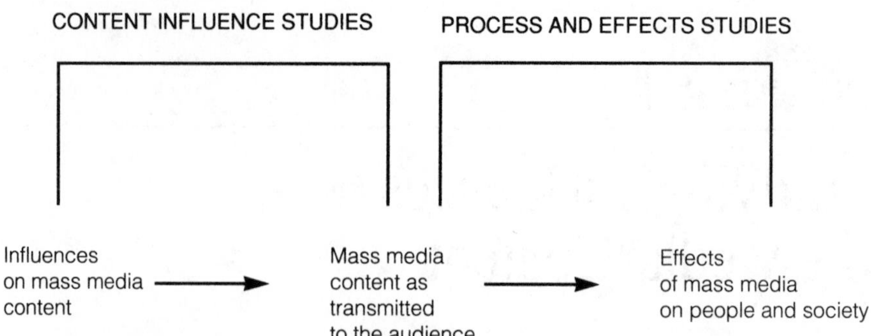

Figure 1.1. Most books on mass media research cover mainly studies dealing with the process through which the audience receives mass media content or with the effects of content on people and society. We believe that it is equally important to understand the influences that shape content.

Some Definitions

Let's begin by defining what we mean by media content. By *content,* we mean the complete quantitative and qualitative range of verbal and visual information distributed by the mass media—in other words, just about anything that appears there. The *quantitative* range of information includes those attributes of media content that can be measured or counted—the number of seconds a television news story lasts, for example, or the number of column inches a newspaper story uses. We can also count such things as the number of newspaper stories about a particular country that appear within a given time period, the number of women who appear in automobile advertisements, the number of situation comedies broadcast in the last ten years, the number of magazine photographs that show U.S. senators, or the number of times a particular sportscaster refers to black football players.

Such measures can provide important information about *amounts* of coverage and some insight into priorities, but they cannot tell us what the coverage was like—the *qualitative* attributes of the content. Two newspapers may run precisely the same number of inches of news about Israel but still provide very different views of what is happening in that country. Knowing how many times a sportscaster refers to black athletes doesn't tell us whether the coverage reflects fairness or prejudice. Measuring the qualitative attributes of media content is difficult, but often far more revealing than looking at quantitative data alone.

Many social scientists who study the media are concerned with the slippery concept of *objectivity*. How close do the media come to representing some objective reality? The problem, of course, is that there is no such thing as an objective observer of reality. All of us use our experiences, personalities, and knowledge to interpret what we see. The best we can do, then, is to compare *media reality* with *social reality*—a view of the world that is *socially derived;* that is, what society knows about itself (Fishman, 1980).

Society offers many sources of information about itself, from personnel files, office memos, and business inventories to book reviews, opinion polls, and media reports. Our assessment of social reality—that is, our best guess about what is actually going on in the world—uses all of the data at our disposal. Generally we find that reality is much too complex to be described objectively by any one source. (For more on the social derivation of reality, see Ichheiser, 1970.)

A RICH HISTORY OF RESEARCH

Media Sociology

The term *media sociology* is sometimes applied to studies that look at influences on media content, but these are not always in fact sociological. For example, studies that look at the socialization of journalists as professionals and at their personal attitudes fall more within the realm of psychology than of sociology. Whether we call these studies media sociology or social psychology, however, they reflect an increasingly popular area of research. A number of researchers who previously studied media effects—including ourselves—now find themselves asking why such effect-producing content exists to begin with.

Although research describing media content has been available since the early part of this century,[1] scientific investigation into the influences on content wasn't extensive until after World War II. Modern studies began with David Manning White's (1950) suggestion that journalists act as *gatekeepers* of media messages—that they select from among the day's events those that will become "news"—and with Warren Breed's (1955) description of how journalists become socialized to their jobs. Since then, an increasing number of studies has focused on the ways in which media workers and their employers, as well as organizational structures and society itself, affect media content. Yet, although the number of such studies has increased, there has been little attention paid to the theoretical links between them.

The Hypothesis Approach

The content studies generated in the last forty years have provided substantially more data than theory, especially as compared with the studies conducted on the "effects" side in Figure 1.1. Few content studies actually define and test a specific theory; rather, the researchers typically present a brief description of what they expect to find and then test one or more *hypotheses,* or relationships between two or more variables that characterize some phenomenon.

An example of a hypothesis is: The more newsworthy an event is judged to be, the more prominently it will be covered by the mass media. The two major variables in this example are *event newsworthiness* and *coverage prominence*. Both are to some extent quantifiable (a national presidential election is objectively more newsworthy than an election for city commissioner; and the placement and amount of coverage devoted to both can be measured). The hypothesis predicts that events of extremely high intrinsic newsworthiness will receive prominent coverage, perhaps on a newspaper's front page or at the beginning of a television newscast; events of only moderate newsworthiness will still be covered, but only on the inside pages of the newspaper or the middle of the newscast; and events that are low in newsworthiness may not be covered by the mass media at all.

Testing several related hypotheses can lead to breakthroughs of theory that help us make better predictions about media content. As these theories grow, they typically also include assumptions that researchers make about their topic, definitions of key concepts, and suggestions for measuring them. In their concentration on data, however, most media content studies lack these kinds of theoretical connections. As a result, the common threads among them have largely been ignored, and the growth of theory inhibited.

A theory may be limited to one hypothesis (like the one in our example above) or to several that deal with the same overall idea but address separate aspects of it. The theory of news content developed by one of the authors of this book, for example, offers eight assumptions and forty-eight hypotheses about how mass media content is shaped (Shoemaker, 1987).

Theoretical Perspectives

Other scholars have organized content research around a variety of theoretical perspectives. Gans (1979) and Gitlin (1980) group these approaches into a handful of categories:

- *Content reflects social reality with little or no distortion.* The *mirror* approach to content research assumes that what the mass media distribute conveys an accurate reflection of social reality to the audience—like a television camera turned on the world. The *null effects* approach similarly suggests that media content reflects reality, but sees this reality as the result of compromises between those who sell information to the media and those who buy it; these forces counteract one another and produce an objective portrayal of events.
- *Content is influenced by media workers' socialization and attitudes.* This *communicator-centered* approach suggests that psychological factors intrinsic to communications personnel—their professional, personal, and political attitudes, and the professional training communicators receive—lead them to produce a social reality in which agreement among social groups is the norm, and in which new ideas or behaviors are treated as undesirable oddities. This approach predicts that communicators will portray deviant people or groups as eccentricities that reasonable people will not take seriously.
- *Content is influenced by media routines.* The *organizational routines* approach argues that media content is influenced by the ways in which communications workers and their companies organize work. News reporters

are taught to write stories in the *inverted pyramid,* for example, putting what they consider the most important information first and organizing the rest in descending order of importance, and the journalist's assessment therefore determines the content of the story.

- *Content is influenced by other social institutions and forces.* This approach suggests that factors external to the communicator and the organization—economic and cultural forces, and audience—determine content. The *market* approach, for example, locates influence in the communicators' desire to give audiences what they want in order to ensure large audiences for sponsors' products; the *social responsibility* approach locates influence in the communicators' desire to give audiences what they need rather than what they want.
- *Content is a function of ideological positions and maintains the status quo. Hegemony* is a broad theoretical approach suggesting that media content is influenced by the ideology of those in power in society. As key parts of the economic system that are controlled by those with economic power, mass media carry an ideology consistent with those interests, which helps ensure that society will continue in its present form.

BUILDING A THEORY OF MEDIA CONTENT

In this book we compare and contrast the existing research in media content, point out similarities among these various theoretical approaches, and thus take the first step in building theory. We begin our look at the factors that shape mass media by comparing our approach with that of the traditional process and effects texts and demonstrating why the important area of media content has been more or less ignored by researchers in mass communication, and why research has been primarily limited to microlevel or individual analysis. We identify several reasons for this, including the history of the field, the cultural preference in American society for the individual over the social focus, and the tendency of scholars to adopt an industry perspective. These arguments compose Chapter 2 in this book.

In Chapter 3 we discuss how media content has been conceptualized and studied over the years, and we question the extent to which media have been thought to reflect reality. We propose an *active* media role in constructing a reality that may be compared with other sources of social reality.

In Chapter 4 we establish the nature of media content, looking at the people, places, and events that make up the media "world." We isolate patterns of media coverage that appear in a variety of studies. (Several studies have shown that news conveys information about the powerful, for example.) We examine the extent to which media content reflects social reality by exploring studies that compare media content with other measures of social reality, and we establish that media do *not* always mirror reality. We describe the systematic ways in which the "media world" differs from the "real world."

Chapters 5 through 9 examine the various influences that affect media content as suggested by the Gans and Gitlin categories above. In Chapter 5, we look at media professionals, in terms of both their personal attitudes and those that result from their professional roles. We investigate claims that communicators' liberal political attitudes affect their work, the difference between "neutral" and "participant" journalists (Johnstone, Slawski, & Bowman, 1972), and how journalists' conceptions of what is news affect the kind of events they cover.

In Chapter 6, we look at how content is influenced by media routines that result from constraints on both newsgathering and transmission. We discuss how media routines like gatekeeping, the beat system, pack journalism, and the reliance on official sources have developed in response to organizational needs to produce a product acceptable to consumers in the most efficent manner.

In Chapter 7, we investigate the influence of media organizations on content, including such areas as political endorsements, editorial positions, and corporate policies. We consider organizational roles, structures, and policies, as well as patterns of ownership and how the economic goals of the organization as a whole affect news content.

Chapter 8 looks at extramedia factors like the economic environment in which the media operate (both macro and micro—circulation, market size, profitability, competition with other media, and the extent to which various media corporations are interlocked through their boards of directors), advertisers and other revenue sources, and cultural and national variables.

In Chapter 9, we review influences on content from the societal-level ideological perspective. We discuss the role of the media in establishing social boundaries between the "normal" and the "deviant," and the links between media content's ideological character and the power centers of society proposed by Marxist scholars. In addition, we describe the relationship between lower-level influences (routines, journalists' values) and their larger ideological functions.

In Chapter 10, we suggest ways in which our content-oriented approach to the study of media can be linked to more traditional process and effects studies. *Effects* studies specify the type of content that produce a particular outcome; our perspective helps predict what arrangement of factors is most likely to produce that type of content—and thus helps to determine the extent of the effect. For example, the hypothesis that "the more people read newspapers, the more likely they are to vote" needs to be qualified by the *kind* of political content the newspaper they read publishes, which is in turn affected by a variety of intra- and extramedia influences. We dispute the usual underlying assumption that mass media content is a channel through which reality passes to audience members, and we suggest that much effects literature is in need of reinterpretation.

Our final chapter synthesizes what we know about influences on media content into a series of assumptions, propositions, and hypotheses. Through such an inductive process we can begin to develop a comprehensive theory of media content.

NOTE

1. For examples of early studies, see Taeuber (1932), Fisk (1933), and Ridings (1934).

REFERENCES

Breed, W. (1955). Social control in the newsroom: A functional analysis. *Social Forces, 33,* 326–335.

Fishman, M. (1980). *Manufacturing the news.* Austin, TX: University of Texas Press.

Fisk, M. (1933). Comparing journalistic and literary English. *Journalism Quarterly, 10,* 202–208.

Gans, H. J. (1979). *Deciding what's news.* New York: Pantheon Books.

Gitlin, T. (1980). *The whole world is watching.* Berkeley: University of California Press.

Ichheiser, G. (1970). *Appearances and realities.* San Francisco: Jossey-Bass.

Johnstone, J. W. C., Slawski, E. J., & Bowman, W. W. (1972). The professional values of American newsmen. *Journalism Quarterly, 36,* 522–540.

Ridings, J. W. (1934). Use of slang in newspaper sports writing. *Journalism Quarterly, 11,* 348–360.

Shoemaker, P. J. (1987). Building a theory of news content: A synthesis of current approaches. *Journalism Monographs, 103.*

Taeuber, I. B. (1932). Changes in the content and presentation of reading material in Minnesota weekly newspapers, 1860–1929. *Journalism Quarterly, 9,* 281–289.

White, D. M. (1950). The "gatekeeper": A case study in the selection of news. *Journalism Quarterly, 27,* 383–390.

CHAPTER 2

Beyond Processes and Effects

Most mass communication theory books concentrate on the process through which messages are received and understood by the audience, and on the effects that those messages may produce. In both cases, the message itself is, in social science terms, the *independent variable,* or cause. The effects of the message are then considered to be *dependent* variables—dependent, that is, on exposure to content. In this book, we define the message itself as a *dependent variable*. We argue that the message, or media content, is influenced by a wide variety of factors both inside and outside media organizations. Before we look at these factors individually, however, we need to understand why they have not been explored in the past as vigorously as questions of audience, process, and effect. In this chapter, we will lay out a framework to help us understand where communications scholars have concentrated their attention—and why.

THE TRADITIONAL FOCUS OF COMMUNICATIONS RESEARCH

To establish the first part of our framework we find it useful to categorize research according to two dimensions—level of analysis and that which is being studied.

Level of Analysis

The levels of analysis in communications research can be thought of as forming a continuum ranging from micro to macro—from the smallest units of a system to the largest. A *microlevel* study examines communication as an activity engaged in and affecting individual people; a *macrolevel* study examines social structures beyond the control of any one individual—social networks, organizations, and cultures. These levels function hierarchically: What happens at the lower levels is affected, even to a large extent determined, by what happens at higher levels.

What Is Studied?

One of the earliest and most often quoted ways of describing the communication process was suggested by Harold Lasswell (1948), who proposed this framework:

Who

Says What

Through Which Channel

To Whom

With What Effect

Mass communication studies have examined all of these elements—the communicator (who); media content (says what); the medium (through which channel); the audience (to whom); and the effects (with what effect)—but most studies have concentrated on the final two elements, audience and effects.

Many studies look at more than one component, but even those that examine several tend to concentrate on one more than the others. To understand how this works, let's look at a classic voting study conducted by Paul Lazarsfeld and his colleagues in Erie County, Ohio, in 1940 (Lazarsfeld, Berelson, & Gaudet, 1944). Three thousand residents were interviewed about their voting intentions, personal characteristics, and the attention they paid to newspaper and radio messages about a particular political campaign. The researchers concluded that media messages *reinforced* (but did not determine) people's political predispositions. Personal characteristics of the audience members were found to determine campaign interest, and audience members used media selectively to filter out political messages contrary to their preexisting political stances. In this study, as in many others, a number of components were involved ("says what"—campaign messages; "through what channel"—radio and newspapers; "to whom"—voters; "with what effect"—reinforcement); however, the primary focus was on the audience.

If we use Lasswell's framework and factor into it our level-of-analysis dimension, we can construct a matrix within which to locate the landmark communications studies of past years. (See Figure 2.1.) Clearly, the largest number of studies (and arguably the most influential) fall into the upper right quadrant of the matrix—under the "To Whom" and "With What Effect" columns, and on the micro or individual row.

The studies we use in Figure 2.1 are those identified by Shearon Lowery and Melvin DeFleur as *Milestones in Mass Communication Research* (1988). Note that, although many of these studies have macrosocietal theoretical implications or deal

Who (communicator)	**Says what through which channel** (media content)	**To whom** (audiences)	**With what effect** (effects)
Micro/ Individual	• *Seduction of the Innocent*, 1954 • *Violence and the Media*, content analysis, 1969 • *Television and Social Behaviors: Media Content and Control*, 1971	• *The Payne Fund Studies: Motion Pictures and Youth*, 1933 • *The Invasion from Mars*, 1940 • *The People's Choice*, 1948 • *Personal Influence*, 1955 • *Television in the Lives of our Children*, 1961 • *Violence and the Media*, audience survey, 1969 • *TV & Social Behavior*, 1971 -*TV in Day-to-Day Life*	• *The Payne Fund Studies: Motion Pictures and Youth*, 1933 • Hovland's *Experiments in Mass Communication*, 1949 • *Communication and Persuasion*, 1953 • *Television and Social Behavior*, 1971 -*Television and Social Learning* -*Television and Adolescent Aggressiveness*
Macro/ Social system		• *The Flow of Information*, 1948	•*The Agenda-setting Function of the Mass Media*, 1972

Figure 2.1. A matrix approach to describing "milestones in mass communication research."

with societywide problems, they are conducted at the individual level of analysis, and we use the measurement variables actually employed in the studies, not their level of theorizing, to locate them on our matrix. Only three of these studies examined media content in any way, and none was devoted solely to communicators. Let's look briefly at each of these "milestone" studies.

Major Communications Studies

On Media Content. Lowery and DeFleur identify only three landmark studies of media content. The oldest of these, Frederic Wertham's *The Seduction of the Innocent* (1954) caused considerable public commotion by linking an analysis of sexual and violent content in comic books with an assumption that such content would negatively affect readers, even to the extent of causing an increase in juvenile delinquency. A more recent and scientific study of content is George Gerbner's analysis of violence in the report of the Commission on the Causes and Prevention of Violence, *Violence and the Media* (Baker & Ball, 1969). (This study also includes research on media professionals (the "who"), but this comprises only two of eleven reports in the volume.) Another content analysis by Gerbner was included in the later surgeon general's report, *Television and Social Behavior* (Gerbner, 1971).

On Audience. Most of the "milestone" studies fall into the "to whom" category. The first of these, the Payne Fund Studies of 1933, comprise twelve separate volumes and are not easily pigeonholed in our matrix (for an overview of these studies, see Charters, 1933). The goals of these studies included measuring film content and audience composition, with the primary object of determining how movies influence children; the resulting research bridges the "audience" and "effects" categories, and the authors conclude that a host of individual and situational factors mediate the effects of film.

The Invasion from Mars (Cantril, 1940) is easier to locate squarely in the "audience" category of our matrix. Cantril explores audience factors associated with panic behaviors through personal interviews with audience members for Orson Welles's famous radio broadcast.

The People's Choice, the Erie County voter study referred to earlier (Lazarsfeld et al., 1948), examines the formation of voting decisions over time, with a primary focus on audience social categories and predispositions. The researchers began with the assumption that voters who changed their voting intentions between May and November did so because of campaign communication, but their study did not bear this out. *Personal Influence* (Katz & Lazarsfeld, 1955) was equally influential in its focus; the researchers surveyed women to determine on whom they relied for various kinds of information. This study hints at a macrolevel analysis by exploring networks of relationships, but measurements are confined to isolated individual respondents.

Schramm, Lyle, and Parker's study of the child audience, *Television in the Lives of Our Children* (1961), was the first large-scale investigation of children and television and was based on comparisons between individual children. The authors focus on children as an active audience, on the uses children make of television, and on the functions television serves for children. The *Violence and the Media* report (1969) mentioned above contains a more general study of the audience for media violence. The Media Task Force survey concentrates on audience norms about violence and media habits; media effects are inferred.

TV in Day-to-Day Life: Patterns of Use (Comstock & Rubinstein, 1971), the fourth in a four-volume series on television and behavior issued by the United States Surgeon General's office, sheds more light on audience uses of television.

Only the last study in this "to whom" category approaches the macrolevel of analysis. *Flow of Information* (DeFleur & Larsen, 1948) examines how information flows through a social system. The authors studied how slogans included in leaflets dropped in a community were retained and distorted by the audience.

On Effects. Justly famous effects studies include those conducted with American soldiers by psychologist Carl Hovland during World War II (Hovland, Lumsdaine, & Sheffield, 1949), which systematically varied content to determine the most persuasive message. Although other components in Lasswell's description of the communication process are included in this study (such as the credibility of the communicator and the structure of the arguments in the messages), these are of interest only in terms of the effects they produce. Later studies by Hovland solidified the central place of persuasion effects in communications research (Hovland, Janis, & Kelley, 1953).

Two other effects milestones were part of the Surgeon General's multivolume report mentioned above (Comstock & Rubenstein, 1971). Volumes 2 *(Television and Social Learning)* and 3 *(Television and Adolescent Aggressiveness)* summarize research and make the strongest case up to that time linking television viewing and aggression.

The final study in our matrix (McCombs & Shaw, 1972) examines media agenda setting. The researchers found that Chapel Hill, North Carolina, residents perceived issues to be important to the extent that the media emphasized those issues; in other words, the media were found to have a potentially persuasive cognitive impact by emphasizing an agenda of issues that tells people not what to think, but what to think *about*. Although specific individuals were interviewed for this study, their responses were combined; the issues ranked important by the Chapel Hill *community* corresponded to those emphasized by the media available to them. Because of this, we place this study toward the macro side of our matrix.

By mapping these studies, identified by communications scholars as landmarks, we can see clearly that the thrust of communications research has been toward the individual, or micro, level and toward a focus on audience and the effects on that audience. When content has been studied, it has typically been in order to make inferences about its potential effects rather than about the people, organizations, and society that produce it.

Textbooks

Before discussing the reasons for this imbalance, we use two final examples to make our point in another way. Most college students have had ample experience in learning from textbooks that convey the common wisdom of a field by summarizing a myriad of studies. Such textbooks must conform to what professors who teach in the field consider the norm—the dominant approach or paradigm. We can, therefore, get a quick reading on how a field has developed by consulting popular textbooks; two in communications theory that may be considered typical are *Mass Communication Theories and Research* (Tan, 1985) and *Mass Media Processes and Effects* (Jeffres, 1986).

Both texts begin with chapters on the nature of theory and research generally and then devote the majority of their remaining space to audience and effects research. Tan devotes sections to communication and persuasion effects, the audience and its needs, socialization, and media and social change (this last approaching the level of macroanalysis). Only 6 percent of the book covers communicators and their environment. Jeffres, as the name of his book suggests, devotes the lion's share of space to effects research—a chapter each on social, political, economic, and cultural effects. A single chapter covers audience, and another content, but much of the latter is devoted to audience perceptions of media content. About 15 percent of the book comprises information about media industries, people, and organizations.

WHY THE TRADITIONAL FOCUS?

Having established that the prevailing focus of communications theory has traditionally been on "to whom" and "with what effect," and that the prevailing level of analysis has been individual or micro, we need to look at the second part of our original question: *Why* has that been the case?

The Social Science Context

Journalism and social science are both systems of information-gathering, and the two have a lot in common. Both are activities that try to represent the world as truthfully as possible; both make claims of objectivity; and yet both by their nature present a restricted view of reality.[1] Neither can be understood apart from the culture that produces and supports it.

Both social science and journalism have *routines*—those habitual, ongoing, patterned procedures that are accepted as appropriate professional practice. For journalists, these include such things as gatekeeping, the beat system, balancing sides in issue stories, and reliance on authoritative sources. For social scientists, they include making systematic observations, formulating hypotheses, and testing these against data. The routines of both social science and journalism were developed to help their practitioners make sense out of the world and interpret ambiguous situations (Tuchman, 1977; Tuchman, 1979; Kidder & Judd, 1986).

Routines like these help the journalist claim accuracy and objectivity and the researcher claim scientific reliability and validity. The journalist interviews credible sources, attributes their remarks, and avoids expressing overt opinions. The social scientist uses methods that invite duplication. In each case, the resulting work can be defended because professional procedures have been followed.

Because they are invoked to defend work, however, does not mean that these routines are perfect. As systems of information-gathering, both journalism and social science have their biases. In fact, no system of information-gathering is ever completely adequate. Instead, we rely on what Kuhn (1962) called *paradigms*—

ways of representing reality based on widely shared assumptions about how to gather and interpret information. These paradigms do not provide truth; they simply give us information that we find useful in ways that we find acceptable.

Paradigms are based on currently shared beliefs and expectations, and as a result, we tend to take them for granted. We lose sight of the fact that beliefs and expectations—and therefore paradigms—change not only over time but from one cultural environment to another. As news consumers, for example, we get used to the routines of the journalistic paradigm. We forget that the information we see and hear has been carefully filtered at several levels.

Scientific knowledge, particularly in the social sciences, is also filtered. It focuses on those questions considered important within the given paradigm. We need to remember, then, that in the social sciences just as in journalism, the answers we find depend on the questions we ask.

What causes some questions to be asked more frequently than others? We need to look more closely at the society in which the questions are being asked. In the remainder of this chapter, we will discuss how social factors like cultural norms have affected what social scientists study and how they study it, and we will identify several influences in mass communications research that have resulted in the individual, audience, and effects emphases in our matrix.

The Focus on the Individual

Three American cultural biases feed into the microlevel orientation of mass communication research: cultural, methodological, and theoretical.

Individualism as a Cultural Bias. The social sciences in America share this country's larger cultural priorities, one of which is to prize the individual over the collective. Our cultural ideal emphasizes self-contained individualism, and we tend to look unfavorably on those who rely too heavily on others (people on welfare, for example) and on the collective society. Conformity has negative overtones in this context of individualism, although conformity may help society work more smoothly. The ideal individual is self-sufficient, self-actualized, and autonomous; the dependent person is considered weak and psychologically underdeveloped. In theory, if not in practice, we value the independent thinker over the organization person.

Individualism is also the religious and social norm in the United States. The dominant Protestant denominations emphasize a personal relationship with God and individual salvation, and the average American prefers a single-family house with a yard and, preferably, a fence around it. Alternative living arrangements that involve interdependency—collectives, communes, and the like—arouse skepticism and suspicion.

Politically, of course, communism is considered patently un-American, and even mild forms of socialism such as government-sponsored medical care are highly suspect. Similarly, our economic system revolves around individual consumption and profit. Naturally, advertisers encourage such consumption—often at the expense of other more collectively beneficial expenditures. Sharing does not create optimum demand and is therefore discouraged. Automobile makers, for example, reap higher profits when each of us owns a car (or two) than when we use mass transit. Consequently, companies like General Motors and Ford have lobbied for Americans' "freedom of transportation" by pushing for more roads, which in turn encourage more cars. No such powerful lobby exists for mass transportation. Thus, urban interstate highways are now clogged with commuters, most of them driving alone.

Individualism as a Methodological Bias. The methods we have developed to study behavior also strengthen this individual bias and work against the study of larger social structures. The statistical techniques we use to analyze data are often based on surveys of individual respondents, so that each person becomes a case; the individual is the unit of analysis.

The same sampling techniques developed for use in manufacturing have been applied to people. The beer bottler discovered early in this century that randomly checking a small number of bottles for quality would give reasonable assurance that the entire batch was good, within certain bounds of probability (see Tankard's description [1984] of W. S. Gosset's work for Guinness Brewery). Before long, someone discovered that this same procedure could accurately measure the behavior of people, and so effective are these techniques that they now form the basis for a huge polling industry.

The beer bottler, however, has no interest in the relationship between and among the bottles; each one is a discrete unit unto itself. The student of human behavior, on the other hand, does need to examine relationships among people in addition to their individual characteristics. Such relationships—sometimes called *social structures*—are less easily studied by performing statistical tests on data collected from individuals. C. Wright Mills (1959) was among the critics of such research, deriding it as "the statistical ritual." Mills argued that we cannot understand larger social structures simply by adding up data on individuals.

Individualism as a Theoretical Bias. We theorize more easily about those things we can measure. Consequently, our methodological biases may also have encouraged the development of theories at the microlevel. Such development of theory is complicated, however, by the fact that any given individual's behavior generally has many causes. We may say, for example, that a juvenile delinquent breaks the law because of a psychological tendency toward crime—an individual explanation for behavior—or because of influence from the gang to which the child belongs—a group-centered explanation. American theorists have tended to prefer the individual explanation, a tendency some have criticized as restrictive. Examples of this abound.

After World War II, communication research incorporated many important areas from its allied field of social psychology—including group dynamics, norms, interpersonal relations, and attitudes—and used them to explain how mass communications were mediated by the audience (Delia, 1987). In spite of this apparent group orientation, however, social psychology has tended to explain the social with reference to the psychological rather than the other way around. Three prominent areas of social psychological research—androgyny, cognitive consistency, and aggression—demonstrate this clearly.

The commonly accepted concept of *androgyny,* for example, is the presence of both male and female traits in an individual personality and is assumed to define a "standard of psychological health" (Bem, 1974, p. 162). Critics like Edward Sampson (1977, p. 772) suggest, however, that a more cooperative, interdependent cultural ideal would not be as likely to favor the self-contained androgynous personality but would regard it as excessively isolated from others. This alternative to our cultural ideal would place greater value on a person who "recognizes his or her interdependency on others in order to achieve satisfaction and completion as a human being." The healthy personality would then be found within a grouping of two or more individuals with complementary traits in a mutually interdependent relationship. Traits like androgyny are not intrinsically healthy, as Sampson points out, but are simply better suited to individual-centered cultures like our own.

In another prominent area of study, cognitive consistency, individuals are said to strive to keep their thoughts and behaviors consistent, and the inability to do this results in an uncomfortable tension, or dissonance (Festinger, 1957). Studies have shown that persons made to suffer in order to reach a goal perceive that goal as more attractive than those who were not made to suffer. Presumably, suffering for an undesirable goal produces dissonance, which can be reduced by changing one's perception of the goal (Aronson & Mills, 1959).

Social psychologists have also looked within the individual for causes of aggression. In one prominent line of research, for example, people were found to respond more aggressively if they were frustrated, particularly if the frustration were seen as "arbitrary" (Pastore, 1952; Berkowitz, 1962).

Some scholars warn, however, that we should not view all behavior as internally motivated. Albert Pepitone (1976) criticizes dissonance and aggression theories for ignoring cultural explanations for behavior. Pepitone suggests, for example, that "dissonant" goal seekers may simply be expressing a shared cultural norm (the Protestant ethic, that goals worth seeking require hard work and sacrifice) or that aggressive individuals may be responding to a breach of contract, an ethical violation of a cultural norm.

These may seem like minor semantic differences in how behavior is interpreted, but such minor differences can make a major difference in how we see and interpret the social world. An individual-centered culture colors the way research is conducted within that culture, and we need to be aware of that coloration in order to avoid a common fallacy; that is, we need to understand that *because we can and do measure the behavior of individuals, we must not conclude that individual-level factors are the sole causes of behavior.*

The Focus on Audience and Effects

Having identified some general reasons for the concentration of research in our matrix (Figure 2.1) at the micro or individual level, we next identify some factors that have tended to limit the topics of study in communications theory research. As we have seen, the dominant focus has traditionally been on the process and effects of communication content as used by the audience, rather than on the organizational, institutional, and cultural roots of that content.

The Social Science Fallacy. Mass communication research shares with other social science research the extent to which it has failed to critically examine the systems around which it developed. The weaknesses in the social sciences observed by Robert Lynd (1939) continue to be a problem today. Economists spend most of their time measuring the operations of the current economic system and evaluating ways to fine-tune it, rather than investigating alternative systems. As Lynd points out, political science tends to be preoccupied with minor adjustments to the political system, rather than the larger impact of the system or, again, possible alternatives. Lynd was particularly critical of large-scale data-gathering bureaucracies, like the former National Bureau of Economic Research, that purport to be objective analyzers of data. Such research "asks no questions that fundamentally call into question or go substantially beyond the core of the folkways" (Lynd, 1939, p. 144).

Lynd's criticisms of economics and political science might also be made of mass communication research, which has concentrated on the day-to-day operation of the mass media and rarely questioned mass media institutions themselves. Of course, social scientists of all disciplines do perform a valuable function by helping us understand the processes that take place within the existing social framework. But to the extent that we take political, economic, and media structures for granted, the structures themselves fail to come under scrutiny. Like the Washington journalists who adopt the values of the political system they cover, scholars are similarly susceptible to the values and priorities of the institutions they study.

Early Institutional Patronage. Even more than in other social sciences, mass communications scholars and the institutions they study are tightly interconnected. Academic concerns have often been those of the large media institutions, and the early history of communications research is inseparable from the history of the mass media. One of mass communication research's key early figures, sociologist Paul Lazarsfeld, spearheaded the Bureau of Applied Social Research at Columbia University, and the word *applied* was not chosen lightly. The bureau actively sought corporate funding for early studies of consumer and voter uses of the media; in return, those studies provided practical "applied" knowledge to their sponsors (Delia, 1987).

Robert Lynd and C. Wright Mills were also on the sociology faculty at Columbia. First Lynd and later Mills attacked the new model of research that they saw emerging from this academic-corporate alliance. Both felt that large-scale data-gathering projects made academic researchers too dependent on large-scale funding. This dependence on money from outside the university, Lynd argued, lured researchers into provisional acceptance of "the system's" definition of problems.

These problems—in other words, the main concerns of the big media organizations—focused on what the audience was doing with media products. Radio in particular had no way of estimating audience size without survey research; television would later share that concern. In the mid-1930s Paul Lazarsfeld worked closely on radio research with Frank Stanton, then research director at CBS. *Life* magazine helped fund the Erie County voting study, which intrigued McFadden Publications *(True Story, True Confessions)* founder Bernard McFadden, who funded Lazarsfeld's follow-up study, *Personal Influence,* on opinion leading in fashion, buying, movies, and politics (Gitlin, 1978).

Government also wanted information about media effects. Carl Hovland's earliest experimental tests of persuasion via a mass medium (Hovland et al., 1949) were funded by a United States government that needed to convince soldiers of the value of fighting Germans and Japanese during World War II. DeFleur and Larsen's *Flow of Information* was also government funded (by the United States Air Force), since dropping leaflets was a common "propaganda" technique, and the military was vitally interested in measuring the method's effectiveness.

This cooperation among government, business, and scholars came at a time of shared national purpose. During World War II, defeating the Axis powers clearly required a concerted effort. Later, widespread prosperity during the Eisenhower years encouraged a general acceptance of the political, economic, and media systems; taking these systems for granted led logically to a research focus on their effects rather than on the systems themselves.

The Relationship Today. Media organizations continue to provide grants for scholars to conduct research, and media professionals continue to serve on boards of colleges and universities. Many professors in departments of communication studies (variously called journalism, mass communication, telecommunication, radio-TV-film, and so on) have themselves worked in the media and often bring the values of their former organizations to their teaching and research. Even so, academic researchers often find themselves under attack from professionals in media organizations for not doing more useful studies of practical problems. Other social science academic departments—sociology or psychology, for example—also rely on external grants for research funding, but they have neither the professional link that communications scholars often have nor the concentrated grant-giving constituency.

Such ties between communication research and the communications industry do not prevent critical questions from being asked. What has concerned critics like Mills and Lynd, however, is the potential development of a systematic tendency for researchers to ask some questions more than others and to ask them from an industry perspective. Studies that clearly will not appeal to grant givers may not even be proposed, let alone funded.

Many scholars find nothing wrong with this arrangement. They point out that working on applied problems can produce interesting results of general theoretical value. This attitude rests partly in the positivist view held by many behavioral scientists, who assume the possibility of eventually gaining a complete understanding of the social world. With enough time, some social researchers argue, a theory of behavior may be developed that is similar in power to those in physical science. To take a simple example, a physics professor who rolls a ball down an inclined plane, and who knows the size and weight of the ball and the angle of incline of the plane, can predict how that ball will behave every time.[2] Some social scientists suggest that, with enough time, human behavior can be equally predictable.

The continuing search for predictive theories in both the social and the physical sciences assumes that, given enough observations, the many discrete research results may ultimately be ordered up into a complete understanding of physical and social life. The development of new knowledge therefore becomes self-justifying; the hope is that, in the long run, it will all make sense.

Mills and Lynd attacked this notion. They saw it as a justification for not addressing the larger questions of power, values, and social structures. It is, however, a notion that is fully compatible with American free-market, laissez-faire capitalism: If all knowledge is good, and if it eventually must be known, then why should the scientist not begin with those questions that also interest big—and wealthy—institutions outside academia, questions that primarily concern media impact on audience buying, voting, and viewing?

SUMMARY

As we can see, a variety of factors have combined to skew communication research in our matrix toward an individual or microlevel approach, and toward questions of media audiences and effects. In this chapter we have attempted to give you a framework for understanding this state of affairs, and to provide you with a little more context than books like this typically offer. Theories and research, after all, do not exist in a vacuum; they are human activities, shaped by the same cultural forces that affect other human activities.

In the remaining chapters, we will turn to the questions that interest us—and that have traditionally been less often asked. Interest in these kinds of questions has been growing in recent years. Media sociologist Herbert Gans (1983) notes a "veritable flood" of studies on the news media since 1970, following a "relative famine" of such research, and he suggests that the rise of television news was partially responsible. In addition, Gans argues that social scientists and journalists began to disagree in their worldviews following the social upheaval of the 1960s and early 1970s, a period marked by civil rights and antiwar protest, racial strife, and the scandal of Watergate. The systems of information-gathering and the communications paradigms developed during previous decades were no longer so widely and unquestioningly accepted.

The increasingly substantial body of research on the organizational, social, economic, and cultural roots of media content (the lower left quadrant of our matrix in Figure 2.1) has rarely been presented within an organized theoretical framework. Yet these influences determine, after all, the available information from which audiences must choose, and are thereby indirectly responsible for the entire range of effects that have traditionally fascinated communications researchers.

NOTES

1. In fact, some journalism educators have advocated applying social science's more systematic techniques (such as survey research) to the practice of journalism (e.g., Tankard, 1976, and Meyer, 1979).
2. Even in physics, however, what is "law" one day can be questioned the next by theoretical physicists. If the physics professor tries to predict which direction a subatomic particle will move after being measured, the task will be very difficult; current theories of quantum physics show that the behavior of the particle is far less predictable than that of the much larger ball.

REFERENCES

Aronson, E., & Mills, J. (1959). The effect of severity of initiation on liking for a group. *Journal of Abnormal and Social Psychology, 59,* 177–181.

Baker, R., & Ball, S. (1969). *Violence and the media.* Washington, DC: U.S. Government Printing Office.

Bem, S. L. (1974). The measurement of psychological androgyny. *Journal of Consulting and Clinical Psychology, 42,* 155–162.

Berkowitz, L. (1962). *Aggression: A social-psychological analysis.* New York: McGraw-Hill.

Cantril, H. (1940). *The invasion from Mars: A study in the psychology of panic.* Princeton, NJ: Princeton University Press.

Charters, W. W. (1933). *Motion pictures and youth.* New York: Macmillan.

Comstock, G., & Rubinstein, E. A. (Eds.). (1971). *Television and social behavior: Media content and control* (Vol. 1). Washington, DC: U.S. Government Printing Office.

Comstock, G., & Rubinstein, E. A. (Eds.). (1971). *Television and social behavior: Television and social learning* (Vol. 2). Washington, DC: U.S. Government Printing Office.

Comstock, G., & Rubinstein, E. A. (Eds.). (1971). *Television and social behavior: Television and adolescent aggressiveness* (Vol. 3). Washington, DC: U.S. Government Printing Office.

Comstock, G., & Rubinstein, E. A. (Eds.). (1971). *Television and social behavior: TV in day-to-day life: Patterns of use* (Vol. 4). Washington, DC: U.S. Government Printing Office.

DeFleur, M., & Larsen, O. (1948). *The flow of information*. New York: Harper and Brothers. Recently reprinted (1987) by Transaction Books, New Brunswick, NJ.

Delia, J. G. (1987). History of communication research. In C. Berger & S. Chaffee (Eds.), *Handbook of communication science* (pp. 20–98). Beverly Hills, CA: Sage.

Festinger, L. (1957). *A theory of cognitive dissonance*. Stanford, CA: Stanford University Press.

Gans, H. (1983). News media, news policy and democracy: Research for the future. *Journal of Communication, 33,* 174–184.

Gerbner, G. (1971). Violence in television drama: Trends and symbolic functions. In G. A. Comstock & E. A. Rubinstein (Eds.), *Television and social behavior: Media content and control* (Vol. 1). Washington, DC: U.S. Government Printing Office.

Gitlin, T. (1978). Media sociology: The dominant paradigm. In G. Wilhoit & H. De Bock (Eds.), *Mass communication review yearbook* (Vol. 2, pp. 73–122). Beverly Hills, CA: Sage.

Hovland, C. I., Janis, I., & Kelley, H. (1953). *Communication and persuasion*. New Haven, CT: Yale University Press.

Hovland, C. I., Lumsdaine, A. A., & Sheffield, F. D. (1949). *Experiments on mass communication*. Princeton, NJ: Princeton University Press.

Jeffres, L. (1986). *Mass media processes and effects*. Prospect Heights, IL: Waveland Press.

Katz, E., & Lazarsfeld, P. (1955). *Personal influence: The part played by people in the flow of mass communication*. Glencoe, IL: Free Press.

Kidder, L. H., & Judd, C. M. (1986). *Research methods in social relations*. New York: Holt, Rinehart and Winston.

Kuhn, T. S. (1962). *The structure of scientific revolutions*. Chicago: University of Chicago Press.

Lasswell, H. D. (1948). The structure and function of communication in society. In L. Bryson (Ed.), *The communication of ideas*. New York: Institute for Religious and Social Studies. Quoted from a reprint of the article in W. Schramm & D. F. Roberts, *The process and effects of mass communication* (pp. 84–99), Urbana: University of Illinois Press.

Lazarsfeld, P. F., Berelson, B., & Gaudet, H. (1948). *The people's choice*. New York: Columbia University Press.

Lowery, S., & DeFleur, M. (1988). *Milestones in mass communication research*. New York: Longman.

Lynd, R. S. (1939, 1964). *Knowledge for what? The place of social science in American culture*. New York: Grove.

McCombs, M. E., & Shaw, D. L. (1972). The agenda-setting function of the mass media. *Public Opinion Quarterly, 36,* 176–187.

Meyer, P. (1979). *Precision journalism*. Bloomington: Indiana University Press.

Mills, C. W. (1959, 1970). *The sociological imagination*. New York, Oxford.

Pastore, N. (1952). The role of arbitrariness in the frustration-aggression hypothesis. *Journal of Abnormal and Social Psychology, 47,* 728–731.

Pepitone, A. (1976). Toward a normative and comparative biocultural social psychology. *Journal of Personality and Social Psychology, 34,* 641–653.

Sampson, E. E. (1977). Psychology and the American ideal. *Journal of Personality and Social Psychology, 35,* 767–781.

Schramm, W., Lyle, J., & Parker, E. (1961). *Television in the lives of our children*. Palo Alto, CA: Stanford University Press.

Tan, A. (1985). *Mass communication theories and research*. New York: Wiley.
Tankard, J. W., Jr. (1976). Reporting and scientific method. In M. McCombs, D. Shaw, & D. Grey (Eds.), *Handbook of reporting methods* (pp. 42–77). Boston: Houghton-Mifflin.
Tankard, J. W., Jr. (1984). *The statistical pioneers*. Cambridge, MA: Schenkman.
Tuchman, G. (1977). Objectivity as strategic ritual: An examination of newsmen's notions of objectivity. *American Journal of Sociology, 77*, 660–679.
Tuchman, G. (1979). Making news by doing work: Routinizing the unexpected. *American Journal of Sociology, 77*, 110–131.
Wertham, F. (1954). *Seduction of the innocent*. New York: Rinehart.

CHAPTER 3

Analyzing Media Content

Why are we interested in content? What part has content played in communication theory, and how has it been studied? In this chapter, we examine these questions and present a framework for thinking about media content in relation to other sources of social reality.

WHY IS CONTENT IMPORTANT?

Media content is the basis of media impact. It is, for the most part, open and accessible for study—the most obvious part of the mass communication process—unlike the behind-the-scenes decisions made by producers, writers, and editors and the behaviors of media consumers.

Communications content is of interest not only in its own right, but also as an indicator of many other underlying forces. Studying content helps us infer things about phenomena that are less open and visible: the people and organizations that produce the content. We can make inferences, for example, about the consumer demands that give rise to certain content, as well as about the organizational and cultural settings that contribute to its production. A quick glance at stories in the *National Enquirer* shows that they are designed to appeal to a different kind of audience than those in the *New York Times*. Comparing editorials in the *Wall Street Journal* with those in the *Washington Post* demonstrates a very different political orientation.

A study of media content also helps us predict its impact on its audience. Media effects researchers have typically, as a first step, determined what messages are available to an audience and, therefore, what messages are available to have an effect on that audience. Bradley Greenberg's *Life on Television* (1980), for example, focuses solely on the content of entertainment television, but he justifies his large-scale research in this area with a social learning perspective; that is, he argues that it is important first to determine what messages are available for viewers to use in learning about their world.

If we assume that the media provide most of the "reality" that people know outside their own personal experience, then studying media content surely helps us assess what reality it is that they consume. Simply establishing that messages are available, however, does not by any means assure that those messages have an effect. Social reformers and special interest group members often assume that media content equals direct effect, and media "monitors" (the PTA on children's television, for example) use content research to support their push for more or less content of specific kinds.

A study of media content alone is not sufficient, however, to understand either the forces that produce that content or the nature or extent of its effects—but content research is a start. Systematic, patterned regularities in content result from stable, underlying structural factors.

CONTENT AND COMMUNICATION THEORY RESEARCH

Categorizing Content

What do communication researchers mean when they talk about *media content?* Are they talking about television or print, news or entertainment? Do these kinds of distinctions matter to our theories of mass media? When we talk about media effects, to what kind of content are we referring? Often the answer is not clear. Different kinds of content have different effects, and result from different audience needs and organizational pressures. Yet most studies do not explicitly examine content; rather they look at the time spent with television as opposed to other activities, the number of newspapers read, and so on. To find useful answers to our questions about content, we need first to suggest a useful framework for discussing it.

There are countless ways in which we could attempt to categorize media content. We might label it based on audience appeal (highbrow/lowbrow), particular effects (prosocial/antisocial), the medium used (television, radio, print), sexual content (pornographic/nonpornographic), or any of a dozen other ways. One common approach is based on the use, or function, that content is designed to serve. Harold Lasswell (1948), in the same essay in which he proposes his components of communication model, identifies three important functions that communication serves in society: (1) the *surveillance* of the environment; (2) the *correlation* of parts of society in responding to the environment; and (3) the *transmission* of social heritage from one generation to another. To these, Wright (1986) adds *entertainment*.

Communication researchers have tended to organize their studies around these functional categories. Let's look more closely at the kinds of content that fit into them.

Surveillance. News content most closely fits the surveillance function. Wright (1986) suggests that news provides "warnings about imminent threats and dangers in the world," and is useful to such everyday activities of the society as the stock market, navigation, and air traffic. News is usually based on some underlying event, and traditionally there is a clear separation between the subjects of the news and its producers; the producers of news, unlike the producers of entertainment, do not have complete control over the events on which their product is based. Also unlike entertainment, news often provides delayed gratification for the consumer, who may have no immediate use for the content presented but may find it helpful eventually in determining political, economic, or other kinds of actions. The milestone studies in political communication listed on our matrix (Figure 2.1) are most concerned with surveillance content: agenda setting (McCombs & Shaw, 1972) and voter behavior (Lazarsfeld et al., 1948).

Correlation. Lasswell's correlation function is less explicit, but Wright (1986) associates it with editorial and propaganda activity—that is, with the production of appropriate responses to problems identified through surveillance content. In one of Lasswell's many analogies, a flock of sheep benefits from having some members act as sentries to warn the rest when necessary; other examples also describe specialized "leaders" who stimulate "followers" to "adapt in an orderly manner to circumstances heralded by the sentinels" (1948, p. 86). Consider that Lasswell published his essay shortly after the end of World War II; in the spirit of the times, the media were perceived as functional instruments that leaders could use to mobilize society toward largely agreed-upon goals.

Correlative content might actually include any content that interprets the news, although it is most often considered to comprise purposive communication that attempts to persuade.[1] Related studies include Hovland's experiments, as well as propaganda analysis. Lasswell does not mention advertising, but we might also consider this correlative content, since it allows consumers to correlate responses to needs.

Transmission. Virtually all forms of content transmit the perceived norms of society in some way. Although Lasswell considered educators to be society's "socializers" (1948, p. 87), virtually all mass media perform this function at some time in some way (and media researchers have examined that phenomenon). Surveillance, correlative, and entertainment content all help transmit lessons to new members of society.

Entertainment. We normally think of entertainment content as that which provides immediate gratification, relaxation, and respite for the consumer, and that which is under the complete control of its producer. Entertainment content may shed light on reality, and represent the human experience and have its origins in real life, but entertainment is usually not designed to convey actual events. Most television content falls into this functional category, and studies of it would include those on television violence conducted by George Gerbner (1971), Wertham's comic book studies (1954), and the children and television research of Schramm, Lyle, and Parker (1961).

Obviously, the functional categories outlined by Lasswell and Wright often blur, but it is basically the first and the last—news (or surveillance) and entertainment—that concern us here.

Our Focus on News and Entertainment

Most early communication research (propaganda analysis, for example) was concerned with correlative content—the overt, persuasive appeal. But correlative content forms only a small part of what the media produce. Entertainment content is not generally designed specifically to persuade (although it may in fact accomplish that purpose), and a small percentage of the available space in daily newspapers or the available time on network or local news broadcasts contains overt editorial viewpoints (Becker, McCombs, & McLeod, 1975). With the obvious exception of advertising messages, news and entertainment are the two types of media content most widely available to audiences, and they therefore form the most far-reaching symbolic pseudoenvironment of social reality.

Content Similarities. Although news and entertainment differ in very important ways, they are also similar in ways that become apparent when we begin trying to categorize content. The often arbitrary distinctions do not hold. For example, most of us would probably agree that the evening network news broadcasts are "news" and the prime-time shows that follow are "entertainment." But where do we classify "reality-based" talk shows like "Donahue" and "The Oprah Winfrey Show," or television's "Lifestyles of the Rich and Famous"? What about more recent "infotainments" like "Inside Edition" and "A Current Affair"? How do we classify *People* magazine or the *National Enquirer?* Television news has often been accused of injecting entertainment values into hard news stories; several networks have been chastised recently for staging reenactments of news events. Even organizational boundaries blur; ABC's morning news show, "Good Morning America," is produced by ABC's entertainment division.

The audience does not always draw the same lines that the researcher does. Viewers are entertained by a television news story about a killer whale giving birth, and they learn important information about AIDS from a made-for-TV movie. Adolescents often look to fictitious characters as role models and learn from them.

The Media's Symbolic Environment. News and entertainment both tell us something about the world, and together they make up a significant symbolic environment. The fact that some are officially labeled "entertainment" does not make them any less potent as cultural forces. Both news and entertainment tell us who is important, how to behave, and what the new trends are in speech, manners, and dress. Both take us to places we've never been before. Many of us have never seen the inside of a hospital operating room, for example, but almost all of us know what one looks like. We've seen it on television—and it makes little difference to us whether it was on a news show or a hospital drama.

With both news and entertainment, the frequency of messages, the production techniques, and the target audiences can be systematically examined. Both types of content may be perceived and explained as resulting from an organizational, cultural, and economic base, as well as from the value systems of the messages' producers. As we'll see below, the same techniques can be used to measure, quantify, and describe both types of content.

MEASURING CONTENT: HOW WE STUDY IT

If as we have agreed we consider *content* everything that appears in the mass media, then our definition takes in an extremely wide range of phenomena—a range almost as all-encompassing as reality itself. Our task, then, is to impose some sort of order on these phenomena in order to grasp their meaning. Part of this ordering process consists of singling out the key features that we think are important, and to which we want to pay attention. Researchers approach content in different ways, using different conceptual and methodological tools. We take what is basically a social science approach to research, but some researchers take another, basically humanistic approach.

Humanistic v. Behavioristic Traditions

Humanists are less likely than social scientists to ask: Do the media reflect reality? They see media content as an *integral part* of a real culture, not as something divorced from that culture. Culture is manifested in many ways, of which media content is one. A humanist examines content for aesthetic meanings. In postwar film analysis, for example, humanist scholars drew from psychoanalysis and cultural anthropology to analyze how film revealed truths about a society or historical culture (Czitrom, 1982), and more recent scholars like Horace Newcomb (1982) have studied television's prime-time and daytime serials to find insights into drama, ritual, and mythology.

Rhetorical analysis, a prominent branch of the humanistic tradition, examines the internal logic of content: What are the rules, forms, thematic unities, ways of storytelling found in content? Nimmo and Combs (1983), for example, examine how the media portray reality through the logic of dramatic representation—actors, acts, style, plot, line, scene, motives, and the sanctioning agent (the principal source that justifies the events, actions, and conclusion of the drama). Robert Smith (1979) studied a number of television newscasts to determine whether they contained a limited number of consistent and predictable narratives; he found that 83 percent could be classified in three categories: "man decides," "suffering," and "villain caught." Smith also found that males and the government were more often shown acting rather than acted upon; the reverse was true for voluntary associations.

This emphasis on the inherent cultural meanings in content differs from that of the social scientist, who has typically been concerned with content to the extent that it produces effects. Humanistic analysis tends to take content as a starting point and work backward, to understand the culture producing it; behaviorists have traditionally taken content as a starting point and worked forward, to examine the effects external to and created by the message.

Quantitative v. Qualitative. Behavioral content analysis is not always or necessarily conducted using quantitative, or numerical, techniques, but the two tend to go together. Similarly, humanistic content analysis naturally gravitates toward qualitative study. Because of their interest in effects, social scientists have sought to quantify content in keeping with behavioral stimulus-response psychology; that is, the more frequently a given stimulus is found, the more potent is its presumed effect. Reducing large amounts of text to quantitative data, however, does not provide a complete picture of meaning and contextual code, since texts may contain many other forms of emphasis besides sheer repetition (Gitlin, 1980).

Quantification nevertheless has great value in summarizing what is to be found in media content, and one of the most popular social science approaches to media research, content analysis, is the "objective, systematic, quantitative and manifest analysis of content" (Berelson, 1952, p. 18).

Analyzing how frequently things, people, and places appear in media content has the advantage of letting us compare media content to some reality benchmark (e.g., the percentage of blacks shown on prime-time television versus the percentage of blacks in the total U.S. population). If we know content patterns, we can try to understand them by looking at the organizations and people behind them.

We are drawn as researchers to those repetitive patterns of widely attended-to mediated messages that have social significance and were produced by media organizations in a routine and standardized way. These systematic repetitive patterns of content make it more likely that content represents some underlying cultural pattern or organizational logic.

DO MEDIA REFLECT EVENTS?

Passive v. Active Conceptualizations

In his book *Public Opinion* (1922), Walter Lippmann describes an island where a handful of French, English, and Germans lived peaceably just before World War I. A British mail steamer provided their only link with the outside world. One day in mid-September, the ship brought news that the English and French had been fighting the Germans for over six weeks. For those six weeks, the islanders, technically enemies, had acted as friends, trusting "the pictures in their heads" (p. 3). Lippmann's compelling allegory has intrigued communication scholars ever since. His simple but important point is that we must distinguish between "reality" and "social reality"—that is, as Lippmann termed it, "the world outside" of actual events and our mediated knowledge of those events—because we think and behave based not on what truly is but on what we perceive to be.

In ancient time, most of the world that people needed to know about was close at hand. They rarely ventured far from their own communities. They lived and died close to where they were born. The complexity and interdependency of modern society, however, mean that people are affected by economic and political forces far beyond their own communities. In fact, we could argue that most of the world that matters to us is beyond our direct grasp and must necessarily be mediated, thus becoming, as Lippmann called it, a "pseudoenvironment." The importance of the mass media as sources for these pictures in our heads leads us logically to question how closely the media world actually resembles the world outside.

The extent to which we see the mass media as distorting the world outside depends on how we envision the media acting. Some conceptions treat the media as passive transmitters of events; others view the media as taking a far more active role in manipulating reality.

A Passive Role for the Media: The Media as Channels

Early models of the communication process implied a passive role for the media in shaping events. Lasswell's model, for example, asks "who/says what/in which *channel?*" The channel idea suggests that the media are nothing more than pipes or conduits through which bits of information flow—neutral transmitters of messages, linking senders to receivers. This approach is perhaps best illustrated in Westley and MacLean's 1957 model of the mass communication process (Figure 3.1), specifically designed with the newsgathering process in mind. They designated channels (the media) as serving "as the agents" of audience members in selecting and transmitting nonpurposively the information they require, especially when the information is beyond their immediate reach. *Nonpurposive* messages are those transmitted without any intent by the communicator to influence the audience. Such a model assumes that nothing important happens to the message while it is in the channel. Any effects on the audience that result from using the mass media must then be due to source or audience characteristics and not to anything that happened to the information while it was in the channel.

Early Studies of Media Effects. Early communication research reflected this view of the media as channels. It was not that these channels were viewed as weak; on the contrary, the ability to communicate to a mass audience was regarded as a powerful instrument that could be used for evil or for constructive social purposes. These early studies of content effects had more to do with human communication theory

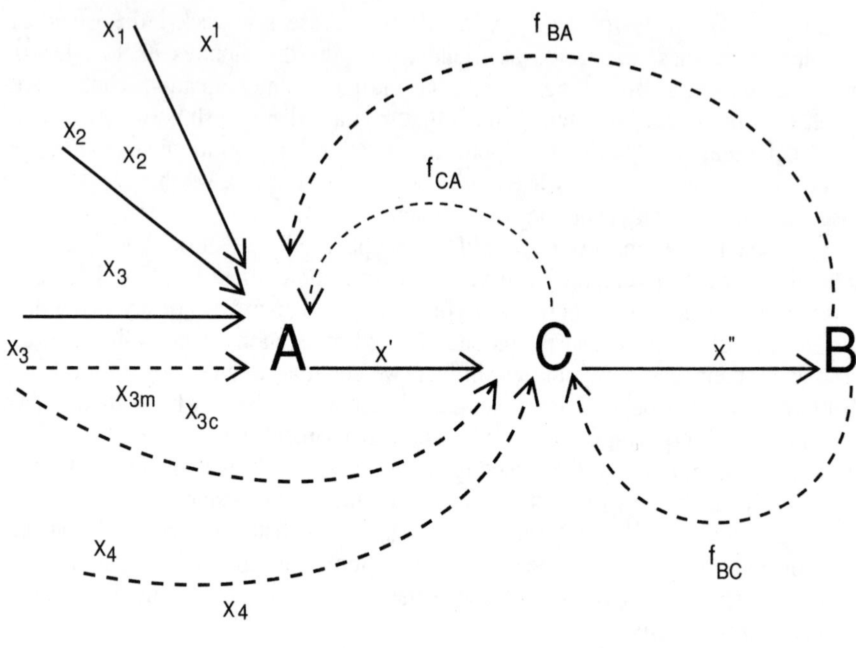

Figure 3.1. Westley and MacLean's (1957) model of the mass communication process. "A" represents the communicator, "C" the channel (the mass media), "B" the public, and the "X_i" the universe of possible messages.

(how audiences respond to specific messages) than they did with *mass* communication theory (what about the media causes the content to be the way it is). They focused on identifying messages that produced effects, or on audience characteristics that mediated those effects. (Which was more persuasive—a one- or two-sided argument? Who was most likely to panic during the "War of the Worlds" broadcast?) The media were seen as instruments for conveying those messages.

Harold Lasswell pioneered the study of propaganda in 1927 with his book *Propaganda Technique in the World War.* The warring nations had used modern communication as an integral part of military strategy, and Lasswell sought to list and categorize these techniques. Propaganda continued as a serious concern until the outbreak of World War II. The Institute for Propaganda Analysis was established in 1937 in response to the apparent success of propaganda in Nazi Germany and helped to publish antipropaganda teaching materials for American schools. These materials told children of the common propaganda techniques like "name calling," "glittering generalities," "plain-folks," and "card-stacking," in the hope of thereby "immunizing" them against their sinister use.

But the U.S. government coveted these same instruments of persuasion to facilitate its war effort. The Army assigned noted director Frank Capra to produce a series of films, called *Why We Fight*. With titles like *Prelude to War, The Nazis Strike, Divide and Conquer,* and *The Battle of Britain,* the films were designed to educate recruits about events leading up to the war. Carl Hovland and his colleagues at Yale (Hovland, Lumsdaine, & Sheffield, 1949) conducted experiments to evaluate the effectiveness of the films. They found the films did convey facts but were ineffective in improving attitudes toward U.S. allies and motivation to fight the enemy. In later research, Hovland looked at other message attributes that might affect their persuasive power, such as one- versus two-sided arguments, source credibility, and fear appeals (Hovland et al., 1949, 1953). These studies assumed that if the right message could be devised, spreading it through mass communication channels would vastly increase its power.

On a larger scale, the studies of Paul Lazarsfeld and others at Columbia's Bureau of Applied Social Research during the 1940s and 1950s also promoted this "media as channels" concept. Their primary purpose was to find how and why people decided to vote, including the role of political propaganda. Finding that the heaviest media consumers were also first to make up their minds, they concluded that the primary effect of the mass media in political campaigns was to reinforce preexisting political attitudes.

In *The Effects of Mass Communication* (1960), Joseph Klapper enshrined this notion in a widely accepted generalization: "Mass communication ordinarily does not serve as a necessary and sufficient cause of audience effects, but rather functions among and through a nexus of mediating factors and influences" (p. 8). In a sense, audience members, like source/persuaders, also were seen as using mass media content as an instrument, to reinforce and justify their own predispositions. An analysis of media content was not considered important, since audience members were assumed to pick and choose the commentators, articles, and other facts that supported their own views. So, in any case, media were viewed as channels, through which purposive messages flowed from persuaders, and from which audience members could select those messages most consistent with and supportive of their views. The media's role in shaping the symbolic environment in which all these decisions were made was largely ignored.

The Neutral Journalist Theory. Another source of the media-as-channel philosophy is the journalist. "We don't make the news; we report it," said Richard Salant of CBS News. "Our reporters do not cover stories from their point of view. They are presenting them from nobody's point of view" (Altheide, 1976, p. 17). Former television newscaster Walter Cronkite's traditional ending for his news program, "and that's the way it is," also exemplifies this perspective. Journalists often defend themselves by pointing out that their role is neutral, to gather and transmit information. The ultimate journalist, then, would be a disinterested, totally independent, all-seeing, and ever-present observer and recorder who never makes a mistake. Media content is assumed to provide an accurate and representative portrait of the world.

The Null Effects Model. A more formal academic model by Young (1981) also predicts that media content is free of distortion. The *null effects model* holds that mass media provide a fair representation of reality with little or no distortion. The reason for the distortion-free content, however, differs greatly from the traditional "journalist as neutral transmitter" approach described above. Young believes that representative content results not because journalists are neutral and noble observers and recorders of reality, but rather because they are pushed and shoved by counterbalancing forces (e.g., liberals versus conservatives, gun control advocates versus the National Rifle Association) into providing a fairly accurate view of the world. The mass media, says Young, simultaneously buy the views of those who have power (news) and sell those views to the working class. The result of this market system—the buying and selling of news—lessens distortion in media content, because distorted content would have a smaller potential audience and would be less lucrative to media owners.

In both the null effects model and the earlier limited effects model, the mass media are viewed as having little or no effect on social change. Control lies within the audience members—both the controlling and working classes—who are active processors of information.

A New Approach. The problem with both these approaches is that they have failed to explain how two or more media channels can be so different in covering the same world. People can easily observe these discrepancies. For example, two newspapers in the same town may provide radically different views of the day's events. People who attend a political rally have a much different idea of what happened from that of those who watched it on television. If the media are mere channels for transmitting reality, then all media should provide the same basic view of an event. If counterbalancing forces from news buyers and sellers result in content that accurately represents the world, then the media version of social reality (such as of the amount of crime in society) ought to conform to that offered by other sources of information (such as police reports). Communication researchers have begun to address these problems by reconsidering the "channel" conceptualization and examining the extent to which the mass media impose their own structure and logic on events in creating a media world.

An Active Role for the Media: the Media as Participants

Media v. Real World: The MacArthur Day Parade. How does a media portrayal of an event differ from the real thing? Walter Lippmann (1922) warned us that people act based on the "pictures" in their heads, but it was three decades before someone took a close empirical look at how the "pictures" we get from the media differ from the world outside. In a now classic study, compelling in its simplicity, Kurt and Gladys Lang (1971) analyzed the 1951 MacArthur Day parade in Chicago. The Langs stationed observers along the parade route and in front of television sets and compared the reactions of those who experienced the parade live with those who saw it on television. People who saw the parade on television thought it was a far more exciting event than did those who saw it in person. The camera followed the action, giving the viewer an uninterrupted picture of excitement; the television viewer went with MacArthur all along the way, whereas the observers stationed along the route got only a brief glimpse of him as he passed by. Unlike viewers, the eyewitnesses saw thinning crowds, making MacArthur's reception appear less glamorous than it appeared on television. People standing along the parade route may also have observed that individuals cheered because they were about to be on television for the first time in their lives, not because they were seeing MacArthur. The Langs concluded that the representation of the world provided by television differed in important ways from personal experience.

Manipulating Reality. If content does not perfectly describe reality, then what does it describe? Media content may be based on what happens in the physical world but it singles out and highlights certain elements over others, and the media's own structural logic is imposed on those elements. Reality is necessarily manipulated when events and people are relocated into news or prime-time stories. The media can impose their own logic on assembled materials in a number of ways, including emphasizing certain behaviors and people and stereotyping. Television can distort people visually through camera perspective and other techniques. Rhetorically, people can be portrayed with different labels (freedom fighter or terrorist). One of the most obvious ways media content structures a symbolic environment is simply by giving greater attention (in the form of more time, greater prominence, and so on) to certain events, people, groups, and places than others. Most content analysis focuses on these features.

Visual v. Verbal Manipulation. Over the years, the primary research emphasis has been on verbal content, on text instead of on pictures. Perhaps we've assumed that verbal content is most open to manipulation, whereas pictures are direct shots of reality. Films and television shows are more ephemeral, harder to study, and have often been deemed less serious-minded than the written word. However, pictures can also be distorted, by cropping, angles, and shot selection. In his study of media treatment of student radicals in the 1960s, Todd Gitlin (1980, pp. 50–51) includes two pictures of an antiwar protest. One picture was made available by UPI but was not used by the *New York Times*. It showed protest marchers holding placards close up in the foreground, relatively more prominent than a group of counterprotesters in the background across the street. Instead the *Times* used another photo, a long shot of both groups, but taken from the side of the street where the counterprotesters marched, thus minimizing the other protesters, both in size and perspective.

Camera perspectives can also manipulate perception. Hans Kepplinger (1982) notes that film can manipulate time and space through, for example, slow motion and extreme camera angles. Newsfilm, he says, claims objectivity and thus hews more closely to reality. Nevertheless, news cameramen he interviewed said it was possible to depict a subject favorably or unfavorably by choosing different camera perspectives.

In analyzing newsfilm from a West German election campaign, Kepplinger found differences in the two candidates' visual images. Helmut Kohl received fewer eye-level shots than Helmut Schmidt (a perspective considered more favorable by the cameramen), and shots of audiences booing, heckling, and holding signs critical of the candidate were seen more often in coverage of Kohl than of Schmidt. Thus, Kepplinger notes, Kohl was portrayed as the candidate most often meeting with voter disapproval.

In some countries, where the major media lack a tradition of objectivity, taking stronger political sides is more overt. For example, the privately owned Mexican television news organization, Televisa, was accused of unfairly depicting the opposition candidate in the 1988 summer presidential elections. They showed him with only a few people around him, implying that few supported him, whereas the government candidate was always shown with large throngs. (They didn't mention that PRI, the government party, paid people to attend.) In another case, Televisa superimposed a picture of Mussolini next to the opposition candidate delivering a speech (Rohter, 1988).

Television news has several other potential visual tricks up its sleeve. During a 1980 presidential campaign story about policies on which Reagan had reversed himself, CBS News put a white "x" on his face every time the reporter said that he had changed his position. CBS apologized the next day, calling it a very bad idea for a graphic (Robinson, 1981, p. 174). In the famous "See It Now" broadcasts of 1954, Edward R. Murrow made famous a more common and powerful visual device. He juxtaposed footage of statements Senator Joseph McCarthy had made at different times and places. Taken as a whole, they proved damaging to McCarthy, because viewers were better able to see the true nature of McCarthy's demagoguery.

SUMMARY

In the next chapter we will review several studies of media content. Many of them compare the media world with the so-called real world. Before we go any further, however, it's important to understand key terms. Philosophers argue about whether there is an objective reality independent of individuals' perceptions. Does a falling tree make a sound if no one is there to hear it? Because we can know the physical world only through our human senses, the limits and nature of our senses limit and shape our knowledge of that world. Practically speaking, then, there is no world apart from our ability to perceive it with our senses. Therefore, questions about the existence of an objective reality apart from our ability to perceive it are moot. What is more, as we discussed earlier, we depend on secondhand sources for our knowledge about that part of the world beyond our immediate perceptual grasp—

which is most of it. Abstract cultural concepts like "Republican," "Democrat," "democracy," and "civil rights" are socially constructed and, to understand these, we must rely on sources outside of ourselves. Our perceptions of an object or event are at the mercy of the accuracy, completeness, and objectivity of those sources.

Fishman (1980) avoids the assumption of an objective external reality by defining social reality as that which a society knows about itself. There are many sources of information about society and/or a specific event. Some are obvious. If you want to know what goes on at the city council meetings in your town, you could get information from the mayor or from another city official, from a citizen who attends the meetings, from the newspaper, from radio or television coverage, from legal notices, from a friend who has information from one of these sources; or you could attend a meeting yourself. Many information sources are not as obvious. Your local telephone directory probably includes some information about city council members—their names, addresses, and telephone numbers, for example. From their names you could infer the number of people on the council and its ethnic or gender makeup. If you could get access to memoranda or other correspondence with the city council members, you could learn still more. What would you learn if you could see the food and drink orders that the city council cafeteria places, personnel files for the city clerks, office-supply inventories, or the council members' trash?

Of the potentially vast number of information sources, each provides its own piece of social reality. Because there are so many, it is impossible for any one source to convey the entire picture. Indeed, the complexity of social reality effectively prevents an objective assessment by any one source (Ichheiser, 1970). To the extent that an individual has access to some of these sources and not to others, his or her social reality (the individual's knowledge of what the world is like) may differ from that of others in the society. All of these assessments of reality are social constructions, and, therefore, each is subjective in its own way. If, as Fishman says, social reality is the fund of what society knows about itself, then distortion arises from a conflict between different sources of information about some feature of society. When the proverbial blind men tried to identify an elephant, one felt its tail and declared it was a rope, while another, feeling a leg, concluded it was a stump, and so on. Like society, the elephant was too large for them to take it all in at once. Like social analysts, they had to rely on their limited senses in examining one portion of the object at a time. Perhaps enough blind men could have pooled what they felt and arrived at a more accurate conclusion.

In the next chaper, we will discuss what kinds of things we may "feel" about social reality from media content. What kind of pictures of the world do media present, and how do they compare with other indicators of reality?

NOTE

1. Wright (1986) sees a journalistic role in correlation, defining it as "selection, evaluation and interpretation of events." It "signifies the relative importance of what is reported . . . through the conventions of headlines, . . . and other devices" (p. 19). These categories are clearly not mutually exclusive.

REFERENCES

Altheide, D. (1976). *Creating reality: How TV news distorts events.* Beverly Hills, CA: Sage.

Becker, L., McCombs, M., & McLeod, J. (1975). The development of political cognitions. In S. Chaffee (Ed.), *Political communication: Issues and strategies for research.* Beverly Hills, CA: Sage.

Berelson, B. (1952). *Content analysis in communication research.* New York: Free Press.

Czitrom, D. (1982). *Media and the American mind.* Chapel Hill: University of North Carolina Press.

Fishman, M. (1980). *Manufacturing the news.* Austin: University of Texas Press.

Gerbner, G. (1971). Violence in television drama: Trends and symbolic functions. In G. A. Comstock & E. A. Rubinstein (Eds.), *Television and social behavior: Media content and control* (Vol. 1). Washington, DC: U.S. Government Printing Office.

Gitlin, T. (1980). *The whole world is watching.* Berkeley: University of California Press.

Greenberg, B. (1980). *Life on television.* Norwood, NJ: Ablex.

Hovland, C. I., Janis, I., & Kelley, H. (1953). *Communication and persuasion.* New Haven, CT: Yale University Press.

Hovland, C. I., Lumsdaine, A. A., & Sheffield, F. D. (1949). *Experiments on mass communication.* Princeton, NJ: Princeton University Press.

Ichheiser, G. (1970). *Appearances and realities.* San Francisco: Jossey-Bass.

Kepplinger, H. M. (1982). Visual biases in television campaign coverage. *Communication Research, 9,* 432–446.

Klapper, J. (1960). *The effects of mass communication.* New York: Free Press.

Lang, K., & Lang, G. (1971). The unique perspective of television and its effects: A pilot study. In W. Schramm & D. Roberts (Eds.), *The process and effects of mass communication* (pp. 169–188). Urbana: University of Illinois Press.

Lasswell, H. (1927). *Propaganda technique in the world war.* New York: Peter Smith.

Lasswell, H. (1948). The structure and function of communication in society. In L. Bryson (Ed.), *The communication of ideas.* New York: Institute for Religious and Social Studies. And in W. Schramm & D. Roberts (Eds.), *The process and effects of mass communication* (pp. 84–99). Urbana: University of Illinois Press.

Lazarsfeld, P. F., Berelson, B., & Gaudet, H. (1948). *The People's Choice.* New York: Columbia University Press.

Lippmann, W. (1922). *Public opinion.* New York: Macmillan.

McCombs, M. E., & Shaw, D. L. (1972). The agenda-setting function of mass media. *Public Opinion Quarterly, 36,* 176–187.

Newcomb, H. (1982). *Television: The critical view.* New York: Oxford.

Nimmo, D., & Combs, J. (1983). *Mediated political realities.* 2d ed., New York: Longman, 1990.

Robinson, M. (1981). A statesman is a dead politician: Candidate images on network news. In E. Abel (Ed.), *What's news.* San Francisco: Institute for Contemporary Studies.

Rohter, L. (1988, July 16). To many, Mexican press is meek. *The New York Times,* p. 6.

Schramm, W., Lyle, J., & Parker, E. (1961). *Television in the lives of our children.* Palo Alto, CA: Stanford University Press.

Smith, R. (1979). Mythic elements in television news. *Journal of Communication, 29,* 75–82.

Wertham, F. (1954). *Seduction of the innocent.* New York: Rinehart.

Westley, B. H., & MacLean, M. (1957). A conceptual model for communication research. *Journalism Quarterly, 34,* 32–35.

Wright, C. (1986). *Mass communication: A sociological perspective* (3rd. ed.). New York: Random House.

Young, J. (1981). Beyond the consensual paradigm: A critique of left functionalism in media theory. In S. Cohen & J. Young (Eds.), *The manufacture of news* (pp. 393–421). Beverly Hills, CA: Sage.

CHAPTER 4

Patterns of Media Content

In this chapter, we focus on the following questions:

- What ideas, people, activities, and views are presented most frequently in the media, and in what fashion?
- In what ways does media content deviate systematically from other sources of social reality?

By reviewing studies in these areas, we see how content as a whole represents a form of cultural mapping, and we discuss these patterns as they relate to social reality and social change.

NARROWING THE FOCUS

Obviously we cannot look at every message distributed on every medium in our attempt to find content patterns. In what content are we most interested? Mass communication studies have traditionally dealt with that mediated content which is widely shared by a large audience. Researchers have paid little attention to small-scale media like memos, cassette recordings, photocopies of speeches, and computer electronic bulletin boards; and we further exclude from our study media like books, billboards, and records that may be important but are less central to our daily lives than other forms of media.

We focus instead on messages in the mass media, and particularly in the major mass media: television, newspapers, and magazines. Although many other media channels exist—and these grow more numerous with new technologies—we choose to focus on those channels that have received the most research attention, as well as the most audience attention. In later chapters, we will narrow our focus even farther, paying particular attention to the major news channels.

Even if we confine ourselves to news and entertainment and to major media, we are still left with a wide range of research to review. We have therefore selected studies that we see as representative of content research. These studies describe *patterns* of media content rather than coverage of a single story or issue. We pick the systematic over the idiosyncratic, and where possible, we include studies that compare content to other social reality benchmarks. We don't divide the studies by medium (television, newspapers, magazines) or by content type; rather we choose to discuss the commonalities of content and save media comparisons for a later chapter.[1]

PATTERNS OF CONTENT

Who do we see in the media? What are their personal characteristics? Where do they come from in the social system? What behaviors do they exhibit? How are they presented in relation to others in society? When we examine a series of representative studies of media content, we begin to see patterns emerging. The following areas have been among the most widely examined.

Political Bias

Most analyses of political content in media have questioned the extent of political bias that exists—that is, specifically partisan, ideological bias. Because of the importance of the news media as partisan forums, many of these studies have been undertaken for adversarial rather than scientific reasons. The conservative movement has been especially active in monitoring content, through groups like Accuracy in Media, to determine if the media are treating some views, parties, and candidates (mainly their own) less fairly than others. Most attention has centered around campaigns, because they inherently lend themselves to this partisan analysis.

Academic researchers have also looked closely at bias, and have generally given the news media good marks for fairness and objectivity. Robinson and Sheehan's (1983) analysis of CBS and UPI 1980 campaign coverage concluded that reporters behaved objectively, rarely making value statements about issues or direct assertions about candidate leadership qualities and policies, sometimes making inferences, but mostly about the campaign's chances or game plan.

Television has received the most criticism (and research attention) for alleged bias, perhaps because Spiro Agnew singled out the networks for his attack on media liberalism in 1969. In general, empirical evidence shows that most news content is neutral, with little evidence of overt partisan bias in favor of one candidate or another. Hofstetter (1978), for example, supports this view, finding no significant partisan bias in the 1972 presidential campaign.

In a more recent study, Michael Robinson (1981) suggests that television campaign coverage is not necessarily biased toward one party or another, but rather is negative toward front-runners and incumbents. In this study, coverage became more favorable when candidates dropped out of the race (as former senator Howard Baker did in 1980). Robinson speculated that the media felt they had an obligation to fully critique any likely winners, but could be magnanimous to those who had dropped out of the race.

The problem with measuring bias is that there are no suitable references with which we can compare media content. A convincing case of bias requires an acceptable standard of fairness, but these are not easy to come by. Journalists are as aware as the media watchdogs of the most simplistic quantitative measures of bias. With ruler and stopwatch they strive to cover candidates evenly in column inches and seconds of airtime. But if we assume that events drive news, then quantitative balance is not a good standard, for events don't always occur in balanced amounts. Nevertheless, bias has been and will remain a hotly contested research issue, examined in a politically charged atmosphere.

Behaviors

Of all the behaviors depicted by the media, aggression must surely be the most widely studied. Because Americans, particularly children, spend so much time with the medium, television has been the predominant focus of content studies of violence. In an extensive program of research, George Gerbner and colleagues at the University of Pennsylvania Annenberg School of Communication have analyzed the violent content of television for over twenty years. They find the incidence of violence, defined as "overt expression of physical force" (p. 11), high and fairly constant from year to year: 70 percent of prime-time shows contain violence, at a rate of 5.7 violent acts per hour, while 54 percent of lead characters were involved in violence. And this high rate of violence is not confined to adult programming: 92 percent of weekend daytime children's shows feature violence (Gerbner, Gross, Morgan, & Signorielli, 1980). How does this compare with real life? One is vastly more likely to encounter violence in the television world than in real life—.32 violent crimes per 100 persons, according to the 1970 census, versus 64 percent of television characters encountering some violence, either committing or receiving (Gerbner, Gross, Eleey, Jackson-Beeck, Jeffries-Fox, & Signorielli, 1977). Note that comparing violent crimes with violence on television (as broadly defined by Gerbner) is not the best comparison. But even if we take his figure of 10 percent of leading characters involved some way in killing (Gerbner et al., 1977, p. 23), it's a wide discrepancy between television and real life.

Violence is common in the news as well, mostly in coverage of criminal acts. Indeed, news shows a preference for violent crime over other types. Crimes against people (e.g., Ammons, Dimmick, & Pilotta, 1982; Fedler & Jordan, 1982) and violent crimes (Antunes & Hurley, 1977) are more likely to get media coverage than crimes against property or nonviolent crimes. Deaths due to violence are more likely to be reported than deaths due to disease (Combs & Slovic, 1979).

This is not confined to the United States. A study of English newspapers by Bob Roshier (1981) showed that reporting of various crimes bore no relationship to their relative frequency in the communities. Overreported crimes were the same across newspapers and over time—serious offenses (crimes against persons, fraud, blackmail, and drug offenses). Murder, including manslaughter, was markedly overreported. The papers focused on solved crimes, and serious punishments, giving an inflated view of the possibility of getting caught and seriously punished.

Although critics often mention "sex and violence" in the same breath, many fewer studies have examined the sexual content of the mass media, and of these, most are of television. For example, one study found that sexual acts occurred once or more per hour of prime time, with intercourse primarily occurring between unmarried people (surely against the actual occurrence in real life) (Greenberg, Graef, Fernandez-Collado, Korzenny, & Atkin, 1980).[2]

Deviance

One way the media tell us what is normal is by showing us what is deviant. The media give importance to some people and groups by portraying them frequently and in powerful positions, and marginalize others by ignoring them or presenting them less advantageously and outside the mainstream. The treatment of deviance is therefore an important feature of media content. For example, Stanley Cohen (1981) notes that in dealing with deviant groups, British news media often "overreport," by exaggerating the seriousness of events, the violence that occurred, and the damage caused.

The psychologically deviant, the mentally ill, are frequently stereotyped by the media as dangerous and as outside the mainstream. An extensive content analysis by Jum Nunnaly (1981) concluded that, although they do not protray them often, "the media of mass communication generally present a distorted picture of mental health problems." He observed that the media deviated from expert opinion (or even public beliefs) on the subject of mental illness, emphasizing bizarre symptoms to make the subject more exciting and appealing to the audience (Nunnaly, 1981, p. 195). On television, more attention has been given mental illness on daytime serials than prime time. Women are three times as likely as men to be portrayed as mentally ill on soaps, but men are shown as more dangerous. Depictions reinforce the image of the mentally ill as evil by associating them with criminal behavior (Fruth & Padderred, 1985).

The treatment of political deviance is central to ideological analyses of the press. James Hertog and Douglas McLeod (1988) examined several features of local media coverage of a march on downtown Minneapolis by members of the Anarchist movement. In articles about the march, the tone was condescending, emphasizing the marchers' appearance over their message. Anarchist actions, such as burning dollar bills in front of a bank, were examined on the basis of criminality rather than their symbolic criticism. More attention was paid to bystanders than the anarchists, and much attention was given to official points of view (police, city attorney, etc.). Visually, the television cameras captured the march from behind police lines, giving viewers the police officers' visual perspective. By treating nonmainstream points of view as unduly deviant, Hertog and McLeod argue, the media restrict the diversity of political discourse.

News Sources and Topics

Before television, most content analyses addressed the print news media. In more recent years, several good media sociology studies have given us a general picture of the common names and activities in the news, with particular interest in the diversity of views expressed. Herbert Gans (1979), in his analysis of CBS, NBC, *Newsweek,* and *Time,* found that news is dominated by the "knowns," people already prominent (71 percent of television stories, 76 percent of magazine columns in 1967). These knowns consist of incumbent presidents, presidential candidates, leading federal officials, state and local officials, and alleged and actual violators of the laws and mores ("well-known people who get in trouble with the law or become enmeshed in political scandal"). The unknowns (representing about a fifth of coverge) consisted of five types: (1) protesters, rioters, strikers; (2) victims; (3) alleged and actual violators of the laws and mores; (4) voters, survey respondents, and other aggregates; and (5) participants in unusual activities.

Leon Sigal (1973), in another frequently cited study, confirmed the prominence of "official" news sources. Sigal examined the *Washington Post* and the *New York Times*. American and foreign government officials accounted for three-fourths of all news sources. Furthermore, he identified almost 60 percent of news stories originating through routine, source-controlled, channels: official proceedings, press conferences, and press releases. The same patterns held true for these papers in 1979 and 1980 (Brown, Bybee, Wearden, & Straughan, 1986).[3]

The major activities in the news followed a similar pattern, according to Gans (1979): a focus on the official, or, if not official, the deviant. The major nonwar domestic activities were government conflicts and disagreements; government decisions, proposals, and ceremonies; protests violent and nonviolent; crimes, scandals, and investigations; and disasters actual and averted.

Geographic Patterns

Domestic. The geographic patterns of news coverage present an appealing opportunity to test the correspondence of that coverage to real world distributions. Dominick (1977) shows an uneven distribution of network news coverage across the United States, with a predominant focus on the two coasts (as do Whitney, Fritzler, Jones, Mazzarella, & Rakow, 1985). In an update of Dominick, Graber (1988) confirms that the Pacific Coast and Northeast are overcovered, while the Midwest is the most undercovered in proportion to population. In her census of 1985–1987 newscasts containing information about individual states, Graber found coverage of the 50 states "quite sparse and extremely uneven." (State news was defined as stories presenting some information about an individual state, excluding stories about, for example, a sports team that just happened to be located in a state.) Although they are among the most populous states, California and New York received proportionately more stories than their population would predict—24 percent of the state stories from mid-1985 to mid-1987. Graber notes that they received nearly as much coverage as the thirty least-covered states. California, New York, Florida, and Texas combined received 39 percent of state news coverage, while constituting only 25 percent of electoral college votes.

International. A large number of studies have examined international news coverage, too many to go into here. Like candidates and corporations, countries are concerned with how they are covered, and, as a result, perceived by others in the world community. This is particularly true for underdeveloped countries. Without large media systems of their own, they often hear about themselves through the media of other nations, particularly the United States. They easily notice disparities between the coverage and reality. Larson (1983) conducted an extensive analysis of network news coverage from 1972 to 1981. Seven of seventeen stories on average were international stories (mentioning some foreign country). He found that the television networks covered the Third World less than industrialized countries. What coverage there was tended to be crisis oriented (27 percent), defined as unrest/dissent; war, terrorism, crime, coups and assassinations; and disasters. Specifically, minimal attention, except for crises, was paid to Latin America, South Asia, Eastern Europe (excluding the USSR), and Africa, which received the greatest proportion of crisis coverage. Developed countries received disproportionately high coverage relative to their population. Sixteen developed countries—14 percent of the world's population—accounted for 35 percent of references, while socialist and developing countries were correspondingly underreported.

Contrary to Larson, Wilhoit and Weaver (1983) found that the number of wire stories on less developed countries exceeded the number on the developed countries. However, compared with coverage of developed countries, a greater proportion of the developing nation coverage concerned conflicts and crises.

According to Herbert Gans (1979), foreign news covers stories relevant to Americans and American interests, with themes and topics similar to domestic coverage (Larson's network news data support this—the United States is referred to in 60 percent of international stories). Gans found that the countries most prominent in foreign news are U.S. allies, and Communist countries and allies. International news concentrates on American activities in a foreign country, foreign activities affecting Americans and American policy, Communist-bloc country activities, changes in foreign government personnel, and political conflict and protest. He notes that U.S. coverage of foreign countries contains more value judgments than would be justifiable in domestic coverage. These values are revealed in the frequent focus on the excesses of dictatorship (the left-wing coups d' état and revolutions are given greater play than their right-wing equivalents). Perry's (1981) study of *Time* and *Newsweek* coverage of international industrial disputes suggests that international coverage responds to the same standards of newsworthiness imbedded in domestic coverage. Coverage of strikes and lockouts corresponded to the magnitude of the problem (measured by lost work days) up to a point. However, strike coverage was relatively less for those countries, like Italy, where labor problems were frequent. Common events (dog bites man) are less newsworthy than rare ones (man bites dog).

Demographic Patterns

Like geographic patterns, demographic statistics give us an unambiguous standard by which to assess coverage. Does it over- or underrepresent people and their roles relative to real-world distributions? Because of its power role in shaping the symbolic environment, many studies have looked closely at television. For example, in occupational patterns, Greenberg (1980) found that professionals are overrepresented on television (over twice the percentage) relative to their prevalance in the population (according to the 1970 census). Clerical and service workers were underrepresented by at least half of their real-world percentage (p. 39). The patterns of occupations seen on television have been stable. A 1964 study by DeFleur shows that upper-middle class occupations were overrepresented, while middle and lower class ones were underrepresented. Dominick (1979) found support for this pattern in a later study. Television overrepresents persons in managerial/professional occupations, and underrepresents others. Of the professionals, Signorielli (1985, p. xvii) notes that doctors, among the most often portrayed professionals, are treated as "demigods," while nurses are seen as subservient to doctors and sometimes as sex objects.

Media portrayals of ethnic groups have been the focus of many research studies. Greenberg (1980) notes that the model prime-time television character is a white male in his late forties to early fifties (p. 186). Minorities are underrepresented across the world of prime time (Signorielli, 1983), particularly so in daytime serials (Greenberg & Heeter, 1983). In fact, Wilson and Gutierrez (1985) find pervasive stereotypical treatment of nonwhite groups in all American entertainment forms. They note that a stereotype is an oversimplified picture that, when combined with prejudiced views toward ethnic groups, treats whites as the desirable reference point. These ethnic stereotypes have given rise to many inaccurate and disparaging media portrayals of American Indians (primitive and savage), Asians (Fu Manchu: corrupt and violent), Latinos (hot-tempered and lazy), and blacks (shiftless and easily frightened). In the case of early movies, these portrayals were designed to appeal to the mostly white movie audience.

Most content analyses of ethnic content have focused on television, and of these, most have examined blacks. From virtual invisibility until the mid-1960s, blacks in more recent years have grown to represent 6 to 9 percent of all television characters (approaching the national percentage of blacks in the population, 10 percent). Compared with whites, however, they tend to play more minor roles in less prestigious occupations, be more often victimized by crime, and be more involved in crime and killing. (It is true that in real life blacks are more likely to be crime victims than whites.) Half of these black characters are concentrated in a few comedy series, where they are more likely to be stereotyped and of a lower socioeconomic status than in integrated casts (the Cosby show is one exception) (cited in Atkin, Greenberg, & McDermott, 1983). Although fewer blacks than whites actually hold higher-level occupations in real life, blacks are still underrepresented in those positions in prime time relative to their real-world numbers (Greenberg, 1980). Greenberg also found that, whereas a majority of black characters were under twenty, most white characters were older. He suggests that producers have felt that blacks would be more palatable to a white audience as young and funny (Greenberg, 1980, p. 21). As for blacks' relations with whites, Signorielli (1985) notes that television studies by Gerbner and his colleagues show white men as most authoritative and least likely to be victimized. Black men were shown as less powerful, and more likely to be victims than victimizers.

In news content, Gans (1979, p. 23) found that the national news featured middle and upper-middle class blacks who had surmounted obstacles to enter the white society. Less affluent blacks become newsworthy as "protesters, criminals, and victims." National news tends to ignore blacks already a part of national institutions or making no attempt to enter them.

The next most examined ethnic group has been Hispanics. Greenberg's (1980, p. 6) content analysis of television prime-time series, 1975–1978, showed a similar pattern of underrepresenting Hispanics. That group comprised only 1.5 percent of speaking characters (versus an estimated 9 percent of the population at that time).

Although women are the numerical majority, their media treatment has much more in common with minority groups. Gaye Tuchman (1981) finds that, since the early days of television, women have been underrepresented in television portrayals (two men for every woman). The proportion has remained relatively constant, notes Tuchman: Males were 60 percent of prime-time characters in 1952, 74 percent in 1973. Among those depicted as employed, an even higher 80 percent were male. Women, like blacks, were concentrated in comedies. When depicted with men, women are most often shown in an inferior capacity (e.g., a male doctor with a female nurse, or a male lawyer with a female secretary). Similarly, she says that commercials neglect or stereotype women in domestic roles. Greenberg (1980, pp. 44–45) confirms this finding: Women are outnumbered three to one, they are young, and overrepresented in lower level jobs, situation comedies, and family dramas, although he sees a trend toward greater diversity. Older men are more apt to be seen on television than older women, directly contrary to the ratio in real life (Greenberg, 1980, p. 45). Nancy Signorielli (1985) notes that the numerous television studies consistently show that women are vastly outnumbered by men, are younger than men, and are featured in traditional, stereotyped roles. This is even more the case on children's programming. Women in daytime serials are more often treated as equals, but women in traditional roles are seen as having an easier time of it (Signorielli, 1985). Women are even stereotyped on television commercials. Men are seen as more authoritative and provide most voice-overs, even for women's products (Signorielli, 1985).

Women television characters are often depicted in dependent or weak positions. For example, two of three women were portrayed as married, compared with one of three men, and women were disproportionately seen as very young or old (Gerbner & Gross, 1976). Greenberg (1980) found that males in television series commit antisocial acts more often then females. Males are involved in physically aggressive acts on television more than twice as often as females (p. 120). Gerbner and his colleagues (1980) confirm this imbalance: Two-thirds of males and one-half of prime-time females were involved in violence. Females were more likely than males to be depicted as victims. Women in minority roles (i.e., old, young, nonwhite and lower class) were more likely to suffer violence than to inflict it. Gerbner interprets these findings from a power perspective, equating symbolic violence with power—that is, who is able to get away with doing something to others? White males are the most likely victimizers, while old, young, and minority women are the most likely to be victims (Gerbner, Gross, Morgan, & Signorielli, 1982).

Even in magazines designed for women, stereotypes are well defined. In a sample of women's magazines, such as *Ladies Home Journal* and *Good Housekeeping,* Helen Franzwa (1974) found that all the women in fiction stories were defined by the absence or presence of men in their lives, furthering a dependent and passive stereotype. As a corollary, work for women was treated as secondary to their home life and even undesirable. Susannah Wilson (1981) analyzed two general interest Canadian magazines, finding that fewer fictional heroines in these publications were employed, compared with the percentage in the population. Few working married women and even fewer working mothers were portrayed (although these roles have become common for women). Few heroines were of low socioeconomic status, held low-status jobs, or belonged to "nondominant" ethnic groups; heroines tended to be young and attractive. Helen Butcher et al. (*sic*) (1981) noted a consistent image of women across several media outlets, all depicting women as oriented toward being mothers, wives, housewives, and sex objects: from a pretty stewardess saying "Fly me" in a television advertisement for an airline, to the Miss World contest on prime time, to popular British press cartoons showing women as illogical, frivolous, and emotional.

When it comes to gender treatment in news, most of the people shown are men. Gans (1979) found that most coverage of women in the seventies has dealt with their entry into the professions and politics (making them, in a sense, newsworthy because of their minority characteristic). Signorielli (1985) notes that women are still underrepresented in television news, appearing primarily in women's issues stories.

The aged may also be considered a minority group. Gans (1979) concludes that national news generally doesn't notice age divisions very much, preferring to cluster age groupings into generations. Nevertheless, daily metro news coverage of aging and the aged was found to be disproportionately low, compared with the number of aged in the population. The papers did not appear to negatively stereotype old people, however (Broussard, Blackmon, Blackwell, Smith, & Hunt, 1980). Greenberg (1980) found a similar imbalance in the television world: People twenty to forty-nine years of age represented two-thirds of television characters, but only a third of the census population at the time. People between fifty and sixty-four years old were represented proportionally to their numbers (p. 27). Signorielli (1985) notes that both very young and very old are underrepresented and negatively stereotyped on television. Even here, though, gender differences remain: Older men are treated more favorably than older women.[4]

UNITY OF CONTENT: POWER/CULTURE MAP?

Of these content studies we've reviewed, some have explicitly compared media patterns with demographic, geographic, and other external benchmarks. For much content, though, there can be no easy way to calibrate it in relation to other standards. What is the standard by which we may judge, for example, news source selection, political bias, or the news agenda? It's easier to compare the media world with the geographic and demographic world. Doing so lets us see whether these worlds differ in predictable, systematic ways. Implicit in such studies, however, is that news and entertainment programming *should* represent the world in amounts proportionate to population, land mass, ethnic distribution, or some other criterion. This would be missing the point, however. A "slice of life" from most of our lives would not attract a large prime-time audience, nor would setting up a camera on a downtown street corner and calling it a news show (although perhaps the C-Span channel on cable television comes closest to this news vérité style). We depend on news to alert us to things that aren't going well. Hearing nothing, we assume they are. It's more efficient for news to alert us to things that have an impact on our lives than those that don't. Similarly, both dramatic forms (the most common entertainment vehicle) and news single out some features of the environment and emphasize them over others. Both drama and news are different from and larger than life, so that they may better tell us about life.

If some features are to be selected over others, how are these selections to be made? Both news and entertainment forms are cultural manifestations and, therefore, represent a reality that is culturally constructed, with people portrayed as they exist in that cultural system. One useful way of thinking about this culture and the patterns we've observed is in terms of power relations. If each person were equally powerful, then we might expect that media attention would be spread according to population and other demographic breakdowns. But each person is not equally powerful, and this gives rise to many of the imbalances we've noted. In any analysis of social relations, power may be considered the most fundamental element, whether it is openly acknowledged or not. Power is an abstract concept, but we can observe the manifestations of it. Power, to use Michael Parenti's definition, is "the ability to get what one wants" (Parenti, 1978, p. 4). A has power over B to the extent that A can get what A wants from B, in spite of B's efforts to resist. We can see the manifestations of this power in the wealth that people are able to accumulate, their ability to benefit from the political and economic system, and other associated indicators.

If we take the power relations imbedded in our culture as the reality in question, then news and entertainment media content comes closer to reflecting it. How are power relations expressed in media content? In television entertainment content, Gerbner has viewed violence as a shorthand way of expressing power: Who has the power to victimize, who is powerless to avoid being victimized? We can look for less overt, physical expressions of power as well. Simply portraying one kind of person more often than another sends a message that the person seen most frequently matters the most; men more than women, Anglos more than ethnics, the younger over the elderly, and so on. In Gerbner's terms, the media have the ability to express lack of power by minimizing people through "symbolic annihilation," by under- or misrepresenting them (Gerbner, 1972).

Which occupations are seen most often? Those associated with the powerful—professional and managerial. The inferior power position of women is shown in their stereotypical media portrayals as dependent on men, as more often married than men, and as having lower-prestige occupations. In the television world, Greenberg (1980, p. 36) concludes that the important people in television are male, white, unmarried, upper-middle class, and between twenty and forty years old.

We can also see the geography of power in media. Which states are mentioned most often? Those on the East and West coasts. New York is the seat of financial power; Washington, D.C., the center of political power; and Los Angeles, the power center of cultural promotion. Internationally, which are the most powerful countries? The Western world and its adversaries, the Communist-bloc countries. The Third World is less powerful, matters less to the First World, and is heard from only when a great calamity breaks through the news threshold. News is about the powerful; therefore, news organizations station their bureaus and reporters to be near the powerful. News media reflect these power relations in the selection of sources, by relying on officials and other wealthy, corporate, and bureaucratic elites. These people are covered routinely. Less powerful people, groups, and causes gain news attention when they become extremists, but then they are taken seriously only as a threat to the status quo, and are often evaluated through establishment sources. When the powerful become deviant by committing so-called white collar crimes, those violations receive less attention than crimes by the powerless. This balance between the routine and the deviant captures the power relations in society—the powerful are presented routinely as representing the normal state of affairs, while the less powerful, when they do intrude into the symbolic environment, do so as deviants or as stereotyped inferiors.

SUMMARY: MOLDING SOCIAL REALITY

The importance of differences between media content and other sources of information about the world lies in the fact that our views of the world, and resulting actions, will be molded by our predominant source of information: the mass media. If you have never traveled to the Soviet Union or talked at length with someone who has, most of what you know about that country—your "social" reality of that country—comes from the mass media in your country. But the media transmit more than just information. Heavy consumers of television entertainment content (such as evening soap operas that were popular on American television in the early 1980s, like "Dallas" or "Dynasty") receive a substantial number of "lessons" about how to make money and get power, how to be an effective political actor, and how to get what they want.

This is not a book about the effects of content, but we are assuming that content has important implications for social change. We'll discuss these in greater depth at the end of this book. For now, though, let us just say that we don't regard content as only a manifestation of culture. Rather we assume that media content is both that *and* a source of culture. That is, media content takes elements of culture, magnifies them, frames them, and feeds them back to an audience. Media impose their own logic in creating a symbolic environment. If we assume that culture must change, adapt, and improve, then media content may serve as either a catalyst for or a brake on this change. By portraying women as homemakers, content may be magnifying a kernel of truth (women used to be found primarily in those roles), but the strength and pervasiveness of those symbols may make it more difficult for women to be accepted in nonstereotypical roles. Media content may take the worst features of a society and blow them up so large that they are reinforced and made difficult to change. Although media portrayals may reflect power relations as they exist, they also may ensure that no other types of relations are conceivable.

The rest of the book examines from several perspectives explanations for the systematic content patterns we have discussed above. These explanations can be found in journalistic routines, journalists' socialization, media practices; media owners' and employees' attitudes and role conceptions; organizational constraints; extramedia factors such as the economic environment, revenue sources, advertisers, and culture; and ideological forces from the powerful or, more specifically, media financiers. Some of these forces working to influence media content have more serious ramifications for social change than others (Shoemaker, 1987). We certainly should not equate a typographic mistake caused by a newspaper reporter with influences on content from government regulations.

In general, influences resulting from media practices (e.g., use of press releases, availability of technology, choice of wire service stories, story type, and editing) may have relatively minor effects on the overall society, since they probably are not factors that would systematically emphasize or exclude certain content to serve institutional imperatives. Influences resulting from individual media professionals may be somewhat broader, but the potential effects of journalists' actions are limited because they are value judgments by individuals rather than institutions at large. When media content is influenced by factors at a higher level of analysis, that is, outside of the media organization, then the opportunity is great for manipulation of media content by extramedia forces seeking to serve their own purposes. Substantial influences on media content from the ideology of the powerful (often referred to as *hegemony*) would indicate broad and pervasive effects on society. We turn next to analyze these influences.

NOTES

1. Of the mass media, some scholars have considered television the most central, and it has certainly received its share of the research. Nancy Signorielli (1985) has compiled a comprehensive bibliography of television studies, whose index gives a rough idea of the topics attracting the most research attention. The heading of "blacks" contained the most listings (111), followed by "family" (52), "occupations" (51), "employment" (39), "violence" (39), "marital status" (38), "social class" (36), "victimization" (30), "aggression" (26), "professionals" (22), "housewives" (20), "Hispanics" (20).
2. Even television portrayals of such routine daily activities as driving a car have been examined. Greenberg and Atkin (1983) concluded that a large number of irregular driving behaviors could be observed in prime time, but few deaths, and few instances of legal fines and seat belt use.
3. When the media break away from the official routine to cover crises, do they portray them accurately? Scanlon, Liuiko, and Morton (1978) conclude that the general impression the media gave about crisis events was accurate, but that there were errors in reporting factual details, such as names, ages, and statistics. Borman (1978) found that few of the facts published about science topics were actually inaccurate, but that there were many omissions of relevant information.
4. Even treatment of insects has not escaped the content analyst. Although 99.9 percent of insect species are not harmful or are beneficial, most magazine articles sampled in one study stressed the negative aspects of insects (the same magazines that carry insecticide ads) (Moore, Bowers, & Granovsky, 1982).

REFERENCES

Ammons, L., Dimmick, J., & Pilotta, J. (1982). Crime news reporting in a black weekly. *Journalism Quarterly, 59,* 310–313.

Antunes, G., & Hurley, P. (1977). The representation of criminal events in Houston's two daily newspapers. *Journalism Quarterly, 54,* 756–760.

Atkin, C., Greenberg, B., & McDermott, S. (1983). Television and race role socialization. *Journalism Quarterly, 60,* 407–414.

Borman, S. (1978). Communication accuracy in magazine science reporting. *Journalism Quarterly, 55,* 345–346.

Broussard, E. J., Blackmon, C. R., Blackwell, D., Smith, D., & Hunt, S. (1980). News of aged and aging in 10 metropolitan dailies. *Journalism Quarterly, 57,* 324–327.

Brown, J., Bybee, C., Wearden, S., & Straughan, D. (1986). Invisible power: Newspaper news sources and the limits of diversity. *Journalism Quarterly, 63,* 45–54.

Butcher, H., et al. (1981). Images of women in the media. In S. Cohen & J. Young (Eds.), *The manufacture of news: Deviance, social problems and the mass media* (pp. 317–325). Beverly Hills, CA: Sage.

Cohen, S. (1981). Mods and rockers: The inventory as manufactured news. In S. Cohen & J. Young (Eds.), *The manufacture of news: Deviance, social problems and the mass media* (pp. 263–279). Beverly Hills, CA: Sage.

Combs, B., & Slovic, P. (1979). Newspaper coverage of causes of death. *Journalism Quarterly, 56,* 837–843, 849.

DeFleur, M. (1964). Occupational roles as portrayed on television. *Public Opinion Quarterly, 28,* 57–74.

Dominick, J. (1977). Geographic bias in network TV news. *Journal of Communication, 27,* 94–99.

Dominick, J. (1979). The portrayal of women in prime time. *Sex Roles,* 5(4), 405–411.

Fedler, F., & Jordan, D. (1982). How emphasis on people affects coverage of crime. *Journalism Quarterly, 59,* 474–478.

Franzwa, H. (1974). Working women in fact and fiction. *Journal of Communication, 24,* 106.

Fruth, L., & Padderred, A. (1985). Portrayals of mental illness in daytime television serials. *Journalism Quarterly, 62,* 384–387, 449.

Gans, H. (1979). *Deciding what's news.* New York: Random House.

Gerbner, G., & Gross, L. (1976). Living with television: The violence profile. *Journal of Communication, 26,* 173–199.

Gerbner, G., Gross, L., Eleey, M., Jackson-Beeck, M., Jeffries-Fox, S., & Signorielli, N. (1977). *Violence profile no. 8, trends in network television drama and viewer conceptions of social reality 1967–1976.* Annenberg report.

Gerbner, G., Gross, L., Morgan, M., & Signorielli N. (1980). The mainstreaming of America: Violence profile no. 11. *Journal of Communication, 30,* 10–29.

Gerbner, G., Gross, L., Morgan, M., & Signorielli, N. (1982). Charting the mainstream: Television's contributions to political orientations. *Journal of Communication, 32,* 100–127.

Graber, D. (1988). *Flashlight coverage: State news on national broadcasts.* Paper presented to the International Communication Association, New Orleans.

Greenberg, B. (1980). *Life on television.* Norwood, NJ: Ablex.

Greenberg, B., & Atkin, C. (1983). The portrayal of driving on television. 1975–1980. *Journal of Communication, 33,* 44–55.

Greenberg, B., Graef, D., Fernandez-Collado, C., Korzenny, F., & Atkin, C. (1980). Sexual intimacy on commercial TV during prime time. *Journalism Quarterly, 57,* 211–215.

Greenberg, B., & Heeter, C. (1983). Television and the social stereotypes. In J. Sprafkin, C. Swift, & R. Hess (Eds.), *Rx television: Enhancing the preventive impact of TV* (pp. 37–52). New York: Haworth Press.

Hertog, J., & McLeod, D. (1988). *Anarchists wreak havoc in downtown Minneapolis.* Paper presented to the Qualitative Studies Division of the Association for Education in Journalism and Mass Communication, Portland.

Hofstetter, C. R. (1978, November). News bias in the 1972 campaign: A cross-media comparison. *Journalism Monographs,* no. 58.

Larson, J. (1983). *Television's window on the world*. Norwood, NJ: Ablex.

Moore, W., Bowers, D., & Granovsky, T. (1982). What are magazine articles telling us about insects? *Journalism Quarterly, 59*, 464–467.

Nunnaly, J. (1981). Mental illness: What the media present. In S. Cohen & J. Young (Eds.), *The manufacture of news: Deviance, social problems and the mass media* (pp. 186–196). Beverly Hills, CA: Sage.

Parenti, M. (1978). *Power and the powerless*. New York: St. Martin's.

Perry, D. (1981). Foreign industrial disputes in Time and Newsweek, 1966–1973. *Journalism Quarterly, 58*, 439–443.

Robinson, M. (1981). "A statesman is a dead politician: Candidate issues on network news." In E. Abel (Ed.), *What's News* (pp. 159–186). San Francisco: Institute for Contemporary Studies.

Robinson, M., & Sheehan, M. (1983). *Over the wire and on TV: CBS and UPI in campaign 80*. New York: Russell Sage Foundation.

Roshier, B. (1981). The selection of crime news by the press. In S. Cohen & J. Young (Eds.), *The manufacture of news: Deviance, social problems and the mass media* (pp. 40–51). Beverly Hills, CA: Sage.

Scanlon, T., Liuiko, R., & Morton, G. (1978). Media coverage of crises: Better than reported, worse than necessary. *Journalism Quarterly, 55*, 68–72.

Shoemaker, P. (1987). The communication of deviance. In B. Dervin (Ed.), *Progress in communication science* (Vol. 8, pp. 151–175). Norwood, NJ: Ablex.

Sigal, L. V. (1973). *Reporters and officials*. Lexington, MA: D. C. Heath.

Signorielli, N. (1983). The demography of the television world. In G. Melischek, K. Rosengren, & J. Stappers (Eds.), *Cultural indicators: An international symposium*. Vienna: Austrian Academy of Sciences.

Signorielli, N. (Ed.). (1985). *Role portrayal and stereotyping on television: An annotated bibliography of studies relating to women, minorities, aging, sexual behavior, health and handicaps*. Westport, CT: Greenwood.

Tuchman, G. (1981). The symbolic annihilation of women by the mass media. In S. Cohen & J. Young (Eds.), *The manufacture of news: Deviance, social problems and the mass media* (pp. 169–185). Beverly Hills, CA: Sage.

Whitney, D. C., Fritzler, M., Jones, S., Mazzarella, S., & Rakow, L. (1985). *Geographic and source biases in network television news: 1982–1984*. Paper presented to Association for Education in Journalism and Mass Communication, Memphis.

Wilhoit, G. C., & Weaver, D. (1983). Foreign news coverage in two U.S. wire services. Journal of Communication, 33, 132–148.

Wilson, C., & Gutierrez, F. (1985). *Minorities and media: Diversity and the end of mass communication*. Beverly Hills, CA: Sage.

Wilson, S. (1981). The image of women in Canadian magazines. In E. Katy & T. Szecsko (Eds.), *Mass media and social change*. Beverly Hills, CA: Sage.

CHAPTER 5

Influences on Content from Individual Media Workers

A lot of people are unhappy with the mass media: Conservatives accuse the media of concentrating on negative news and expressing a liberal bias. Liberals accuse the media of kowtowing to conservative presidents. Films and television shows are accused of including too much sex or violence or not enough socially significant story lines. And a lot of people put the blame for media content squarely in the hands of communication workers such as journalists, filmmakers, photographers, and advertising and public relations practitioners. Characteristics of these *individual* communicators are the subject of this chapter. As Figure 5.1 shows, the individual level of analysis is the first we will discuss.

The number of journalism jobs increased by more than 60 percent between 1971 and 1982, when the total news work force in daily and weekly newspapers, newsmagazines, television, radio, and news services was calculated to be 112,072 by Weaver and Wilhoit (1986a, p. 13). In fact, the outlook for communication jobs is in general good: Employment for communicators is expected to increase at a faster-than-average rate through the year 2000 (Bureau of Labor Statistics, 1988).

Using somewhat different categories than Weaver and Wilhoit, the U.S. Bureau of Labor Statistics in 1986 estimated the number of people engaged in communication jobs, whether full time, part time, or on a free-lance basis:

- 75,000 reporters and correspondents, 70 percent of whom work for newspapers.
- 214,000 writers and editors, nearly 40 percent of whom work for newspapers, magazines, and book publishers.
- 61,000 radio and television announcers and newscasters.
- 87,000 public relations specialists.

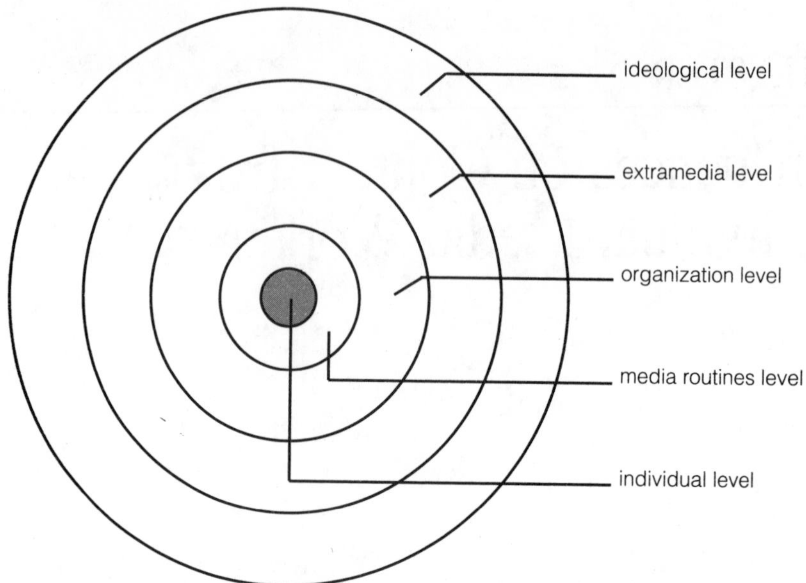

Figure 5.1. Individual influences on media content in the hierarchical model

- 323,000 marketing, advertising, and public relations managers.
- 109,000 photographers and camera operators, about half of whom are self-employed.
- 73,000 actors, directors, and producers.

In this chapter, we discuss potential influences on mass media content from factors that are *intrinsic to* the communication worker: First, we look at the characteristics of communicators and at their personal and professional backgrounds to see how, for example, the journalists' education may influence their stories. Second, we consider influences from communicators' personal attitudes, values, and beliefs—those attitudes that individual communicators hold as a result of their backgrounds or personal experiences, for example, political attitudes or religious beliefs. Third, we investigate the professional orientations and role conceptions that communicators hold at least partly as a function of being socialized to their jobs, for example, whether journalists perceive themselves to be neutral transmitters of events or active participants in developing the story.

Figure 5.2 shows the relationships among these factors. The communicators' characteristics (such as gender and ethnicity) and their personal backgrounds and experiences (such as religious upbringing and their parents' socioeconomic status) not only shape the communicators' personal attitudes, values, and beliefs, but also direct the communicators' professional backgrounds and experiences (such as whether the communicator goes to journalism or film school). These professional experiences (including those from communication jobs) then shape the communica-

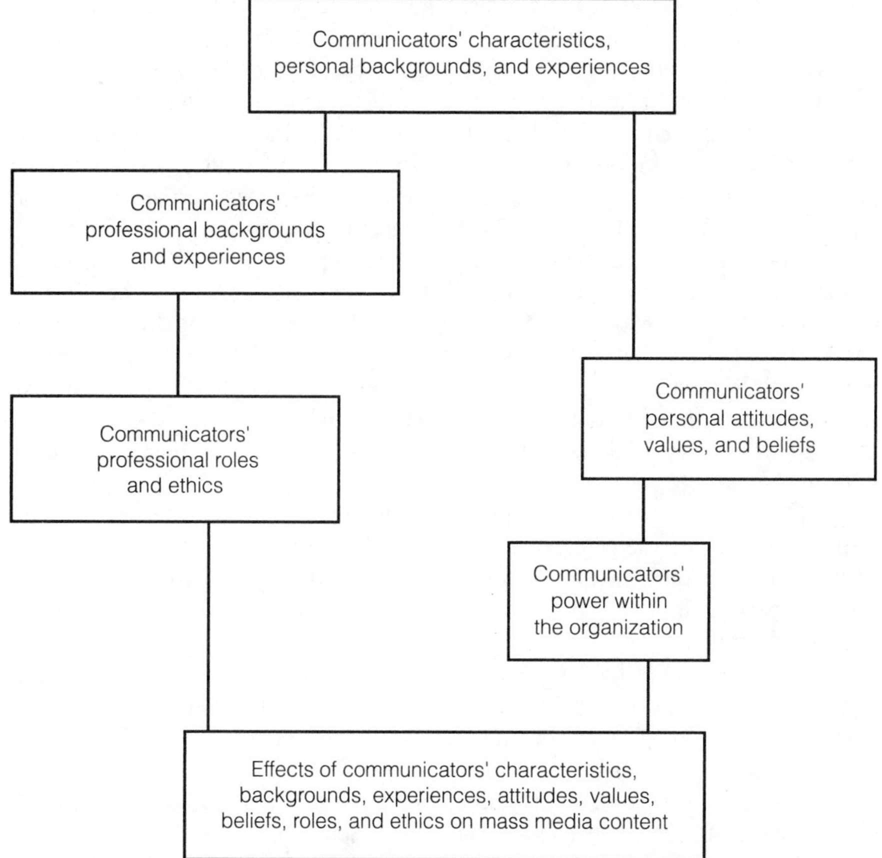

Figure 5.2. How factors intrinsic to the communicator may influence media content.

tor's professional roles and ethics. These professional roles and ethics have a direct effect on mass media content, whereas the effect of personal attitudes, values, and beliefs on mass media content is indirect, operating only to the extent that the individuals hold power within their media organizations sufficient to override professional values and/or organizational routines (such as we discuss in Chapters 6 and 7).

BACKGROUND AND CHARACTERISTICS

What kind of person goes into mass communication? Weaver and Wilhoit's 1982–1983 survey of U.S. journalists discovered that, although there is substantial variability, "the 'typical' U.S. journalist is a white Protestant male who has a bachelor's degree, is married and has children, is middle-of-the-road politically, is thirty-two years old, and earns about $19,000 a year" (1986a, p. 12).[1]

Women are gaining ground, however, especially in the broadcast media (Weaver & Wilhoit, 1986a, pp. 38–39). In 1983, about one-third of journalists were female, up from one-fifth in 1971 (p. 19). Although this represents a substantial increase in opportunities for women, the percentage of women in journalistic jobs still lags behind the percentage of women in the U.S. labor force—nearly 43 percent in 1981. With women accounting for about 60 percent of journalism and mass communication students (pp. 38–39), the percentage of women can be expected to continue increasing; however, this will not necessarily mean more women reporters. Many female students are training for careers in public relations or advertising, mass communication jobs that are not included in Weaver and Wilhoit's statistics. In fact, Becker, Fruit, and Caudill's (1987, p. 56) study of journalism education shows that female students "are less likely to pick news editorial study and more likely to pick public relations than [are] male students."

As their numbers increase, women are also beginning to make inroads into media management. The percentage of women who are supervising editors (such as desk editors in newspapers or news producers in television and radio) has increased from 12 percent in 1971 to 28 percent in 1982. Women also account for an increasing proportion of top management positions; in 1982, 20 percent of newspaper managing editors, 8 percent of television news directors, and 18 percent of radio news directors were women (Weaver & Wilhoit, 1986a, pp. 70–71). Stone's 1986 survey of television and radio news directors shows that the trend is continuing (1987, p. 749).

As more women work in journalism, the large salary discrepancies observed in 1970 by Johnstone (Weaver & Wilhoit, 1986a, pp. 82–83) are narrowing substantially. Weaver and Wilhoit found that, in 1981, there was no salary disparity between entry-level male and female journalists, although men still make more than women at other levels—a disparity partially explained by differences in experience.

Unfortunately, the successes of women in journalism have not been accompanied by similar successes of minorities (Weaver & Wilhoit, 1986a, pp. 38–39). Although the absolute number of blacks, Hispanics, and Jews in U.S. journalism increased between 1971 and 1982, these groups accounted for a smaller percentage of journalists in 1982 than in 1971. Blacks, Hispanics, Jews, and Orientals accounted for about 22 percent of the U.S. population in 1980, but in 1982 only about 10 percent of journalists came from one of these groups (p. 23). Although Hispanics made up 7.9 percent of the U.S. population in 1987, only about 1.7 percent of journalists were of Hispanic origin (Lawrence, 1988, p. 1).

There is some evidence that this may be changing: About 11 percent of new hires by newspapers and wire services in 1986 and 1987 were minorities, compared with about 17 percent in radio and television ("Of 1987 J-graduates," 1988). Today about 10 percent of journalism graduates are minorities (McCombs, 1988, p. 103). Nonwhite students are more likely to pick broadcasting as their emphasis in journalism school than are white students (Becker, Fruit, & Caudill, 1987, p. 56).

Average or Elite?

One of journalism's myths is the conception of the early newspaper editor as a courageous, rough-and-tumble character who braved the frontier, learned his profession at the knee of the local printer, and dared to speak out in defense of people just like himself—working people, immigrants, or the needy. Not everyone idealized journalists, however. Sociologist Max Weber said journalists were members of a "pariah caste" (Hess, 1981, and in the late 1800s, Harvard University president Charles William Eliot described reporters as being "drunkards, deadbeats, and bummers" (Weaver & Wilhoit, 1986a, p. 6). Journalism certainly was not a very lucrative profession: As late as the mid-1800s, many journalists were paid only $12 to $20 a month, with fringe benefits that included board and washing (Weaver & Wilhoit, 1986a, p. 5).

By the late nineteenth century, however, American journalists had more in common with the corporate elite than with the working class. When Hart (1976) studied the backgrounds of 137 newspaper editors between 1875 and 1900, he found that they did not have much in common with poor immigrants or even with the average American, although older editors did tend to have humbler origins than the younger ones. Older editors began as printer's apprentices and worked their way up to be newspaper owners. Younger nineteenth-century editors were more likely to come from elite families in which the father was successful in business. The younger editors generally started their journalism careers as reporters and were less likely than their predecessors to buy a controlling interest in the newspaper they worked for.

This pattern of recruitment and education remains the norm in today's newspapers, even though one occasionally still reads that as recently as twenty to thirty years ago journalists' origins were closer to the working class. Studies of Washington, D.C., journalists by Rosten in 1936, Rivers in 1951 (both cited in Hess, 1981), and Hess in 1981 all show that journalism has become, in the words of Daniel Patrick Moynihan, "if not an elite profession, a profession attracted to elites" (Hess, 1981, p. 116). In the 1930s, 80 percent of journalists had at least some college education. About a third of Washington reporters since the 1970s have been graduates of highly selective universities (Hess, 1981). Among college students majoring in journalism, students from families in which their fathers held managerial positions were more likely to pick news editorial study as their emphasis than were students from lower occupational backgrounds (Becker, Fruit, & Caudill, 1987, p. 56).

Researchers' conclusions about whether journalists represent the "average American" or the "elite" depends on which journalists are studied. Weaver and Wilhoit (1986) conclude from their study of journalists from a representative sample of U.S. news media (daily and weekly newspapers, newsmagazines, news services, radio, and television stations) that U.S. journalists come primarily from "the established and dominant cultural groups in the society" (p. 22). Lichter, Rothman, and Lichter (1986) studied only journalists at what they call the "elite" media—the *New York Times,* the *Washington Post,* the *Wall Street Journal, Time, Newsweek,*

U.S. News and World Report, and CBS, NBC, ABC, and PBS (p. 20)—and conclude that "the typical leading journalist is the very model of the modern eastern urbanite" (p. 294).

The Evolution of Communication Careers

Journalism has always been a relatively easy career to get into—no license or test is necessary; you don't even need a college degree in journalism. Because most people think that they can write (whether they can or not), they often think that they would make good journalists. The result is that a lot of people try journalism as a first career and then move on to something else. Low salary and benefits are the most-cited reasons for leaving journalism (Weaver & Wilhoit, 1986a, pp. 38–39).

This turnover makes journalism primarily a young person's career: The median age of journalists is slightly lower than the median age of all U.S. civilian workers (Weaver & Wilhoit, 1986, p. 20). More than half of U.S. journalists are under thirty-five years old, and only about 10 percent are fifty-five or older (p. 19). Hess (1981) reports that 38 percent of journalists working in Washington, D.C., are in their thirties, 25 percent in their forties, and only 16 percent are over fifty.

Youthfulness is associated with excitement, and a sense of excitement and discovery makes a good journalist. Washington-based columnist Stanley Karnow says that "journalism is the only profession in which you can stay an adolescent all your life" (Hess, 1981, p. 128). Most television reporters seem especially young and attractive, whether because of youthful excitement or prejudice on the part of management. Although the prevailing wisdom remains that men age more gracefully than women, you don't see an abundance of older men on television, and there are virtually no unattractive reporters of any age or gender. There are notable exceptions, of course. Charles Kuralt, who for years traveled America doing stories "on the road" for CBS, says that being "fat and bald" helps him put people at ease: "People look at me and they say, 'if that guy can look like that and talk like that, then I can just be myself" (Kuralt, 1986, p. 5).

Journalists who lose their youthful sense of excitement or who want higher salaries generally get out of journalism. Those most likely to leave tend to have the most education and experience; they tend to be between thirty and forty-five years old (Weaver & Wilhoit, 1986a, p. 103). Specialty reporters sometimes leave work in their area of expertise; we know of an award-winning environmental reporter who went to work for an environmental group, apparently frustrated about being on the sidelines of environmental battles. Some reporters who cover politics become advocates for candidates or causes and leave their media jobs to become political actors instead of watchers.

Sometimes journalists just get bored or burned out by the repititious nature of the job (not another election story about the candidate's supportive spouse!) or by the cynicism that often accompanies the journalist's role as a passive observer of events: David Wise, a former Washington bureau chief for the *New York Herald Tribune,* says that reporters spend "an awful lot of time sitting around marble corridors waiting for the grown-ups inside to tell them what's happening" (Hess, 1981, p. 123). In addition, as journalists age, they can become dismayed by the fact that they know more about the secretary of transportation's job than does the newly appointed (and probably younger) cabinet member.

Such knowledge is essential for reporters covering technical beats, however. The typical newspaper science writer is older and better educated than the average general assignment reporter (Storad, 1984). Science writers need quite a bit of scientific training if they are to translate technical reports into language that the layperson can understand. An apocryphal story about a newspaper photographer assigned to cover an anniversary of the first sustained nuclear reaction at the University of Chicago illustrates the dangers of limited knowledge: "Arriving on campus, the photographer addressed himself to the assembled scientists, including Yannevar Bush, Enrico Fermi, Arthur H. Compton, and Harold C. Urey. 'Now, fellows,' he said, 'I got three pictures in mind. First you guys putting the atom in the machine. Then splitting the atom. And finally all of you grouped around looking at the pieces' " (Braden, 1981, p. 248).

There is a fair amount of movement between journalism and other mass communication jobs. Some journalists leave their newsgathering jobs to work as television writers and producers. In her study of the Hollywood television producer, Cantor (1988) identifies three types of producers, two of which are occasionally associated with journalism backgrounds. The *filmmaker* producers are the youngest, generally having a college education in mass communication. Although most of the filmmakers started in the bottom ranks of a major Southern California studio, some had also worked as journalists or radio disc jockeys. The *writer-producers* tend to be middle-aged, but have backgrounds similar to the filmmakers. Their university degrees generally involve writing—mostly journalism or English, but sometimes theater. As writers, they had generally held mass media jobs before becoming television producers, such as radio writers, news editors, or movie script writers. In contrast, the *old-line producers* are less likely to have university degrees and are often the oldest and most successful producers in television.

The Education of Communicators

Another aspect of communicators' backgrounds is the amount and type of education they have. Communication departments have flourished in universities under a number of different names—journalism, mass communication, radio-television-film, speech communication, advertising, communication arts, and communication sciences. The formal origins of journalism education were in 1869 at a short-lived journalism program at what is today Washington and Lee University, and in the late nineteenth and early twentieth centuries, several land grant colleges established journalism programs (Dennis, 1988, pp. 10–11). Today more than 340 universities give bachelor's degrees in journalism and mass communication (Weaver & Wilhoit, 1986b, p. 6), and these programs continue to grow. In 1985, more than 20,000 bachelor's degrees were awarded in journalism and mass communication—more than six times the number awarded just twenty years earlier (McCombs, 1988, p. 101).

A 1987 survey of full-time mass communication faculty from four-year and graduate programs revealed that 98 percent have professional media experience; the average is nine years. Although faculty members holding Ph.D. degrees have less professional experience than other faculty (who average twelve years of experience), the media experience of Ph.D.'s still averages more than six years (Weaver & Wilhoit, 1986b, p. 16). It should not be surprising, then, that mass communication faculty are similar to working journalists in many ways, including geographic distribution, ethnic and religious origins, undergraduate college major, and use of the mass media (Weaver & Wilhoit, 1986b, p. 38).

How They Got Started

Benjamin Bradlee, executive editor of the *Washington Post,* got his first journalism job at sixteen years of age as a copy boy for the *Beverly Evening Times* in Massachusetts. After working on his college newspaper, he chose journalism as a career.

Benjamin Bradlee

Janet Chusmir, executive editor of the *Miami Herald,* decided to become a journalist at eleven after getting an A on a composition. Although she attended journalism school, she says that she "learned very little that was worthwhile." She started as an editor/reporter for the life-style section of the *Miami Beach Sun.*

Janet Chusmir

James Dowling, president and chief executive officer for Burson-Marsteller, is a journalism graduate who worked for *Newsweek,* United Press, and Associated Press after college. A brief stint in public relations for Mobil Oil convinced him to pursue a PR agency job. He joined Burson-Marsteller when it was still small and quickly rose through the management ranks.

Guillermo Garcia, reporter for the *Austin* (Texas) *American-Statesman,* settled on journalism as a second choice—as a child he wanted to be a U.S. ambassador. He studied journalism in college, and his first job was at KYOZ radio in Laredo: For an hour each day he did rewrites for the news director.

Carol Reuppel, news director at WTKR-TV, Norfolk, Virginia, was an English major in college. After a one-year stint at advertising a high school newspaper, she got a job as a television reporter and news producer. She worked at several stations around the country before becoming news director at WTKR.

Bernard Shaw, an anchor for Cable News Network, started in journalism as a reporter for WYNR (Chicago). He decided to become a journalist at age

Bernard Shaw

thirteen, having been impressed with Edward R. Murrow. After four years in the Marine Corps, his college major was history.

Compiled from the following sources: (1) Great careers, modest beginnings (1988); (2) Fink (1990); (3) information from the journalists. (Photos courtesy of the *Washington Post,* the *Miami Herald,* and Cable News Network.)

Today, the majority of media professionals have communication degrees, whereas earlier they came primarily from English, creative writing, political science, American Studies, or other disciplines (Weaver & Wilhoit, 1986a, p. 63). Not all media people value a journalism education, however; CBS writer/editor Charles Kuralt says that he would rather hire an American Studies graduate than someone from journalism school: "Journalism is not so complicated that you can't learn it on the job, but America is complicated, and deserving of much contemplation" (Kuralt, 1986a, p. 6). Nonetheless, the vast majority of new hires at newspapers are journalism graduates (McCombs, 1988, p. 101). A movement of communication graduates into management over the past couple of decades could account for the increases in communication graduate hires.

The best approach to mass communication education is a subject for some debate. Many journalists are critical of their journalism education (Burgoon, Burgoon, & Atkin, 1982). While some professionals like Kuralt want liberal arts educations with a strong orientation in research, theory, and critical thinking, others want highly technical, skills-oriented programs. This disagreement shows up in mass communication textbooks and in the types of materials that journalism faculty read. After reviewing thirty-one textbooks, Shoemaker (1987) concluded that mass communication texts are designed either to socialize students to being mass communication "insiders" or to teach them to look critically at all social institutions, including the mass media (the "outsiders"). The insiders would learn how to be successful media professionals, but they would not be encouraged to contemplate the role of the mass media in society. Insiders are trained to be critical of every social institution *except* the mass media.

Through their choice of textbooks, faculty have ample opportunity to introduce their students to either the insider or outsider point of view. The decision probably reflects the faculty members' own orientation toward mass communication. Weaver and Wilhoit (1986b, pp. 33–34) found that, although 40 percent of mass communication faculty keep up with both academic and media industry knowledge, about 30 percent read only industry publications and about 20 percent read only scholarly journals. About 10 percent of faculty don't seem to keep up with either.

In his assessment of "exemplary journalism schools," Footlick (1988, p. 69) writes that good journalists must "know more than a little about a lot of things, from mathematics to foreign policy, from courthouse politics to art history. They must care about a lot of things. They must be able to learn quickly. They must write well, and cherish that ability. To most professionals, the exemplary journalism schools are the ones that give students the best opportunity to begin mastering these fundamental qualities."

Most mass communication departments are organized along media lines, in news-editorial, magazine, broadcast, photojournalism, public relations, or advertising "sequences." Students take very few courses in common, concentrating on the acquisition of specialized knowledge from their sequence. Trinity University, San Antonio, Texas, has tried to counter criticism of professional journalism education by abandoning its traditional sequence organization for a more general curriculum that includes four areas: media study and theory, media management and research, media writing, and media production (Christ & Blanchard, 1988). In schools that retain the traditional sequence organization, advertising and public relations sequences are growing the fastest. Students are increasingly rejecting the news-editorial sequences because of "negative perceptions of what newspaper professions have to offer," including low salaries and lack of creativity (Mann, 1988, p. 60).

Another recent debate has centered on how much liberal arts education journalism students should have. The traditional guidelines by the Accrediting Council on Education in Journalism and Mass Communication has been about 25 percent courses inside the journalism or mass communication department and 75 percent in liberal arts and science courses. Some educators want their students to take more courses within the major in order to meet the demands of their increasingly complex profession.

The tie between liberal arts and communication disciplines will undoubtedly remain close. After all, most communication students would probably be liberal arts majors (especially in English) if they weren't in communication. Even with journalism school graduates taking over more and more journalism jobs, there still remains a significant core of liberal arts graduates in the profession. Thomas Winship (1988, p. 24) says that "most gifted journalists I know stumbled into the business because they were liberal arts deadbeats."

Effects of Media Professionals' Backgrounds on Media Content

"In terms of demographics, if there is an average Washington reporter and an average American, they do not look much like each other. . . .Does this make a difference in how the news is reported? In some instances the answer is yes" (Hess, 1981, p. 117). Yet, to say that there is an influence on content is not to conclude that the influence is negative. Journalists are better educated than the average American. They are better writers than the average American. Are these differences negative? Would the world be a better place if journalists were less literate or less educated?

Still, there is a tendency for our backgrounds to affect how we see the world. Our families, our schools, and all of our life experiences shape our priorities, expectations, and dreams. This is no different a process for communication professionals than it is for construction workers, physicians, or social workers.

But how strong are such influences? Weaver and Wilhoit say that the effect of journalists' demographics on news values and content is probably minor, given the importance of organizational routines and constraints (1986a, p. 25). Therefore, it is possible that increasing numbers of women and minorities within the mass media will not result in any significant changes in media content; education, socialization, and organizational constraints may negate most individual differences between communicators. This is an empirical question, however, and can be addressed by research. For example, Farley (1978) found that female magazine publishers gave more favorable coverage to the Equal Rights Amendment than did their male counterparts.

Such an influence may be most obvious when demography is related to expertise as in the changing nature of foreign correspondents. Scott Shuster (1988), a former free-lance foreign correspondent, says that budget trimming among U.S. media is making it more practical to hire foreign journalists as "foreign" correspondents than to send American journalists abroad. "There is an army of foreign journalists out there, ready to put an end to the ancient and ridiculous practice of sending speak-only-English American reporters halfway around the world to pretend to be experts on places they have never seen before" (p. 43). And, fiscal responsibility aside, these foreign journalists can probably do a better job: Because they know more about the local environment, they "should be able to depict foreign reality more accurately than a 'parachuting' foreign correspondent" (p. 43). David Lawrence, Jr., publisher of the *Detroit Free Press,* advocates hiring U.S. Hispanics as journalists, saying that the fact that most Hispanics are bilingual and bicultural will help them "communicate with and understand the perspectives of 400 million people south of the border" (1988, p. 1).

Similar arguments are sometimes made by Hispanic leaders who criticize local newspapers that hire Anglos to cover the Hispanic community, according to a study by Greenberg, Burgoon, Burgoon, and Korzenny (1983). Even when Hispanic personnel were recruited, they "tended to be hired from places other than the local community and consequently failed to identify and focus on those issues perceived by the Hispanic constituency as important" (p. 64). As a result, "employment patterns and traditional stereotypes were said to cause an overemphasis on negative news" (pp. 64–65).

As in all careers, the population of communication professionals is self-selected—you "volunteer" to be a journalist; you aren't drafted—and people who choose the same career tend to have characteristics in common. Hess (1981, p. 124) says that there is a "personality type" in journalism and that the study of journalists' personalities "may be the most promising field of study for explaining why news is as it is." He says that journalists like excitement and dislike abstractions. Their love for excitement leads them to prefer covering the Senate rather than the House of Representatives and politics rather than management.

PERSONAL ATTITUDES, VALUES, AND BELIEFS

Charges that mass communicators are politically liberal, antireligion, and unlike "most Americans" have been common in recent years. Concern with mass communicators' attitudes and values are based on the assumptions that a journalist's attitudes influence his or her stories.

Personal Values and Beliefs

U.S. journalists (and many other Americans) generally hold what are called the "motherhood" values—they favor family, love, friendship, and economic prosperity; they oppose hate, prejudice, and war (Gans, 1979, p. 42). In addition to these basic values dealing with human kindness (or the lack of such), journalists also hold values more typical of the American Progressive movement of the early twentieth century (Gans, 1979). Paletz and Entman (1981) say that these include individualism, free enterprise, competitiveness, and materialism. Gans (1979) identifies these as ethnocentrism, altruistic democracy, responsible capitalism, small-town pastoralism, individualism, moderatism, social order, and national leadership.

Ethnocentrism refers to journalists' tendency to value U.S. practices above all others—other countries are judged against an American standard.

Altruistic democracy is the label Gans uses to indicate most journalists' belief that the news should "follow a course based on public interest and public service" (1979, p. 43). This value underlies stories about corrupt politicians and others who deviate from some unstated democratic ideal, government waste, and the failure of citizens to fully participate in their democratic society.

Responsible capitalism is what most journalists expect business people to practice—fair competition without unreasonably high profits or the exploitation of workers, and respect for small and family-owned businesses. In fact, Peterson, Albaum, Kozmetsky, and Cunningham (1984) found that newspaper business editors are more favorably disposed toward capitalism than is the general public.

Small-town pastoralism is a journalistic ideal, representing rural areas and small towns as centers of virtue, craftsmanship, and cohesive social relationships. Stories about urban areas emphasize crime, the hectic pace, racial unrest, economic problems, and threats to the environment.

Individualism is prized by journalists, who fill feature stories with "rugged individualists"—people who work for the good of society, but in their own way. The individual is the hero who wins despite overpowering odds. This value also applies to stories about technology and large organizations that rob people of their individualism.

Moderatism acts as a check on excessive individualism—the hero must not break the law or existing norms. Fanaticism of any sort is treated as suspect, as is conspicuous consumption and fervent political ideology.

Social order is valued highly by journalists, leading them to include many stories on unrest and threats to the establishment. By pointing out instances where people disrupt social order or act contrary to established social values, journalists help define what is acceptable and unacceptable behavior.

Leadership is also prized by journalists, because leadership is required to deal with social order. This leads to stories about politicians who are lacking in honesty or morality and explains why journalists are suspicious of powerful people who may influence elected officials. Ettema (1988, p. 3) illustrates how investigative reporting can be a conduit for the journalist to express "righteous indignation not merely at the individual tragedy [being investigated] but also at the moral disorder and social breakdown which the tragedy represents." The journalist's outrage is often aimed at the "incompetence, indifference, or illegal behavior of public officials and agencies" and frequently results in demands for social reform.

As Gans (1979) points out, some of these values reflect an underlying conservative ideology and others reflect liberalism. Journalists' defense of "responsible capitalism" could be described as "right-leaning liberalism," whereas journalists' respect for tradition, nostalgia for pastoralism and rugged individualism, defense of the social order, and faith in leadership are conservative (p. 68). Although individual journalists may agree more or less with each of these, Gans argues that these values—typical of the reformist Progressive movement—come through clearly in the news. Perhaps people who wish to improve society gravitate to journalism as a career because of the opportunities that journalism gives them to expose social evils.

Personal Political Attitudes

Popular wisdom during the early 1980s held that journalists were predominantly liberal, thanks to a study of journalists from major Northeast U.S. media organizations (Lichter, Rothman, & Lichter, 1986, p. 294), quickly picked up and spread by conservative organizations such as Accuracy in Media:

> Today's leading journalists are politically liberal and alienated from traditional norms and institutions. Most place themselves to the left of center and regularly vote the Democratic ticket. Yet theirs is not the New Deal liberalism of the underprivileged, but the contemporary social liberalism of the urban sophisticate. They favor a strong welfare state within a capitalist framework. They differ most from the general public, however, on the divisive social issues that have emerged since the 1960s—abortion, gay rights, affirmative action, et cetera. Many are alienated from the "system" and quite critical of America's world role. They would like to strip traditional powerbrokers of their influence and empower black leaders, consumer groups, intellectuals, and . . . the media. [ellipsis in original]

Their data have been used by many conservatives to justify criticism of the media: Herbert Schmertz, vice president of public affairs for Mobil Oil, says that journalists' views "are in direct opposition to prevailing American values" and that "if [journalists] use the press to 'crusade' on behalf of these beliefs . . . they do the public a great disservice" (Gans, 1985, pp. 29–30).

So just how liberal are journalists? What is behind their political orientations? We have already discussed the fact that journalists tend to be better educated than the average American—a difference that has been tied to charges that journalists are more politically liberal than most Americans (Gans, 1985). A college education is not necessarily tied to liberalism, however. Whereas college students of the 1960s and early 1970s tended to be more liberal than their parents, college students in the 1980s have shown a tendency to be more conservative.

This trend is reflected in how journalists' political attitudes changed between 1971 and 1982 (Figure 5.3): Although 38 percent of journalists described themselves as liberal in 1971, only 22 percent did so in 1982. The big increase in 1982 was in the percentage of journalists who described themselves as politically moderate (57.5 percent)—an increase of 19 percent since 1971 (Weaver & Wilhoit, 1986a, p. 26).

Although journalists were not as conservative as the U.S. population in 1982 (nearly 18 percent of journalists rated themselves as conservative, compared with 32 percent of U.S. adults), this did not manifest itself in a clear journalistic preference for liberalism. The proportion of journalists who reported liberal political attitudes in 1982 was almost identical to the proportion of U.S. adults favoring liberalism. Instead of favoring either liberal or conservative ideologies, a majority of journalists in 1982 said that they were "middle of the road" politically.[2]

The arguments have not centered around the average journalist, however, but rather around what Lichter, Rothman, and Lichter (1986) describe as media "elites"—those journalists who work for the most prestigious and influential U.S. media. Between 1979 and 1980, they found that 54 percent of elite journalists are politically liberal and 17 percent are conservative (see Figure 5.3). Of those elite

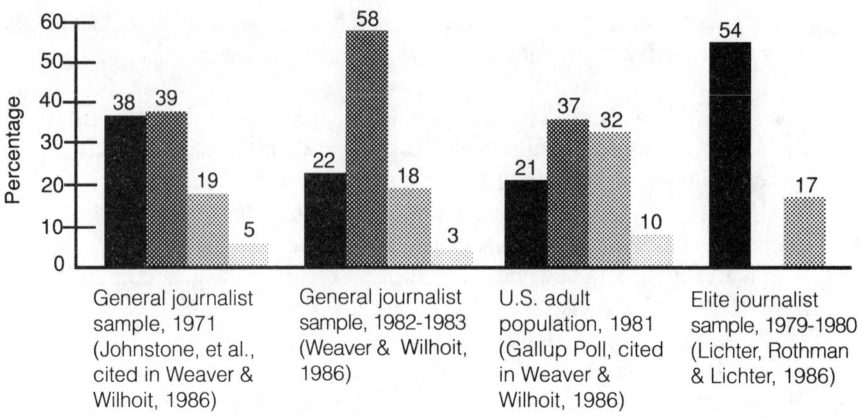

Figure 5.3. Although U.S. journalists in general report being less liberal in 1982 than in 1971, elite journalists are still more liberal than the U.S. adult population.

journalists who voted in presidential elections between 1964 and 1976, more than 80 percent voted for the Democratic candidate in each year (1986, p. 30). This compares with Weaver and Wilhoit's data gathered from a probability sample of U.S. journalists (not just from elites), that show that in 1982–1983, 45 percent of journalists were Democrats, 25 percent were Republicans, and 30 percent were independents (1986, p. 29).

Whether true or not, many individuals persist in their perception of journalists as politically more liberal than the general population, and journalists are not immune to this: In his study of the "elite" Washington press corps, Hess (1981) found that, although Washington journalists also perceive the news corps to have a liberal bias, they rate themselves as being more conservative than this image (p. 115). Hess concluded that elite Washington journalists are more apolitical than press critics imply.

Personal Religious Orientations

Closely tied to arguments about journalists' political orientations is the extent to which journalists are for or against Christianity, Judaism, or other religions. Olasky (1988) says that, although journalism was Christian up until the mid-1800s, modern journalists have been "influenced by anti-Christian humanism and pantheism [and have] abandoned their Christian heritage" (p. xi).

Lichter, Rothman, and Lichter (1986) studied journalism at ten "elite" national media organizations (all headquartered in the Northeast United States), finding that 20 percent are Protestant, about 13 percent are Catholic, and 14 percent are Jewish. About half of the elite journalists studied said that they had no religious affiliation, and 86 percent of elite journalists reported that they "seldom or never attend religious services" (p. 22).

These elite journalists turn out to be considerably more secular than journalists as a whole. Weaver and Wilhoit's (1986a) survey of a random sample of 1,001 journalists from all over the United States in 1982 and 1983 shows a substantially different picture than the one presented by Lichter, Rothman, and Lichter. As Figure 5.4 shows, U.S. journalists as a whole "almost perfectly match the overall society in general religious background," with about 60 percent of journalists saying they are Protestant, 27 percent Catholic, and 6 percent Jewish. Only 7 percent of journalists reported either another or no religious affiliation (Weaver & Wilhoit, 1986a, p. 24).

Influences of Personal Attitudes, Values, and Beliefs on Content

One of the most controversial questions facing those who study mass media content is the extent to which communicators' attitudes, values, and beliefs affect content.

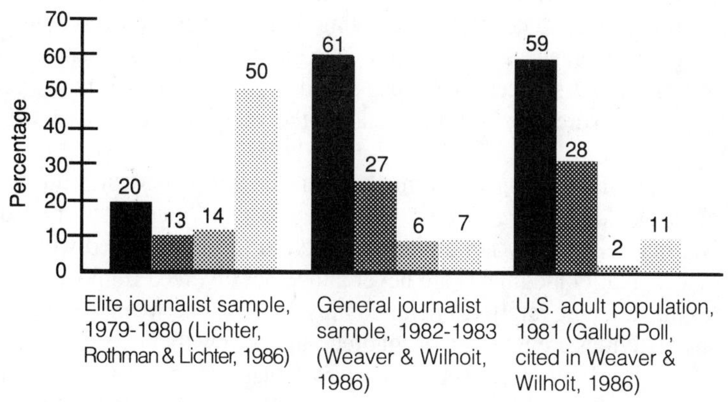

Figure 5.4. Although U.S. journalists in general have religious orientations similar to U.S. adults, journalists in elite media organizations are quite different from U.S. adults.

The existence of an attitude does not necessarily translate directly into behavior: "Bias that counts must be in the copy, not just in the minds of those who write it" (Robinson, 1983, p. 56).

Some critics suggest that journalists consciously bias their news reports in line with their personal attitudes. Although conservative critics charged that journalists treated Ronald Reagan unfairly during his presidency, NBC news commentator John Chancellor says that the press fell under the spell of "the Reagan enchantment" ("A TV newsman's view of Reagan," 1988, p. 69): "The media started out by routinely pointing out inaccurate statements Reagan made in press conferences. But after about 25 such sessions, the President's goofs became routine even for the press. . . . And in the kind of mindless way that journalism has, it wasn't news any more." Bruce Buchanan suggests that journalists were easier on Republicans than Democrats *because of* charges that the media were liberally biased. "I observed in the Reagan administration what I thought was an effort by the media to restrain itself [sic] in direct response to allegations of liberal bias," Buchanan says. "There are observers who believe that this self-restraint continue[d] in the treatment of George Bush during the 1988 campaign" (Tindol, 1988, p. 2). Robinson's 1983 study of how journalists in the eastern United States reported on the 1980 elections supports Buchanan's contention. He found that the supposedly liberal journalists treated Democrats worse than Republicans.

Other scholars believe that the influence of personal attitudes, values, and beliefs is even less direct. These critics suggest that journalists' "worldviews"—their perceptions of social reality—may influence their work. In response to criticism from Herbert Gans about the Lichter-Rothman-Lichter study, Robert Lichter wrote, "We are certainly not saying that attitudes are everything, nor that journalists are ideologues. We're simply saying that news judgment is subjective and decisions about sources, news pegs, and . . . language will partly reflect the way a journalist perceives and understands the social world" ("Face-off," 1987, p. 31).

Gans may have changed his mind about the extent of such influence. In his 1979 book *Deciding What's News,* Gans wrote that "journalists try hard to be objective, but neither they nor anyone else can in the end proceed without values. Furthermore, reality judgments are never altogether divorced from values. . . . The values in the news are rarely explicit and must be found between the lines—in what actors and activities are reported or ignored, and in how they are described" (1979, pp. 39–40). By 1987, however, Gans wrote that organizational constraints and professional norms effectively remove the effects of most journalists' attitudes and values:

> Of course, there are some individuals whose attitudes do matter. Henry Luce had some influence on what *Time* said while he was the editor-in-chief and the owner. William Buckley, another fairly highly opinionated editor, has a great deal of influence, I'm sure, on what the *National Review* puts out. But for rank-and-file journalists, whether they are

> reporters or writers or even news executives, personal attitudes do not affect their work except in unusual circumstances. Moreover, they try to be objective and leave their values at home. ("Face-off," 1987, p. 31)

Another issue involves observed conflicts between the personal attitudes and values held by elite journalists and those held by journalists at large: Do elite journalists have a substantial impact on media content different from the impact of most journalists? Weaver and Wilhoit say that "it is questionable how much influence [the elite journalists] exert over the hundreds of smaller news organizations throughout the country. Certainly with regard to local and regional news, the influence of these media 'elites' is likely to be minimal or nonexistent" (1986a, p. 25). But, as Reese and Danielian (1989) have shown, there may be substantial media "convergence" on issues of national concern. In their study of how five newspapers, three television networks, and two newsmagazines covered cocaine during 1985 and 1986, Reese and Danielian show that when one elite medium picks up a particular story, other media are quick to follow. In the case of cocaine during the mid-1980s, the *New York Times* set the news agenda for the television networks. Thus elite journalists' opinions may in fact have a wider influence than Weaver and Wilhoit assume.

When it comes to filmmakers, however, the expression of values within movies may be more important due to differences in the distribution of movies and television shows compared with news. Actor/director/producer Alan Alda says that some filmmakers try to produce shows that reflect "a responsible set of values" (Newcomb & Alley, 1983, p. 17). Some producers are more aware than others of how their values influence their work. In the early years of his career, producer Norman Lear denied that he was "trying to say" anything with his programs:

> But gradually I began to realize that I was not being honest with myself. . . . Then I began to realize that I was 50 years old, a grown man, with responsibilities and attitudes, and why wouldn't I have thoughts and why wouldn't my work express them? And of course it did! Then it became a question of openly saying, "yes, as a full grown human being with children and concerns and attitudes, who reads a couple of newspapers a day and pays a lot of attention to what is happening to the younger generations, there is much to talk about, much that interests me." (p. 177)

Empirical tests of the extent to which communicators' personal attitudes, values, and beliefs influence their work provide conflicting results:

- Shoemaker (1984) showed that general attitudes about special interest and other political groups can affect how a group is covered by the news media. She correlated data from a content analysis of how legitimately the *New York Times* covered eleven political groups[3] with a survey of U.S. journalists' attitudes toward the groups. The more deviant journalists thought the groups were, the less legitimately the *Times* portrayed the groups.

- Rainville and McCormick (1977) showed that racial prejudice can influence communication. They compared the descriptions of black and white football players by sports announcers. White players got more praise and were more likely to be described as the executors of aggression—a desirable trait in football. Blacks were more likely to be referred to negatively and to be unfairly compared with other players.
- Pasadeos and Renfro (1988) showed that owners can influence newspaper content. They compared the content of the *New York Post* before and after its purchase by media baron Rupert Murdoch, finding that the amount of space devoted to visuals increased substantially and that the *Post* tended to cover stories more sensationally.
- Flegel and Chaffee (1971) found that reporters' stories were influenced more by their personal opinions than by their editors and readers. Even more interesting, this influence was apparently conscious.
- Drew's (1975) study found that students' attitudes toward a source were not related to how favorably their stories treated the source.
- Peterson, Albaum, Kozmetsky, and Cunningham (1984) studied newspaper editors' attitudes toward capitalism as a way of explaining the alleged antibusiness sentiment of the press. They found that newspaper business editors were more favorably disposed toward capitalism than were the general public.

Because of these mixed research findings, we are unable to make any sweeping statements about the influence of communicators' personal attitudes, values, and beliefs on media content. It seems clear that some communicators' attitudes, values, and beliefs affect some content at least some of the time, but such a weak assertion is practically worthless. It is possible that when communicators have more power over their messages and work under fewer constraints, their personal attitudes, values, and beliefs have more opportunity to influence content (see Figure 5.1). As Gans (1985) points out, the routines and constraints imposed by the media organization *may* negate the influence of personal attitudes, values, and beliefs. But we must also realize that the power of organizational routines and constraints varies from organization to organization, probably inversely with the effects of the individual communicator's attitudes, values, and beliefs. Organizational influences are dealt with in Chapters 6 and 7.

PROFESSIONAL ROLES AND ETHICS

Finally we consider how mass media content may be affected by communicators' professional roles and ethical frameworks. We treat these job-related orientations separately from communicators' personal attitudes, values, and beliefs, which are primarily shaped by forces outside of mass communication, such as their personal characteristics, backgrounds, and experiences. By contrast, communicators' professional and ethical orientations are primarily shaped on the job (or in professional education), through a process that Breed (1960) describes as socialization:[4] The new journalist "discovers and internalizes the rights and obligations of his status and its norms and values" (Breed, 1960, p. 182).

In his study of the socialization of newspaper journalists, Breed (1960) describes how journalists learn what their organizations want by observation and experience. As young journalists read the newspapers they work for or watch their television stations' newscasts, they learn a lot about the norms of the community and how reporters cover controversy. Are Democratic and Republican candidates treated in the same way? What about Libertarian or Socialist party candidates? They also learn from the editing process, which gives new journalists direct feedback about what is acceptable in stories. If your editor consistently deletes references to a politician's personal life, then you quickly learn that "policy" discourages it. Sometimes policy is conveyed through gossip, as journalists get together after work and discuss their superiors' actions. New journalists quickly learn what the boss likes from more experienced staffers.

Breed adds that direct communication of policy from the editor or publisher/manager is rare. New employees learn "by osmosis" (p. 182), such as by listening to their superiors discuss the pros and cons of various news stories. Policy information is carried not only by what executives say, but also by what they don't say.

The rewards for quickly learning and following policy are from coworkers and employers within the media organization—not from the audience. Socialization to your medium's policies gives you what Sigal (1973, p. 3) calls "a context of shared values" with those around you. These values shape the context in which events are viewed and the selection of the aspects of each event that will become the news.

Professional Roles

Is journalism a profession? The answer depends on which set of criteria you use. One defines a profession as having the following characteristics (Lambeth, 1986, p. 82):

1. *It is a full-time occupation.* This is certainly true of a large proportion of journalists.
2. *Its practitioners are deeply committed to the goals of the profession.* Journalists are probably not as committed to journalism as physicians are to medicine. Although an early commitment to social reforms may lead people to journalism as a career in early adulthood, many people leave journalism for other fields.
3. *Entrance to and continuance in the profession are governed by a formal organization that has established professional standards.* There is no licensing authority for journalists, and, although codes of ethics and

professional standards are recommended by many journalism organizations, one need not adopt any of these to be a journalist. To be a journalist requires only that someone hire you.

4. *Its practitioners are admitted to the profession following prescribed formal schooling and the acquisition of a specialized body of knowledge*. Although most journalists today have college training in journalism, no journalism degree (or any other degree, for that matter) is required. Not only do journalism school curricula differ dramatically, but it can also be said that no specific body of *knowledge* exists to be mastered by potential journalists. Aside from mastering writing and production skills, journalists are educated as generalists; they are expected to know a little about a lot of areas. Although most journalism schools require courses in communication law, ethics, theory, and history, these are often barely tolerated by journalism students, who see them as peripheral to learning skills.
5. *It must serve society*. Although critics suggest that the business aspects of the mass media eclipse their service role, more journalists would agree that the mass media (at least the news media) service society through transmitting information, providing a context for events, socializing new members of society, and entertaining.
6. *Its members must have a high degree of autonomy*. Although some journalists have more autonomy than others, journalists as a group are subject to a wide range of organizational constraints that dictate what they do and when they do it.

Journalism doesn't fit these professionalism criteria very well. Although most journalists work full time, are (at least for a while) committed to their jobs, and perform services that aid society, there is no mechanism for enforcing professional standards or for prescribing formal schooling and the acquisition of a body of knowledge, and journalists' autonomy is limited by organizational constraints.

Whether journalism meets such criteria is for all practical purposes irrelevant—many journalists think of themselves as professionals, and they share conceptions of what a professional journalist is supposed to be like. But do journalists' feelings about their professionalism affect the stories they write and edit? Weaver and Wilhoit conclude that media organizations exert many bureaucratic controls over the production of media content, and these controls limit the influence of individual journalists' professional orientations. Thus, journalists are "*of* a profession but not *in* one" (1986a, p. 145). They may not be able to attain professionalism in the same way that physicians do.

Attempts at devising an index to measure journalists' professionalism have had mixed results. Indices developed by McLeod and Hawley (1964), Wright (1976), Weinthal and O'Keefe (1974), and Idsvoog and Hoyt (1977) do not appear to be measuring the same things, leading to different conclusions about professional journalists' demographic characteristics and attitudes (Henningham, 1984).

Johnstone, Slawski, and Bowman (1972) found that some journalists consider themselves "neutrals," seeing their jobs as mere channels of transmission, and that others see themselves as "participants," believing that journalists need to sift through information in order to find and develop the story. Neutral journalists see their jobs as getting information to the public quickly, avoiding stories with unverified content, concentrating on the widest audience, and entertaining the audience. Participants see their jobs as investigating government claims, providing analysis of complex problems, discussing national policy, and developing intellectual/cultural interests. In the Johnstone study, participant journalists tended to be younger than neutrals, they had more education, and they worked for larger media organizations.

In their 1982–1983 extension and replication of the Johnstone study, Weaver and Wilhoit added two items to the media role index—serving as adversary of government and of business—wondering if the participant role would extend to this adversary relationship. Weaver and Wilhoit thereby identified three journalistic role conceptions (1986a, pp. 112–117):

- The *interpretive* function—investigating official claims, analyzing complex problems, and discussing national policy—is the dominant professional role of modern U.S. journalists. More than 60 percent of surveyed journalists scored very high on the interpretive scale. Print journalists tended to see it as somewhat more important than did broadcast journalists.
- The *dissemination* function—getting information to the public quickly and concentrating on the widest audience—is also very important, with more than half of U.S. journalists scoring very high on this scale. About a third of journalists scored high on both the investigation and dissemination functions. Although print and broadcast journalists agreed about the need to get news out quickly, radio journalists tended to value wide audiences the most, and newsmagazine journalists the least.
- The *adversary* function—serving as an adversary of officials or of business —is a relatively minor role. Only 17 percent of U.S. journalists scored very high on the adversary scale, and there was little overlap between the adversary function and the other two. Print journalists were the most likely to value the adversary role, with radio journalists valuing it least.

Because of the substantial overlap among the roles—only 2 percent of journalists in 1983 fell into one category exclusively, compared with 18 percent in the 1971 Johnstone study—Weaver and Wilhoit conclude that "a large majority see their professional role as highly pluralistic. . . . The modern journalist attempts to blend the classical critical role of the journalist—as interpreter or contemporary historian—with the technical requirements of disseminating great volumes of descriptive information" (1986a, p. 144).

Ethical Roles

Journalists' beliefs about what is ethical can exert an overt influence on media content. Although journalism as a whole lacks an enforceable code of ethics, this is not for lack of possibilities. In 1988, more than 58 percent of newspapers had published standards governing how their staffs should operate ("Two recent studies," 1988, p. 5). For example, the *Milwaukee Journal* published its "Rules and Guidelines" in 1978 to explain that its news-editorial employees are to avoid participating in community activities that could create a conflict of interest "or give the impression of one" ("Rules and Guidelines," 1978, p. 3). Employees also are forbidden to work in public relations and/or for a political candidate.

Society of Professional Journalists Code of Ethics

SOCIETY of Professional Journalists, believes the duty of journalists is to serve the truth.

We BELIEVE the agencies of mass communication are carriers of public discussion and information, acting on their Constitutional mandate and freedom to learn and report the facts.

We BELIEVE in public enlightenment as the forerunner of justice, and in our Constitutional role to seek the truth as part of the public's right to know the truth.

We BELIEVE those responsibilities carry obligations that require journalists to perform with intelligence, objectivity, accuracy, and fairness.

To these ends, we declare acceptance of the standards of practice here set forth:

I. Responsibility:

The public's right to know of events of public importance and interest is the overriding mission of the mass media. The purpose of distributing news and enlightened opinion is to serve the general welfare. Journalists who use their professional status as representatives of the public for selfish or other unworthy motives violate a high trust.

II. Freedom of the Press:

Freedom of the press is to be guarded as an inalienable right of people in a free society. It carries with it the freedom and the responsibility to discuss, question, and challenge actions and utterances of our government and of our public and private institutions. Journalists uphold the right to speak unpopular opinions and the privilege to agree with the majority.

III. Ethics:

Journalists must be free of obligation to any interest other than the public's right to know the truth.

1. Gifts, favors, free travel, special treatment or privileges can compromise the integrity of journalists and their employers. Nothing of value should be accepted.

2. Secondary employment, political involvement, holding public office, and service in community organizations should be avoided if it compromises the integrity of journalists and their employers. Journalists and their employers should conduct their personal lives in a manner that protects them from conflict of interest, real or apparent. Their responsibilities to the public are paramount. That is the nature of their profession.

3. So-called news communications from private sources should not be published or broadcast without substantiation of their claims to news values.

4. Journalists will seek news that serves the public interest, despite the obstacles. They will make constant efforts to assure that the public's business is conducted in public and that public records are open to public inspection.

5. Journalists acknowledge the newsman's ethic of protecting confidential sources of information.

6. Plagiarism is dishonest and unacceptable.

IV. Accuracy and Objectivity:

Good faith with the public is the foundation of all worthy journalism.

1. Truth is our ultimate goal.

2. Objectivity in reporting the news is another goal that serves as the mark of an experienced professional. It is a standard of performance toward which we strive. We honor those who achieve it.

3. There is no excuse for inaccuracies or lack of thoroughness.

4. Newspaper headlines should be fully warranted by the contents of the articles they accompany. Photographs and telecasts should give an accurate picture of an event and not highlight an incident out of context.

5. Sound practice makes clear distinction between news reports and expressions of opinion. News reports should be free of opinion or bias and represent all sides of an issue.

6. Partisanship in editorial comment that knowingly departs from the truth violates the spirit of American journalism.

7. Journalists recognize their responsibility for offering informed analysis, comment, and editorial opinion on public events and issues. They accept the obligation to present such material by individuals whose competence, experience, and judgment qualify them for it.

8. Special articles or presentations devoted to advocacy or the writer's own conclusions and interpretations should be labeled as such.

V. Fair Play:

Journalists at all times will show respect for the dignity, privacy, rights, and well-being of people encountered in the course of gathering and presenting the news.

1. The news media should not communicate unofficial charges affecting reputation or moral character without giving the accused a chance to reply.

2. The news media must guard against invading a person's right to privacy.

3. The media should not pander to morbid curiosity about details of vice and crime.

4. It is the duty of news media to make prompt and complete correction of their errors.

5. Journalists should be accountable to the public for their reports and the public should be encouraged to voice its grievances against the media. Open dialogue with our readers, viewers, and listeners should be fostered.

VI. Mutual Trust:

Adherence to this code is intended to preserve and strengthen the bond of mutual trust and respect between American journalists and the American people.

The Society shall—by programs of educational and other means—encourage individual journalists to adhere to these tenets, and shall encourage journalistic publications and broadcasters to recognize their responsibility to frame codes of ethics in concert with their employees to serve as guidelines in furthering these goals.

CODE OF ETHICS (Adopted 1926; revised 1973, 1984, 1987)

The *Minneapolis Star* "Code of Conduct" (cited in Dennis, 1981), warns staff members against holding stock in local companies. Although it is sometimes considered ethical to receive tickets and meals from sources, other gifts and free trips generally are not acceptable (*Los Angeles Times'* Code of Ethics, cited in Itule, 1987; *Washington Post* Standards and Ethics, cited in Fedler, 1984). The preceding code of ethics adopted by the Society of Professional Journalists and its members addresses journalists' responsibilities to the public, freedom of the press, ethics, accuracy and objectivity, and fair play.

Sometimes it easn't easy to avoid ethical problems. Conflicts of interest can arise from the very nature of the journalists' assignments. For example, crime reporters must gain enough trust from their police sources to elicit cooperation, but such a cooperative relationship could create a conflict of interest in stories about wrongdoing in the police department. Chibnall (1981) says that crime reporters "are obliged to defend and promote the interests of police unless they can be clearly shown to be in conflict with the interests of the public. . . . Such beliefs reinforce already existent predispositions to construct public accounts which are generally favourable to agencies of social control" (p. 93).

Some journalists take a simpler view toward ethics, equating it with objectivity (Merrill, 1985). Still others may equate ethical behavior with truth telling, but which truth? Definitions of truth shift over time and between sources (Christians,

Rotzoll, & Fackler, 1987). Some journalists take refuge in what Tuchman (1972) calls "objectivity as strategic ritual," devising a set of rules that, once followed, allow the journalist to protect himself/herself against criticism. Institutionalized ethical strategies such as directly quoting what others say (whether true or not) and presenting "both sides" of an argument will be discussed at length in the next chapter.

Some journalists oppose the publication of written standards because such standards may make journalists "more vulnerable to liability in libel cases." Even if a mass medium has not published its own standards, however, "codes of professional groups or testimony by expert witnesses may be introduced into a case in an at tempt to prove malice or negligence by a newspaper" ("Two recent studies," 1988, p. 5).

In the final analysis, however, no code of conduct can prescribe behavior in every possible situation; interpretation of ethical standards and specific decisions must be made by individual journalists. Editors were presented with such a decision when Pennsylvania treasurer R. Budd Dwyer committed suicide during a news conference in 1987. Both still photos and video of Dwyer putting the gun in his mouth and pulling the trigger were available. Although some local television stations broadcast the actual suicide, none of the national networks did. Although neither ABC nor CBS used video of the press conference, NBC and CNN showed footage of Dwyer reading his statement and waving his gun—they cut away the actual shooting. In explaining the decision, CNN spokeswoman Judi Borza said, "We didn't feel it was necessary to actually show the man putting the gun in his mouth and shooting himself." NBC spokesman Andrew Freedman said, "We feel it is too unsettling for our viewers" ("Graphic suicide," 1987).

Such decisions are often made after consideration of whether the publication of sensational photographs will cause additional suffering to victims or to their families. The media's traditional justification of "the public's right to know" has increasingly been questioned as public complaints increase and lawsuits charging invasion of privacy are filed (Clark, 1988).

Weaver and Wilhoit (1986a, pp. 128–132) addressed such ethical decisions in their national survey of journalists. Only 5 percent of journalists could see any justification for divulging a confidential source, whereas 20 percent approved claiming to be someone else in order to get a story. Just over one-fourth of journalists approved of paying people for confidential information or using personal documents such as letters without permission. Around half of journalists thought that badgering unwilling informants or using confidential business or government documents without authorization are justified. About two-thirds of journalists accepted going undercover as an employee of a company in order to gain inside information about it. Older journalists were less likely to approve such practices; journalists working for large organizations were more likely to approve them.

In the same study, about three-fourths of journalists credited newsroom socialization or their family upbringings with influencing their ethical standards. Half or more said that fellow journalists or college professors had influenced them (Weaver & Wilhoit, 1986a, p. 135).

Effects of Professional Roles and Ethics on Content

It seems clear that the way journalists define their jobs will affect the content they produce. Journalists who see themselves as disseminators/neutrals should write very different accounts of an event than those who see themselves as interpreters/participants. Some evidence for this was provided by Starck and Soloski's (1977) study of student reporters: Journalism students who saw themselves as neutrals wrote the least fair and comprehensive stories. The most objective and accurate stories were written by students who saw themselves as midway between the extreme neutral and the extreme participant role.

The role of ethical judgments is easier to assess. Whether a decision to publish a certain photograph is based on published codes of conduct or on an individual's personal decision, the decision has a concrete effect on media content. More interesting, however, are situations when ethical standards may clash with one another or with values. Breed pointed out in 1964 that ethical standards can clash with other values, such as public decency, respect for convention, and orderliness. "Accurate reporting is sometimes sacrificed to these other virtues of respect, decency, and order, that is, the mass media have often placed more emphasis on some value other than truth" (p. 183).

SUMMARY

We have investigated how communication workers' characteristics, personal and professional backgrounds, personal attitudes, and professional roles can influence media content. Although it is easy to show that the "average" journalist and the "average" adult American don't look entirely alike, it is difficult to determine what influence journalists' characteristics have on their work. For example, although women and minorities are gaining ground in communication careers, many people believe that the media's practices and routines effectively suppress effects on content due to gender or ethnicity.

Certainly, the fact that journalists are well educated affects media content, but in at least one favorable way—the public would be little served by illiterate journalists. Still, journalists' education (as well as their other background experiences and characteristics) may influence the way in which they see the world, a potentially far-reaching effect on what is selected to report and on how it is reported.

Figure 5.2 shows how factors intrinsic to the communicator may interact to influence media content. We believe that there is no direct influence of communicators' characteristics, backgrounds, and experiences on media content, but content may be affected to the extent that such factors influence both personal and professional attitudes and roles. Of these two sets of attitudinal variables, we believe that communicators' professional roles and ethics have more of an influence on content than do their personal attitudes, values, and beliefs. Not only is the suppression of personal attitudes, values, and beliefs part of the professional communicator's role; the exertion of personal will within a mass media organization takes more power than most communicators can wield. Even the power of publishers and television station owners can be limited by boards of directors, audiences, and advertisers. However, even communicators who are not in ownership or managerial positions can sometimes influence the direction of content. For example, a reporter for a West Coast newspaper who is based in Washington, D.C., has substantially more control over the selection and direction of stories than the reporter working out of the newspaper's main offices, under the direct supervision of management.

Professional roles, on the other hand, determine what the communicator thinks is worth transmitting to his or her audience and how the story should be developed. As we will see in the next two chapters, such organizationally defined factors have direct impact on mass media content.

NOTES

1. Weaver and Wilhoit's figures are based on people who work in news-related jobs at daily and weekly newspapers, newsmagazines, news services, and radio and television stations. They do not include workers in public relations, advertising, or entertainment jobs.
2. A survey of Texas and Louisiana high school students in 1983 showed similar results. High school journalists' attitudes were no more liberal than those held by nonjournalists (Johnson, 1987).
3. The groups included (from least to most deviant) were League of Women Voters, Sierra Club, Common Cause, NAACP, NOW, NRA, Moral Majority, Jewish Defense League, Communists, KKK, Nazis.
4. Professional roles can also be learned in journalism school, according to Becker, Fruit, and Caudill (1987), but early job experiences tend to alter the professional roles learned in school.

REFERENCES

Becker, L. B., Fruit, J. W., & Caudill, S. L. (1987). *The training and hiring of journalists.* Norwood, NJ: Ablex.

Braden, W. (1981). LSD and the press. In S. Cohen & J. Young (Eds.), *The manufacture of news: Deviance, social problems and the mass media* (pp. 248–262). Beverly Hills, CA: Sage.

Breed, W. (1960). Social control in the newsroom: A functional analysis. In W. Schramm (Ed.), *Mass communications* (pp. 178–194). Urbana: University of Illinois Press. Reprinted from *Social Forces, 33* (1955), 326–335.

Breed, W. (1964). Mass communication and sociocultural integration. In L. A. Dexter & D. M. White (Eds.), *People, society, and mass communications* (pp. 183–201). New York: Free Press.

Bureau of Labor Statistics. (1988, April). *Occupational outlook handbook.* (U.S. Department of Labor). Washington, DC: U.S. Government Printing Office.

Burgoon, J. K., Burgoon, M., & Atkin, C. K. (1982). *The world of the working journalist*. New York: Newspaper Advertising Bureau.

Cantor, M. G. (1988). *The Hollywood TV producer: His work and his audience*. New Brunswick, NJ: Transaction.

Chibnall, S. (1981). The production of knowledge by crime reporters. In S. Cohen and J. Young (Eds.), *The manufacture of news. Deviance, social problems, and the mass media* (pp. 75–97). London: Constable.

Christ, W. G., & Blanchard, R. O. (1988). Pro education: Who needs it? *Journalism Educator, 43*, 62–64.

Christians, C. G., Rotzoll, K. B., & Fackler, M. (1987). *Media ethics: Cases and moral reasoning*. New York: Longman.

Clark, R. P. (1988). Covering crime: Journalists face difficult choices. *Crime victims and the news media*. Forth Worth, TX: Fort Worth Star-Telegram.

Dennis, E. E. (1981). *Reporting processes and practices: Newswriting for today's readers*. Belmont, CA: Wadsworth.

Dennis, E. E. (1988). Whatever happened to Marse Robert's dream? The dilemma of American journalism education. *Gannett Center Journal, 2*, 1–22.

Drew, D. G. (1975). Reporters' attitudes, expected meetings with social and journalistic objectivity. *Journalism Quarterly, 52*, 219–224.

Ettema, J. S. (1988). *The craft of the investigative journalist*. Chicago: Institute of Modern Communication, Northwestern University.

Face-off. (1987, September). *Washington Journalism Review*.

Farley, J. (1978). Women's magazines and the equal rights amendment: Friend or foe? *Journal of Communication, 28*, 187–192.

Fedler, F. (1984). *Reporting for the print media*. San Diego, CA: Harcourt Brace Jovanovich.

Fink, C. C. (1990). *Inside the media*. New York: Longman.

Flegel, R. C., & Chaffee, S. H. (1971). Influences of editors, readers, and personal opinions on reporters. *Journalism Quarterly, 48*, 645–651.

Footlick, J. K. (1988). Eleven exemplary journalism schools. *Gannett Center Journal, 2*, 68–76.

Gans, H. J. (1979). *Deciding what's news*. New York: Pantheon.

Gans, H. J. (1985, November–December). Are U.S. journalists dangerously liberal? *Columbia Journalism Review*, pp. 29–33.

Graphic suicide pictures stir newsroom debates. (1987, January 23). *Austin American-Statesman*, p. A6.

Great careers, modest beginnings. (1988). *Gannett Center Journal, 2*, 33–48.

Greenberg, B. S., Burgoon, M., Burgoon, J. K., & Korzenny, F. (1983). *Mexican Americans and the mass media*. Norwood, NJ: Ablex.

Hart, J. R. (1976). Horatio Alger in the newsroom: Social origins of American editors. *Journalism Quarterly, 53*, 14–20.

Henningham, J. P. (1984). Comparisons between three versions of the professional orientation index. *Journalism Quarterly, 61*, 302–309.

Hess, S. (1981). *The Washington reporters*. Washington, DC: Brookings Institution.

Idsvoog, K. A., & Hoyt, J. L. (1977). Professionalism and performance of television journalists. *Journal of Broadcasting, 21*, 97–109.

Itule, B. D. (1987). *Newswriting and reporting for today's media*. New York: Random House.

Johnson, S. (1987). A comparison of attitudes and backgrounds of high school journalists with high school non-journalists. *Southwestern Mass Communication Journal, 3,* 103–113.

Johnstone, J. W. C., Slawski, E. J., & Bowman, W. W. (1972). The professional values of American newsmen. *Public Opinion Quarterly, 36,* 522–540.

Kuralt, C. (1986). *The view from the road: The Red Smith lecture in journalism.* South Bend, IN: University of Notre Dame.

Lambeth, E. B. (1986). *Committed journalism: An ethic for the profession.* Bloomington: Indiana University Press.

Lawrence, D., Jr. (1988, August/September). Hispanics: An overlooked minority? *Minorities in the newspaper business,* p. 1.

Lichter, S. R., Rothman, S., & Lichter, L. S. (1986). *The media elite.* Bethesda, MD: Adler & Adler.

Mann, R. (1988). Students reject news-ed due to negative views. *Journalism Educator, 43,* 60–62.

McCombs, M. E. (1988). Test the myths: A statistical review 1967–86. *Gannett Center Journal, 2,* 101–108.

McLeod, J. M., & Hawley, S. E., Jr. (1964). Professionalism among newsmen. *Journalism Quarterly, 41,* 529–538.

Merrill, J. C. (1985). Is ethical journalism simply objective reporting? *Journalism Quarterly, 62,* 391–393.

Newcomb, H., & Alley, R. S. (1983). *The producer's medium.* London: Oxford University Press.

Of 1987 J-graduates hired by newspapers, only 7.8 percent minorities. (1988, June). *Presstime,* p. 100.

Olasky, M. (1988). *Prodigal press: The anti-Christian bias of the American news media.* Westchester, IL: Crossway.

Paletz, D. L., & Entman, R. M. (1981). *Media, power, politics.* New York: Free Press.

Pasadeos, Y., & Renfro, P. (1988). Rupert Murdoch's style: The New York Post. *Newspaper Research Journal, 9,* 25–34.

Peterson, R. A., Albaum, G., Kozmetsky, G., & Cunningham, I. C. M. (1984). Attitudes of newspaper business editors and general public toward capitalism. *Journalism Quarterly, 61,* 56–65.

Rainville, R. E., & McCormick, E. (1977). Extent of covert racial prejudice in pro football announcers' speech. *Journalism Quarterly, 54,* 20–26.

Reese, S. D., & Danielian, L. H. (1989). Intermedia influence and the drug issue: Converging on cocaine. In P. J. Shoemaker (Ed.), *Communication campaigns about drugs: Government, media, public* (pp. 29–46). Hillsdale, NJ: Lawrence Erlbaum.

Robinson, M. J. (1983, February/March). Just how liberal is the news? 1980 revisited. *Public Opinion,* pp. 55–60.

Rules and guidelines. (1978, February 12). *Milwaukee Journal,* p. 3.

Shoemaker, P. J. (1984). Media treatment of deviant political groups. *Journalism Quarterly, 61,* 66–75, 82.

Shoemaker, P. J. (1987). Mass communication by the book: A review of 31 texts. *Journal of Communication, 37,* 109–131.

Sigal, L. V. (1973). Reporters and officials: The organization and politics of newsmaking. Lexington, MA: D. C. Heath.

Shuster, S. (1988, May/June). Foreign competition hits the news. *Columbia Journalism Review,* pp. 43–45.

Starck, K., & Soloski, J. (1977). Effect of reporter predisposition in covering controversial story. *Journalism Quarterly, 54,* 120–125.

Stein, M. L. (1985). *Getting and writing the news.* New York: Longman.

Stone, V. A. (1987). Changing profiles of news directors of radio and TV stations, 1972–1986, *Journalism Quarterly, 64,* 745–749.

Storad, C. J. (1984). Who are the metropolitan daily newspaper science journalists, and how do they work? *Newspaper Research Journal, 6,* 39–48.

Tindol, R. (1988, October 24–30). Liberal bias allegations in media. *On Campus* (University of Texas at Austin), p. 2.

Tuchman, G. (1972). Objectivity as strategic ritual: An examination of newsmen's notions of objectivity. *American Journal of Sociology, 77,* 660–679.

A TV newsman's view of Reagan. (1988, June). *Presstime, 10,* p. 69.

Two recent studies explored newsroom standards. (1988, February). *The Editors' Exchange, 11,* p. 5.

Weaver, D. H., & Wilhoit, G. C. (1986a). *The American journalist: A portrait of U.S. news people and their work.* Bloomington: Indiana University Press.

Weaver, D. H., & Wilhoit, G. C. (1986b). A profile of JMC educators: Traits, attitudes, and values. *Journalism Educator, 43,* 4–41.

Weinthal, D. S., & O'Keefe, G. J. (1974). Professionalism among broadcast newsmen in an urban area. *Journal of Broadcasting, 18,* 193–209.

Winship, T. (1988). Genes, romance, and nepotism: And other essential qualifications for the journalist. *Gannett Center Journal, 2,* 23–32.

Wright, D. K. (1976). Professionalism levels of British Columbia's broadcast journalists: A communicator analysis. *Gazette, 22,* 38–48.

CHAPTER 6

Influence of Media Routines

In order to better understand mass media workers, we must next look at the routines that go with their jobs. Karl Mannheim, a German sociologist, wrote that "strictly speaking it is incorrect to say that the single individual thinks. Rather it is more correct to insist that the individual participates in thinking further what others have thought before" (Mannheim, 1936/1964, p. 29). In other words, people are social creatures and participate in patterns of action that they themselves did not create. They speak the language of their group, think as their group thinks. As individuals in groups, they have developed styles of thought from an endless pattern of response to common situations.

We refer to something similar with the term *routines,* those patterned, routinized, repeated practices and forms that media workers use to do their jobs. From Mannheim's perspective we can view these routines as a set of constraints on the individual media worker (see Figure 6.1). Routines form the immediate context, within and through which these individuals do their job.

To illustrate, consider the *gatekeeper* label commonly applied to mass media decision makers. This term bridges the inner core and the outer ring of our model in Figure 6.1 and helps remind us that the individual is filling a role and serving a function within a larger system of gates. Whether in news or entertainment industries, the media gatekeeper must winnow down a large number of potential messages to a few. The book publisher chooses from many possible titles, the network programmer selects from among several ideas for sitcoms, serials, and dramas to compose a prime-time schedule, and the newspaper editor must decide on a handful of stories to run on the front page. These decisions directly affect the media content that reaches the audience. But are those decisions made at the whim of the individual?

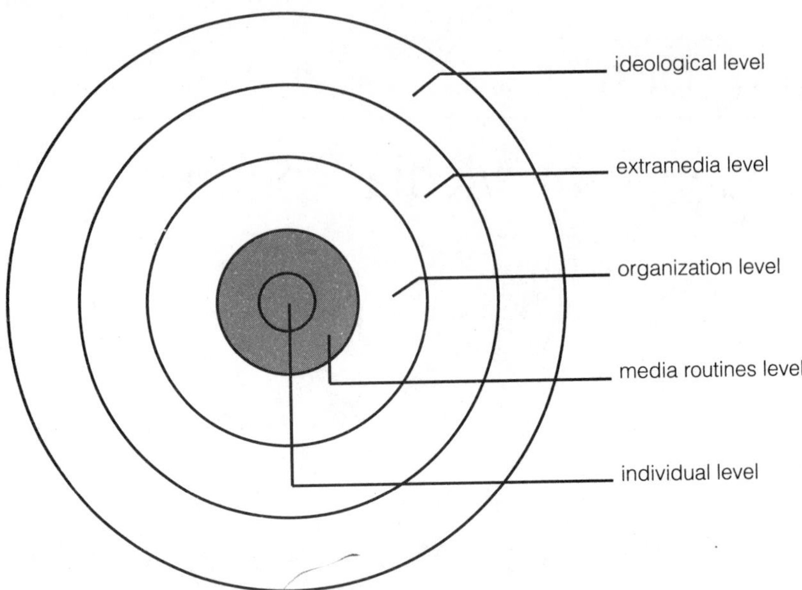

Figure 6.1. Influences of media routines on media content in hierarchical model

Perhaps. The popular notion is that they are. The public knows the personal side of gatekeepers best. Journalists are often romanticized as crusading editors or as fearless investigative reporters like Bob Woodward and Carl Bernstein, whose work helped bring down a president and was popularized in the movie *All The President's Men*. The library shelves are packed with journalists' memoirs, telling of their hobnobbing with the great and near-great.

These gatekeepers, however, represent their respective professions and organizations. As such, the occupational setting limits their decisions. To understand these limits we have to consider the media system within which people work, including the routines and craft norms that are so much a part of systematic information-gathering. The standardized, recurring patterns of news and entertainment content result in large part from these routine practices. These routines ensure that the media system will respond in predictable ways and cannot be easily violated. They form a cohesive set of rules and become integral parts of what it means to be a media professional. Tuchman (1977a), for example, notes that reporters who have mastered routine modes of processing news are valued for their professionalism (what questions to ask, how to handle hard and soft stories, what techniques are appropriate to each). Routines may be considered means to an end, but often these means, having become institutionalized, take on a life of their own.

The study of media routines is linked to an organizational perspective on the mass media. In recommending that approach, Paul Hirsch (1977) says that the mass media may serve different functions, but they share many organizational similarities that outweigh many of the differences. For example, Hirsch notes:

> This perspective finds clear analytical similarities among the constraints on and organizational context in which reporters, writers, artists, actors, directors, editors, producers, publishers, executive vice-presidents, and others learn and carry out activities characteristic of the respective roles, crafts and occupations. (p. 15)

Thus, whether news or entertainment, print or broadcast, from the *New York Times* to the *National Enquirer,* we can ask: What are the stable, patterned sets of expectations and constraints that are common to most media organizations? All these messages are symbolic content, produced according to practical considerations. Routines develop in response to these considerations and help the organization cope with the tasks at hand. Although entertainment and news organizations may be thought of in much the same way, in the remainder of this chapter we focus primarily on journalists. Much more research has been directed at this group than at their entertainment counterparts.

In analyzing this impact, most attention has been directed at the day-to-day activities of lower level media workers: reporters, editors, writers. The routines of media practice constitute the immediate environment of these media workers. Although publishers and news vice presidents are also bound by routines, higher-level media workers like these are perhaps given greater range of movement (we address their influence later). (Note that media routines correspond to what Paul Hirsch [1977] calls the occupational level, within which attention is directed to the socialization of media workers and their interactions with the larger organization.)

In addition to the gatekeeper, another familiar metaphor helps illustrate how different organization needs dictate different routines and the tensions that often exist between the media worker and the needs of the larger organization. Although we don't normally think of newswork as a blue-collar occupation, the production of television news is, in many respects, organized like a factory. All organizations desire routinization to improve efficiency, but some require it more than others. In observing a local television news station, Charles Bantz and his colleagues found that several factors produced routinization in television news. Television newspeople change jobs more often than print journalists, creating a continual turnover in personnel, which makes easily learned routines essential for smooth organizational continuity. Television news requires careful coordination of complex technologies (such as videotape editing, microwave and satellite transmissions) requiring specialized roles, scheduling, and other routinized procedures to bring it off smoothly. In addition, competition has led stations to rely on news consultants who prescribe formulaic guidelines for the number of stories and their length. These factors, according to Bantz and colleagues, emphasize "technically uniform, visually sophisticated, easy to understand, fast-paced, people-oriented stories that are produced in a minimum amount of time" (Bantz, McCorkle, & Baade, 1981, p. 371).

Bantz argues that a television newsroom resembles a "news factory" that divides tasks into chunks at different stages along the "assembly line": from story ideas to presenting the newscast. This highly routinized structure often lacks flexibility. A microwave van operator, for example, told to help with a live remote report on an unexpected snowstorm, angrily complained: "It wasn't planned." For the newsworkers, the highly specialized factory structure means they lack personal investment in and control over the final news product. Furthermore, the factory environment does not encourage such professional values espoused by newsworkers who are evaluated on their productivity—doing the assignment on time, rather than necessarily well, as epitomized by the "quick and dirty" story. Thus, the routines of the news organization don't always mesh with the individual professional goals of its members.

Ultimately, routines are important because they affect the social reality portrayed by the media. As Altheide (1976, p. 24) says, "the organizational, practical, and other mundane features of newswork promote a way of looking at events which fundamentally distorts them." Indeed, sociologists like Tuchman (1977a) even suggest that routines make news by allowing everyday occurrences to be recognized and reconstituted. Similarly, sociologists like Molotch and Lester (1974) argue that there are no free-standing newsworthy events "out there," but rather occurrences, promoted to the status of "events" by either sources or the media. To understand what becomes news we must understand the routines that go into its construction.

SOURCES OF ROUTINES: PROCESSOR/CONSUMER/SUPPLIER

As we have already suggested, media routines don't develop randomly. Given finite organizational resources and an infinite supply of potential raw material, routines are practical responses to the needs of media organizations and workers. The job of these media organizations is to deliver, within time and space limitations, the most acceptable product to the consumer in the most efficient manner. Since most media are profit-making enterprises, they strive to make a product that can be sold for more than the costs of production. A media organization can be described much like any other business that strives to find a market for its product. Media must obtain and process "raw product" (news, comedy), usually obtained from "suppliers" (officials, playwrights) outside the organization, then deliver it to "consumers" (readers, viewers, and listeners). At each stage, the organization must adapt to constraints—limitations on what it can do.

With this in mind, we can think of media routines as stemming from constraints related to these three stages. These routines help the media organization address the following questions: (1) What is acceptable to the consumer (audience)? (2) What is the organization (media) capable of processing? (3) What raw product is available from suppliers (sources)? In a newsroom, for example, an editor must consider all three questions in deciding which stories to publish: What stories are available, which ones would appeal to an audience, and which satisfy the needs of the organization (space requirements, etc.)?

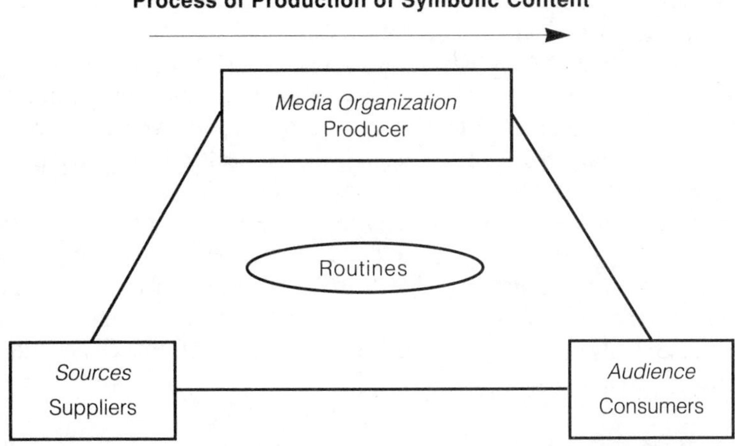

Figure 6.2. Media routines as related to three sources of constraints

These three stages are represented in Figure 6.2. Each media routine can be visualized as fitting somewhere in the triangle formed by these three stages. Depending on the needs that they serve, routines may be closer to one than the others. Of course, these often overlap. A routine may serve both audience and organization requirements. Newspaper stories, for example, are often written in an *inverted pyramid* style, with facts listed in order of decreasing importance. Readers can stop after a few paragraphs, knowing that they've read the most important information; an editor can trim such stories from the bottom up to fit available space, without having to rewrite the entire story. In the early days, it was said that telegraph operators strove to get the most important facts over the wire first, in the event that the transmission was lost before they finished tapping the whole story (Schudson, 1978). Thus, the inverted pyramid routine relates to needs of both the organization and the audience. It has relatively little to do with sources/suppliers. Conceptually, a routine located in the exact middle of the triangle would serve all three needs equally. Each routine may be said to strike some balance between all three constraints—none of which can be ignored completely.

AUDIENCE ORIENTED: CONSUMER

The mass media spend a lot of money finding out about their audiences. Newspapers keep a close watch on their circulation figures. Broadcasters rely on companies like Nielsen and Arbitron to tell them the ratings and audience shares of their programs. The media are keenly interested in the size and demographic characteristics of their audiences (as we'll discuss in Chapter 8). Most of this information, though, is gathered so advertisers will know where to place their messages so as to reach their target audiences. These audience data help gauge public acceptance after the fact but are not of direct help in guiding the countless choices that go into producing media messages.

Given the nature of the product, "what's news?" is inherently a more difficult question than "what sells?" Perhaps that is why we puzzle more over defining news than entertainment. Entertainment producers have a more direct link to the audience than their news counterparts. By watching the best-seller lists, the top grossing movies, and the highest-rated television programs, they know "what sells." Unlike news producers, movie studios can even try out different endings with preview audiences. An editor, for example, can't consult audience members before making selections. Audience research may give media workers ideas about general interests of viewers, listeners, and readers, but it doesn't come often enough to help much in the many other daily choices. And other forms of audience feedback are minimal.

News Values

Lacking this feedback, audience needs have long ago been incorporated into stable, enduring craft norms. As Schlesinger (1978) says,

> Production routines embody assumptions about audiences . . . "the audience" is part of a routinized way of life. . . . When it comes to thinking about the kind of news most relevant to "the audience" newsmen exercise their news judgement rather than going out and seeking specific information about the composition, wants or tastes of those who are being addressed. (pp. 115–116)

This news judgment is the ability to evaluate stories based on agreed-on news values, which provide yardsticks of newsworthiness and constitute an audience-oriented routine. That is, they predict what an audience will find appealing and important, and, in practice, direct gatekeepers to make consistent story selections.

Over the years, these news values have become fairly predictable and are included with little variation at the beginning of most journalism textbooks. In one way or another, the following news values distill what people find interesting and important to know about. They include importance, interest, controversy, the unusual, timeliness, and proximity (from Stephens, 1980; but also see Baskette, Sissors, & Brooks, 1982; Dennis & Ismach, 1981).

1. *Prominence/importance*. The importance of a story is measured in its impact: how many lives it affects. Fatalities are more important than property damage. Actions of the powerful are newsworthy, because what the powerful do affects people.
2. *Human interest*. In addition, though, people are interested in lots of things that don't have any direct effect on their lives: celebrities, political gossip,

and human dramas. Stories with a human element elicit this kind of interest. That's why television news, in particular, illustrates issues through the people affected.

3. *Conflict/controversy*. Why are we so interested in controversy? It signals conflict, and alerts us to important issues. Conflict is inherently more interesting than harmony. Maybe we assume that most of the time things are harmonious, but when they aren't we want to know about it.
4. *The unusual*. The unusual also interests us. We assume that the events of one day will be pretty much like the next, and the unusual is the exception to that rule.
5. *Timeliness*. News is timely. We have limited attention and want to know what's happening now. Timely events are also more likely to require action.
6. *Proximity*. Finally, events that happen nearby are considered more newsworthy. Local events usually have more effect than distant ones. Local media seek local angles in national stories, so as to better interest the audience.

We can see that these news values stem largely from the limited attention and interest of the audience. Even if the media could tell everything that went on in a day, it would not be very useful. If a friend returned from a week's vacation and asked you what happened during that time, you would probably start with the most important things first and work your way down. If you had time, you might throw in something unusual or funny. You would assume that your friend knows the sun normally rises and sets and would not include that in your narrative. The most important news would be that which deviated from the norm, or that would directly affect your friend (tornado sightings, tuition going up).

The media are often accused of carrying too much "bad" news. But bad news often means a problem that needs action. We can easily see that this is more efficient than if the media dwelled only on what was going right. Periodically, newspapers are published that report only good news. They don't usually last long. Totalitarian states, like the Soviet Union or China, often use the media to spread positive messages: a farm collective exceeding its harvest projections, or the opening of a new tractor plant. But these announcements are designed to suit the state, not the audience. Interestingly, news workers in Western societies can easily spot this distinction. British Broadcasting Corporation news producers, for example, have little respect for Eastern European news film, available to them through Intervision. They described these offerings as "all fraternal solidarity meetings" and "definitely no riots or good crashes" (Schlesinger, 1978, pp. 91–92).

Defensive Routines

If news values help gatekeepers select content for its appeal, other routines help prevent offending the audience. The routine of objectivity is a prime example, and can be viewed as serving a defensive function. Objectivity, although a cornerstone of journalistic ideology, is rooted in practical organization requirements. In this sense, objectivity is less a core belief of journalists than a set of procedures, which journalists willingly conform to in order to protect themselves from attack. Their editors and publishers are equally concerned with jeopardizing their own positions.

Michael Schudson (1978) notes that at the turn of the century, newspapers, in competing for circulation, tried to conform to the public's standards of truth, decency, and taste. Reporters believed they had to be lively and entertaining while factual at the same time. Indeed, editors and reporters were preoccupied with facts to avoid public criticism and embarrassment for the newspaper. Gans suggests that objective style, by keeping personal values out, allows reporters autonomy in choosing the news. Otherwise every story would be subject to attack. Similarly, Daniel Hallin (1989, p. 67) argues that objectivity helps legitimate the media. Because they are large, privately owned, and heavily concentrated, with a great deal of power, the media ensure public support through objectivity by claiming that their power has been put in a "blind trust." The Associated Press is also credited with a strong role during that same period in strengthening the objectivity norm. A uniform style helped it sell its product to a diverse set of client papers, which in turn needed to reach a mass and diverse audience for their mass advertising. Thus, the objectivity routine helps organizations in a number of ways to maximize their audience appeal.

From the organization's point of view, Tuchman (1977b) argues that objectivity is a ritual that serves primarily to defend the organizational product from critics. Because newsworkers have little time to reflect on whether they have gotten at the "truth" in their stories, they need a set of procedures, or strategies, that if followed will protect them from occupational hazards, like libel suits and reprimands from superiors. These procedures include relying on verifiable facts, setting statements off in quotation marks, including many names in a story to keep the reporter's views out, and presenting supplementary evidence for a "fact." Often, verifiable facts are not available, leading reporters to report the truth-claims of sources. Because they often lack time to verify such statements, they cannot claim they are factual. They can, however, report conflicting statements, allowing them to say both sides of the story have been told. Both statements may be false, getting the reporter no closer to the truth, yet the procedure helps fend off criticism.

Attributing statements to sources is a key element of the objective ritual and protects reporters against accusations that they were manipulated. When Mark Hertsgaard asked CBS News White House reporter Bill Plante to defend himself against the charge that the press was a passive conduit for Ronald Reagan's version of reality in the 1984 campaign, Plante argued that the president's views all had been carefully attributed:

> Do you convey Reagan's version of reality, or do you convey what Reagan says is reality? We certainly conveyed what he said was reality. . . . [Shifting the blame back to the audience, he continued] . . . Now it may be true that most people don't make that distinction.

> They should. We ought to start off in grammar school, or junior high, with a course on reading the newspaper and watching television: how to understand attribution. (Hertsgaard, 1988, p. 73)

The objectivity routine also leads to omitting seemingly harmless information. Lemert, Mitzman, Cook, and Hackett (1977) found that news stories were less likely to contain *mobilizing* information (instructions on what to do, where to go for a cholesterol screening, what time the political rally will be held) if they were negative, controversial, or nonlocal, or in a main news section or on the editorial page. They speculated that mobilizing information is routinely kept out to avoid accusations of partisanship.

The objectivity routine has led to abuses over the years. One of the most famous was the ability of Senator Joe McCarthy to make wild accusations during the anti-Communist witch hunts of the 1950s. They were dutifully carried in the press, properly attributed, but contained falsehoods few of the reporters believed. Although these reporters were angry at being obliged to report McCarthy's untruths, they did not abandon the resilient objective routine, and reporting patterns remained intact.

Audience Appeal and Story Structure

Not only do gatekeepers select information for its newsworthiness, or audience appeal, they present it in ways designed to meet audience needs. In a newspaper the stories must be readable, the photos arranged properly on the pages, the headlines composed to direct reader attention. Television messages must be visually appealing and hold audience attention. These presentation techniques and formats become important routines of media work.

One of the most enduring routines is the story structure. To appeal to an audience, media content often takes this form. The story must have an inherent appeal for humans, considering the prominence in culture of myths, parables, legends, and oral histories. Perhaps because it is closer to the oral tradition, television news has embraced the story form most easily. Television news producers regularly exhort reporters to "tell stories," not reports. Reuven Frank summed it up in a memo to his staff at NBC:

> Every news story should, without any sacrifice of probability or responsibility, display the attributes of fiction, of drama. It should have structure and conflict, problem and denouement, rising action and falling action, a beginning, a middle and an end. These are not only the essentials of drama; they are the essentials of narrative. (Epstein, 1974, pp. 4–5)

Thus, the story represents a routine way of processing "what happened" and guides the reporter in deciding which facts to include in transforming events into a news commodity.

Some stories are made part of a larger continuing drama. Nimmo and Combs (1983) observe that the Iranian hostage crisis story, beginning in November 1979 when U.S. citizens were captured at the American embassy and held hostage for 444 days, was treated like a melodrama by the networks. The hostages were heroes, the hostage families were victims, and the Iranian militants were clear villains. Melodramatic language had the hostages riding an "emotional roller-coaster," and facing trial before a "hanging judge." Visual symbols featuring a logo of a blindfolded hostage heightened the melodrama. Nimmo and Combs suggest that this emphasis on dramatic principles kept reporters from giving a more comprehensive picture of conflicting Islamic and Iranian factions and the history of U.S.-Iranian involvement. The dramatic thrust of the story theme necessitated an anti-Iranian, anti-Khomeini, anti-Islamic, pro-shah, and pro-U.S. government orientation (Nimmo & Combs, 1983).

Of course, reality cannot always be neatly packaged, with a beginning, middle, and end. Following this routine carries its own form of distortion. The story format constrains the reporter to organize facts to fit the plot line. One of the most famous examples is the CBS documentary "The Uncounted Enemy: A Vietnam Deception," broadcast in January 1982. CBS had promoted the show with an ad in the *New York Times* that referred to "a deliberate plot . . . " ("Uncounted enemy," 1982, January 22). At the beginning of the program, correspondent Mike Wallace said evidence would be presented to show "indeed a conspiracy at the highest levels of American military intelligence—to suppress and alter critical intelligence on the enemy in the year leading to the Tet offensive ("Uncounted enemy," 1982, January 23).

William C. Westmoreland was charged with trying to mislead political officials and the public by suppressing enemy troop counts. The distortion in the program, brought out in the general's subsequent libel suit, can be traced in large part to the producer's need to construct a show compelling enough to compete with prime-time programming. That required finding a clear villain, and painting an exaggerated picture of a conspiracy to mislead. As CBS's own internal investigation concluded, the producer violated several CBS News guidelines, including failing to pursue information contrary to the program's thesis. In effect, organizational norms were violated to produce a clear plot line.

Audience Routines v. Other Routines

The audience is included in Figure 6.2 as the ultimate consumer of the media product. Many would argue, however, that the audience figures least prominently in the many routines of the media, particularly in news. Before proceeding further, we consider two indicators why we should pay close attention to other routines, beyond those associated with the audience. It would be a mistake to conclude that news has evolved into its present form because it most perfectly suits the audience—that the public gets what it wants. How could we explain the fact that per capita newspaper subscription is declining, and that only a small percentage of the public keeps up with the news in any serious way? A closer examination of our list of news values also undermines the notion of audience appeal. Because these values have been derived from analyzing actual news content, they represent a post hoc explanation. They rationalize those selections already made. One way to test the influence of news values as a routine is to question whether other stories satisfied these criteria, yet did not receive coverage.

Each year a group of media experts from academia and the press do just that. They compile a list of stories for Project Censored, which includes the most important news stories underreported or overlooked by the American media ("Top 10," 1989). The following stories were among those recently selected:

- *Nuclear accidents.* The Chernobyl nuclear power plant disaster in the USSR became a big story in April 1986. But many other accidents have gone unreported: In 1986 there were 3,000 documented incidents, up 24 percent since 1984. Not reporting them, the project charges, strengthened the industry's undeserved reputation for safety.
- *Biological warfare.* The Reagan administration dramatically raised funding for biological warfare research during its term, up to $42 million by 1986. There was little reporting on this surge, nor on the risks associated with the research, including safety and security of labs at major universities where it was carried out.
- *Space shuttle carries plutonium.* NASA made plans to launch the Project Galileo shuttle space probe with highly radioactive plutonium. One pound is said to be capable of giving everyone on the planet a fatal case of lung cancer if evenly distributed. The shuttle was to carry 49.25 pounds. NASA minimized the chances of an accident on launch or reentry. But then NASA estimated the chance of a shuttle accident before the Challenger disaster as 1 in 100,000. Later estimates put it at 1 in 25.

Other "censored" stories included decline in genetic diversity, Third World toxic dumping, and torture in El Salvador. These stories were important and timely, yet did not receive the attention that their importance might have predicted. Thus, it is more accurate to say that to be included in the news, stories must have news value, but that is not sufficient in itself. If these "censored" stories had news value, and yet were not reported, why were they excluded? We must go beyond audience appeal routines to fully understand these decisions.

Another piece of evidence leading us toward the other two stages of our media production model comes from the observational study of newswork. In practice, media workers spend less time than one might think considering the audience. Studies of newsroom activity show that occupational and organizational considerations far outweigh any constraints imposed by audience needs and interests. The low importance of audience-oriented routines in newswork can also be seen in the attitudes of newsworkers toward their audience. In his study of the BBC, Philip Schlesinger found that these communicators labeled those who tried to contact them as "cranks," in keeping with the conviction that the "bulk of the audience reaction is from cranks, the unstable, the hysterical, and sick" (Schlesinger, 1978, pp. 107–108). Journalists write primarily for themselves, for their editors, and for other journalists.

Indeed, journalists studied by Gans (1979) were highly suspicious of audience research, being reluctant to accept any encroachment on their professional autonomy and news judgment: "When a network audience-research unit presented findings on how a sample of viewers evaluated a set of television news films, the journalists were appalled because the sample liked the films which the journalists deemed to be of low quality and disliked the 'good stories' " (p. 232).

MEDIA ORGANIZATION: PROCESSOR

Turning to the second stage of our model in Figure 6.2, we ask: What are the routines that are most related to helping the organization itself in processing information? Like people, organizations develop patterns, habits, and ways of doing things. The media organization must find ways of effectively gathering and evaluating its raw material. Most of these routines have become part of the news business, giving workers clearly defined and specialized roles and expectations. As with the audience-oriented routines, we assume these routines have developed to meet the needs of the system, and they have become standardized, institutionalized, and understood by those who use them.

Understanding Mr. Gates

To understand how media routines work, researchers have spent a lot of time directly observing how people in these organizations do their job. One of the earliest and most frequently cited efforts is the "gatekeeper" study by David Manning White (1950). It focused, however, on individual rather than routinized judgment, and started a long tradition of examining the criteria media decision makers use to select information. White kept track of the stories selected by the last in a chain of gatekeepers, a newspaper wire editor he called "Mr. Gates," and later questioned him about his decisions. White obviously felt that much could be learned by knowing the subjective, idiosyncratic reasons why the editor chose one story over another: "not interesting," "B.S.," "don't care for suicide stories" (p. 386).

However, we can find many indications of routine constraints on Mr. Gates. For example, he said he preferred stories slanted to conform to his paper's editorial policy (p. 390) and White questioned whether Mr. Gates could refuse to play up stories if his competition was doing likewise. Thus, although he took an individual approach, White did recognize the importance of constraining routines, noting that "the community shall hear as fact only those events which the newsman, as the *representative of his culture,* believes to be true" (p. 390) [our emphasis]. In fact, in a later study of several such editors at sixteen Wisconsin daily newspapers in 1956, Walter Gieber (1960) found little difference among the papers in story selection and display, just in their explanations of their decisions. He concluded that the "task-oriented" telegraph editors had the pressures of the newsroom bureaucratic routine in common.

In recent years, scholars have emphasized the concentric rings of constraints around Mr. Gates. This perspective is encouraged by the strong similarities in the news agendas across media, despite the fact that each organization is staffed with its own "subjective" gatekeepers. In a reanalysis of White's data, Hirsch (1977) shows that Mr. Gates selected stories in roughly the same proportions as they were provided by the wire service. That is, the menu of crime, disaster, political, and other stories was duplicated on a smaller scale in the editor's selections (also McCombs & Shaw, 1977). Thus, Mr. Gates exercised personal choice, but only within the format imposed on him by the wire service routine. Did Mr. Gates and the wire service simply hold the same individual values as to the relative importance of the various categories, or was the wire menu dictating his "agenda"?

To find out, Whitney and Becker (1982) experimentally presented one group of editors with a set of stories distributed unevenly across seven categories (labor, national, international news, etc.). Another group received the same number of stories in each of these categories. The editors closely followed the proportions contained in their source copy where the proportions varied. They used more subjective judgments when given equal numbers of stories in the categories. When story proportions varied, the wire routine had an impact by cluing the editors in making their selections.

Routines and the Organization

The wire service menu may limit the choices made by an editor, but that structuring is precisely what a media organization finds desirable. By subscribing to the Associated Press or other news services, a paper can ensure a steady, predictable stream of a quality product and reduce the amount of news for which it is responsible. This routine is but one of many that help media organizations operate smoothly. For example, the more constraints a reporter operates under, such as deadlines and geographic location, the narrower is the range of sources relied on for stories (Fico, 1984). While constraints affect content, routines help explain how that content is shaped in response to those limits.

As rational, complex organizations with regular deadlines, the news media cannot cope with the unpredictable and infinite number of occurrences in the everyday world without a system. These occurrences must be recognized as newsworthy events, sorted, categorized, and classified (e.g., hard versus soft news). Organizations must routinize work in order to control it. This is particularly important for news organizations, which must, in the seemingly contradictory phrase used by Tuchman (1973, p. 111), report "unexpected events on a routine basis." These routines impose their own twist on the social reality they help produce.

Many routines are designed to help the organization cope with physical constraints. The very term *gatekeeper* suggests the idea of adapting to physical limits. That is, given the number of stories and the limited space, decisions must be made, to funnel many news events down to a few. From the start, only a small part of the world can be dealt with. Although media space is limited, it is usually fixed from day to day. Regardless of how much is going on, a network newscast has a half-hour format to fill every night. A newspaper is more flexible in the number of pages it prints, but the news hole stays relatively stable from one edition to the next. The gatekeeper must choose some minimal number from among many messages. Because of this steady appetite for information, bureaucratic routines help ensure a steady supply. For example, lacking the ability to be everywhere at once, news organizations establish bureaus at those locations likely to generate news events. Beats for reporters are established, for the same reason, at institutions where reliable news can be gathered (police, fire, courts, etc.).

Time may also be considered a physical constraint, represented by the news organization's deadline schedule. Deadlines force journalists to stop seeking information and file a story, and reporters must adjust their schedule accordingly. Tuchman (1977a) notes that this causes temporal gaps in the news net (in addition to geographic and institutional): Occurrences falling outside normal business hours, for example, have less chance of being covered. As Michael Schudson (1986) observes, the news organization

> lives by the clock. Events, if they are to be reported, must mesh with its temporal spokes and cogs. Journalists do not seek only timely news if, by "timely," one means "immediate" or as close to the present as possible. Journalists also seek coincident and convenient news, as close to the deadline as possible. News must happen at specified times in the journalists' "newsday." (p. 2)

Politicians are particularly mindful of this and schedule press "events" early enough in the day to get on the evening newscasts, or on late Friday if they want to minimize coverage. This focus on timely stories often doesn't allow for adequate treatment for slowly developing stories. It also makes media unsuitable for advocacy journalism: Reporters can address a problem but cannot dwell on it. They must move on to more timely issues.

Requirements of the News Perspective

As we've suggested, media routines, while helping fit the flow of information into manageable physical limits, impose their own special logic on the product that results. News organizations are not just passive recipients of a continuous stream of events lapping at the gates. News routines provide a perspective that often explains what gets defined as news in the first place. Before it even gets to the first gate, newsworkers "see" some things as news and not others. Through their routines, they actively construct reality.

In this view news is what an organization's routines lead it to define as news. Tuchman (1973), for example, finds that newsworkers "typify" unexpected events based on how the organization must deal with them. Thus, the hard news/soft news distinction is less a function of the nature of the content than how the event is scheduled. Hard news is most often based on "prescheduled" events (trials, meetings, etc.) or "unscheduled" events (fires, earthquakes). In either case, the news of the event must be gotten out quickly. Soft news, also called feature stories, is "nonscheduled." That is, the news organization can determine when to carry it, such as in the fat Sunday editions. Nonscheduled stories can help fill in those holes where prescheduled stories are slack.

Tuchman uses the term *news net* to refer to a system of reporters deployed to institutions and locations expected to generate news events. Once deployed, this net tends to, at the expense of other events, reinforce and certify the newsworthiness of those happenings that fall within it. Reporters covering these beats promote their daily stories to their organization, which uses them, if for no other reason than that it has an economic investment in them—the reporter's salary has already been paid. In his observations of a local newspaper beat system, Fishman (1980) found that even when a reporter and editor agreed that nothing was happening on a beat, the reporter was still obliged to write something.

By directing newsworkers to take facts and events out of one context and reconstitute them into the appropriate formats, routines yield acceptable news stories. But in doing so, this process inevitably distorts the original event. A predefined story "angle," for example, provides reporters a theme around which to build a story. Reporters work most efficiently when they know what their interview sources will say. This sounds counterintuitive, but it helps explain why reporters rely on familiar sources—they can predict in advance who will give them the information needed to flesh out their angle.

David Altheide (1976), in his study of a local news channel in Arizona, observed that reporters usually approached stories with predefined options that fit their view of what was significant in an event. Such expectations led them to seek out supportive sources and details. Thus, Altheide concluded that the short time reporters often had to work on stories could not be blamed for distorted coverage; more time would have produced a more detailed but not necessarily more complete story. He observed one Phoenix television reporter who set out to do a story on solutions to traffic jams. The reporter had apparently already decided that more freeways were the best solution before interviewing the following source, an economics professor and transportation specialist:

REPORTER: How many miles of freeway do you think we need in Phoenix?

PROFESSOR: Well I don't know that. Because, you see, this is the purview of the engineer. So I don't really know how many miles we need. . . . I am an economist and we don't get into the actual matter of how many people use a given mile, etc. . . . So I can't answer that one.

REPORTER: In general, would you say we could use more freeways?

PROFESSOR: Yes, well certainly. I think there is a place that the through, freeway-type of highway has got to play . . . and it probably is one in which we can move people more efficiently on an intermediate basis than if we talk about fixed rail.

REPORTER: But you're still going to need more freeways anyway, aren't you . . ? (pp. 103–104)

Even when covering less ambiguous actual events, reporters often have an anticipated "script" as to how the story will unfold. The power of this script can be seen in an incident one evening in 1983 when a television news camera crew was called to a deserted Alabama town square. An unemployed drifter had called the station to announce that he was setting himself on fire as an act of protest. The television crew anticipated a routine story of police work; they would arrive at the square in time to film the police subduing the drifter and carting him off to jail. When police were delayed, so strong was the anticipated script that the camera crew commenced filming anyway. By doing so, the crew was criticized for inciting the man to set himself on fire, and then filming him running off in a ball of flame. Critics argued that as human beings the crew, in the absence of authorities, should have tried to prevent the man from hurting himself, but the powerful routine script overrode individual judgment (Bennett, Gressett, & Haltom, 1985).

News is commonly thought to revolve around events. An "event" routine is helpful for the organization because, compared to more abstract processes, it is more easily and less ambiguously defined as news. Events are more defensible as news. According to Molotch and Lester, public life consists of an infinite number of "occurrences," some of which are promoted into full-blown news "events" by sources or the media themselves. News organizations find these happenings useful as points of reference in the temporal world, to "break up, demarcate, and fashion lifetime, history, and a future" (1974, pp. 101–102). Television in particular needs events to give the camera something to record. The visual nature of the medium demands that something happen. Even more general issue stories are often centered around a concrete news event "peg." Events are useful to news media in providing both a focus for their attention and a schedule of meetings, elections, and other events around which to plan and allocate resources. The organization can schedule coverage, because it usually knows when and where they will take place. (The Radio/Television News Directors Association, for example, plans its annual meetings to fall in December every even-numbered year to avoid conflicting with election coverage.) Events are so seductive that the press will often cover them, even if news value would predict otherwise: train crashes in France, gas leaks in Canada, apartment fires in distant cities. These stories may not be proximate or important but they appeal to news producers by fitting an unambiguous news event model.

When events are combined with a dramatic story, so much the better. When eighteen-month-old Jessica McClure fell down a well in Midland, Texas, in October 1987, the national media converged on the town. During the fifty-eight-hour rescue drama, the "baby in the well" story rivaled many big national issues in coverage. The story was ideal for the media: It had a clearly defined location and victim; it contained dramatic elements of suffering, heroism, and suspense; and the event had an unambiguous life span—one way or the other it would come to an end. Of course, many children are victims of longer-term life-threatening conditions, but cannot be depicted in this compact event structure—unless, that is, they require transplants or other dramatic operations that provide an event focus for media and public attention. Of course, trying to fit news stories into familiar forms may blind reporters to other features of the story. Issues don't always lend themselves to the event model. A president's visit to a national park, for example, may obscure the fact that no substantial action has been taken to protect the environment.

Routine Reliance on Other Media

Journalists rely heavily on each other for ideas, and this reliance constitutes an important organizational routine. Indeed, many blame this groupthink, or "pack mentality," for making the news so similar across media. Leon Sigal (1973) says that in covering an ambiguous social world, newsworkers seek certainty in consensus:

> So long as newsmen follow the same routines, espousing the same professional values and using each other as their standards of comparison, newsmaking will tend to be insular and self-reinforcing. But that insularity is precisely what newsmen need. It provides them with a modicum of certitude that enables them to act in an otherwise uncertain environment. (pp. 180–181)

Mark Hertsgaard (1988) observed how carefully the three networks monitor each other's coverage: When U.S. jets intercepted the alleged hijackers of an Italian cruise ship, Achille Lauro, President Reagan announced that he was sending a message to terrorists everywhere: "You can run but you can't hide." After some argument, one network decided to lead with video of that statement.

> As it happened, the other two networks also opened *their* broadcasts with the identical piece of Reagan's video. In the postmortem meeting after the broadcast, the producer's colleagues pointed to their competitors' leads as evidence that their initial news judgment had indeed been correct. (p. 79)

Thus, lacking any firm external benchmarks against which to measure the product, journalists take consistency as their guide: consistency with other news organizations, and even with themselves. Electronic news retrieval systems, like

Nexis, now make it much easier for reporters to rely on their own past work for guidance. Big city daily newspapers, for example, rely heavily on material previously published in their own newspaper (Hansen, Ward, & McLeod, 1987). This inbred reliance contributes to the closed-system nature of much reporting, yet provides an essential function. It reduces the risk for the organization by ensuring that its product is the correct product.

One much-studied and highly visible version of this routine is the tendency of reporters to cover news in packs. Television and print reporters are often seen crowding around newsmakers with outstretched microphones and miniature cassette recorders. Not only do reporters tend to cover the same people and stories, but they rely on each other for ideas and confirmation of their respective news judgments. In his often-cited study, Timothy Crouse (1972) observed the way reporters covering the 1972 presidential campaign relied heavily on each other, particularly on the AP reporter, for help with how to construct story leads. The "boys on the bus," as Crouse called his book, knew that their editors would question their stories if they deviated too far from the wire service version of an event. Following a primary debate between Hubert Humphrey and George McGovern, pressroom reporters immediately checked with AP reporter Walter Mears. He said he was leading with the candidates' statement that neither would accept George Wallace as a running mate, and most of the reporters followed his example:

> They wanted to avoid "call-backs"—phone calls from their editors asking them why they had deviated from the AP or UPI. If the editors were going to run a story different from the story in the nation's 1,700 other newspapers, they wanted a good reason for it. Most reporters dreaded call-backs. Thus, the pack followed the wire-service men whenever possible. Nobody made a secret of running with the wires; it was an accepted practice. (p. 22)

A more recent study (Martindale, 1984) compared newspaper reports of campaign events but found that they were not as similar as Crouse's observations might have suggested. Perhaps media organizations now strive to provide a service more complementary to the wires. At any rate, the tendency of reporters to follow each other, although strong, is most likely when the stories are based on regular beats and highly predictable events or during crisis coverage when reliable information is scarce (Nimmo & Combs, 1983). Media analyst David Shaw reports that the tendency of the pack to follow the common wisdom has gotten even stronger since Crouse's book, due in part to technology that provides instant access to other reporters' work (CNN, computer data services, etc.) (Shaw, 1989).

The importance of "intermedia" influence as a routine is demonstrated in its importance in so many different settings. In their observation of Wisconsin statehouse reporters, Shields and Dunwoody (1986) found that, although media organizations urge their reporters to regard each other as competitors, in practice they "routinely" share information among themselves, particularly those reporters who had spent many years at the capitol (star reporters and the inner club). All reporters were expected to answer questions about the accuracy of information. A study of Michigan statehouse reporters found that "broadcast and newspaper reporters were more similar in their information gathering and source citation priorities than different." Atwater and Fico (1986) suggest that this pattern of similarities suggests a common value system across organizations—a system reinforced by close proximity, sharing information, and observing the work of other reporters.

Reliance on other media is no less important when journalists aren't in direct contact. They still rely on each other's reporting, as an institutionalized practice, for story ideas and to help confirm their own judgments. Warren Breed (1980), in his classic study of the newsroom, observed that newspapermen (they were mostly men in those days) avidly read other newspapers. For beat reporters, these papers provide a valuable resource. David Grey (1966, p. 422) observed a courts reporter for the now defunct *Washington Evening Star*. After entering his basement office in the court building and calling his paper to check in:

- 9:45—Takes off suit coat and sits back in swivel chair. Starts reading the morning *Washington Post*. Flips and scans pages.
- 9:47—Sees article on (then) Justice Goldberg speaking at a Unitarian church. Tears article from paper.
- 9:50—Throws *Post* into nearby wastebasket and starts skimming the *New York Times*.
- 9:54—Throws *Times* into wastebasket.
- 9:56—Leaves office with pencils for sharpening and "to see if I can find out any clues."

Editors are avid readers too. Breed (1980) found that editors of small papers in particular used larger city papers to guide them, "as if the editor of the small paper is employing, in absentia, the editors of the larger paper to 'make up' his page for him" (p. 195). Herbert Gans (1979, p. 91) noted that editors read the *Times* and *Post* before entertaining story ideas. If these respected judges of news value have carried a story, it has been judged satisfactory, "eliminating the need for an independent decision by the editor" (p. 126). For "trend" stories in particular, Gans found that a reporter stood a better chance of selling it to an editor if it had already been reported elsewhere (p. 170). In 1986, for example, the *New York Times* helped certify the "cocaine issue" by giving it prominent coverage early in the year. Other media followed in a "feeding frenzy" as the networks and newspapers converged on the story throughout the summer and early fall (Reese & Danielian, 1989).

Certain media have special influence. The *New York Times* has strong influence for international stories, the *Washington Post* for national domestic issues. Even smaller publications can sometimes exert influence on others. *Rolling Stone,* for example, regarded as a leader for counterculture antiestablishment stories, triggered national media attention when it ran a story on Americans kept in Mexican prisons on drug charges (Miller, 1978). In general, though, the *New York Times* is considered the final arbiter of quality and professionalism across all the news media. Indeed, in the ambiguous world of journalism, "if the *Times* did not exist, it would probably have to be invented" (Gans, 1979, p. 181).

The Pack v. the Exclusive

The organization must balance the benefits derived from pack routine with the benefits of the "exclusive." To understand why a news organization would usually rather run with the pack than scoop the competition, we have to understand the different yet related functions these routines serve. Exclusives do little to enhance the audience appeal of an organization. Most people read only one paper or see one newscast. Yet, newspapers will, for competitive reasons, develop exclusive stories such as the *Miami Herald*'s exposé of presidential candidate Gary Hart's affair with Donna Rice in 1988, or other high-profile multipart series designed to attract the attention of Pulitzer Prize judges. The very fact that these are exceptional and noteworthy, however, shows them to be the exception to the more common pack coverage.

If the mainstream media all go after the same stories, how is one organization permitted to lay claim to special excellence? Through the scoop. Getting first what everyone else will want is the standard in the highly ambiguous process of deciding what news is. Network journalists covering political conventions pride themselves on getting information even a few seconds before the competition. Exclusives also provide a standard of performance by which organizations can evaluate their employees. Schudson notes that "the race for news—a race whose winner can easily be determined by a clock—affords a cheap, convenient, democratic measure of journalistic 'quality' " (1986, p. 3). And yet the reporter does not want to get too far in front of the pack. In coverage of presidential campaigns, for example, national attention is directed at the same candidates and events, and as a result reporters are perhaps in greatest synchronization. The desire to be unique is far outweighed by the risk in being different and perhaps wrong in full view of the nation. (Of course, producers of entertainment content are prone to the same pack mentality. Just look at the similarities in television prime-time programming, and made-for-television movie themes, radio formats, and tabloid television.)

Television v. Newspapers: How Do They Differ?

Clearly, different media must create different structures to carry out their functions. The print and broadcast media, for example, differ in the technology they use to gather and transmit messages, their economic support, how frequently they publish or air their product, and their political relationships (with the FCC, etc.). One way to identify organizational differences that make a difference is to observe how workers differ in their behavior and attitudes. Many of these differences can be traced to the nature of the organization they work for. (Different routines are mentioned here to the extent that they can be traced to organizational differences.)

Although they belong to a common profession, reporters differ in the ways they deal with their sources. Because television news stations typically have smaller staffs than newspapers in comparable communities, reporters are subject to constant demand for daily stories. This plus the other technological baggage of television news reporters often make them subservient to their sources (Drew, 1972) and dependent on public relations control efforts (Dunwoody, 1978).

Comparing source reliance of Michigan statehouse journalists, Atwater and Fico (1986) found that broadcast reporters relied more on routine activities, such as news conferences, which produced the more visually dramatic stories, while print reporters relied most on personal sources (experts, legislative leaders, etc.), which produced good background information. Shields and Dunwoody (1986) found that in the Wisconsin statehouse pressroom, the broadcast reporters occupied the lowest level in the journalists' own hierarchy. The lack of their organization's commitment to a steady statehouse presence, not the fact they were broadcasters, prevented these reporters from "paying their dues" and reaching the "inner club."

Broadcast reporters are less likely to say they have regular beats and to say they have freedom to select the stories they work on. They are less likely than print reporters to say they have their work edited (Becker, 1982). Broadcast reporters report having more editorial decision-making power than their print counterparts (Ismach & Dennis, 1978). Television news reporters have fewer layers of editorial oversight. Practically speaking, it is much harder to change a reporter's video package than to edit newspaper copy. Once the reporter has done a story, however, he or she must relinquish control to others. Because of the presentation aspects of television news, much effort goes into getting the show out, and the reporter's work becomes one element within the larger production.

The routines discussed here serve the convenience and needs of media organizations as they produce their product. Of course, the media do not exert complete control over the raw material that goes into that product. To complete the picture of routines we consider next those that are a function of the suppliers, or sources.

EXTERNAL SOURCES: SUPPLIERS

In manufacturing symbolic content, the media rely on external suppliers of raw material, whether speeches, interviews, corporate reports, or government hearings. These suppliers, or *sources* as we'll call them, have a major influence on media content (as will be discussed more fully in Chapter 8). Here, in this final section, we consider how these sources dictate routines for media organizations. In other words, these routines can be viewed as an adaptation by media to the constraints imposed by their sources. In some cases, media and sources have adapted to each other's requirements, making it hard to determine which came first.

In some cases, source-oriented routines are hardly visible. For example, even highly enterprising investigative reports, like those on "60 Minutes," often rely on lawsuits in progress for stories. Notice the number of potential sources in such stories that can't (or won't) comment due to impending litigation. Lawsuit-based issues are convenient for journalists to cover. The legal system has essentially laid the groundwork for the reporter and set the routine. Willing sources (usually on the plantiff side) are available and committed to a clear point of view. Articulate lawyers are more than willing to advance their client's case. The adversarial format fits the news model, although it may give a distorted view of the case. Other source-based routines are more obvious. Photo opportunities and press conferences show more clearly the routines employed by sources to get into the news. In recent years, the public has become wise to many of these strategies, as indicated by the entry of terms like *media event, sound bite,* and *spin doctor* into popular jargon.

The rise of public relations played a major role in routinizing and making more systematic the link between the press and other institutions. During the early twentieth century, Michael Schudson (1978) notes, newspapers encouraged public relations efforts by using the handouts and copies of speeches supplied by press agents, even though scorning those who provided them. Overall, Martin and Singletary (1981) found that nearly 20 percent of press releases were used verbatim (more by the relatively resource-poor nondailies than dailies). The rise of the press release and press conference reduced the ability of reporters to get scoops and inside stories. At the same time, it made journalists more easily manipulable due to their dependence on the news flow of public relations–generated information.

Routine Channels

Theoretically, the news media have countless resources available to them as a raw product, including firsthand observation, libraries, and polling. Practically, though, they depend heavily on interviews with individuals for their information. Stephen Hess (1981), for example, found that the Washington press corps made very little use of documents in doing their research, preferring to rely on sources and each other. Reliance on sources reduces the need for expensive specialists and extensive research. Sigal (1973) found a clear tendency for *New York Times* and *Washington Post* reporters, members of organizations that could presumably afford to gather news through whichever channels they chose, to rely on routine channels of information. He defined *routine channels* as (1) official proceedings (trials, legislative hearings, etc.), (2) press releases, (3) press conferences, and (4) nonspontaneous events (speeches, ceremonies, etc.). Informal channels were (1) background briefings, (2) leaks, (3) nongovernmental proceedings, like professional association meetings, and (4) reports from other news organizations, interviews with other reporters, and editorials. Enterprise channels included (1) interviews conducted at reporters' initiative, (2) spontaneous events witnessed firsthand (fires, etc.), (3) independent research, and (4) reporters' own conclusions and analysis (p. 20).

Of the page one stories in the *New York Times* and *Post,* of all channels included in these stories, informal channels accounted for 15.7 percent, enterprise

25.8 percent, and routine channels more than double that at 58.2 percent. Of the enterprise channels, interviews with individual sources accounted for 23.7 percent of the 25.8 percent figure. This ratio became even more skewed when Sigal examined stories with Washington datelines and tabulated only those "primary channels" constituting the lead or the major part of a story. Of the channels used, 72.3 percent were routine, 20.1 percent informal, and 7.7 percent enterprise. Sigal concluded that "the predominant use of routine channels in Washington newsgathering seems to reflect efforts of official news sources everywhere to confine the dissemination of news to routine channels, as well as reporters' reliance on them" (p. 123). This same pattern of reliance on routine channels has been found in more recent research (Brown, Bybee, Wearden, & Straughan, 1987), confirming the importance of this practice. Of course, Washington is not the only place where news is gathered routinely. Sachsman (1976) found reporters and editors relied heavily on press releases for information about the environment, because they provided a convenient source of information.

Official Channels

The centralization of government power following World War II only enhanced its ability to control information. With that increased ability came routines for institutionalizing that control. These routines imposed by official sources, especially those in Washington, have drawn the most scholarly attention. Certainly, though, newsmakers in business and the professions also attempt to routinize their relations with the press: Corporation executives hold press conferences to announce a new product, movie actors release press kits through their publicist. The newsmaking activity of government has nevertheless been of greatest interest. Official behavior is more open to view and study. Corporate directors don't write as many memoirs as ex-politicians. The attempts of business to manipulate information, being more diffuse and secretive, provoke less attention than the more easily located government agencies, with their greater tradition of openness and public accountability. Although all sources are becoming more sophisticated in their media relations, official relations have achieved a formalized and institutionalized state.

In Chapter 4 we observed how, in particular, news content consists largely of statements from official sources. By relying on these official sources, reporters receive most of their information through routine channels. Clearly, official sources prefer to release information through these channels. Doing so allows them to set the rules and exert greater control over the information. The press release and press conference allow them to regulate the release of information and do so more efficiently than speaking to everyone in turn. Although press conferences give the appearance of exposing officials to adversarial exchanges, in practice these "events" are often well choreographed by the sponsoring official. Questions can be planted, hostile reporters ignored, friendly ones recognized, difficult questions ignored, or evasive responses given.

Informal background briefings may not be a routine channel, as Sigal defines it, but are regular channels through which officials transmit information. In that sense, they constitute a source-dictated routine. These briefings are common in Washington, and are governed by generally accepted conventions. Briefings can be "off the record," on "deep background," or "background." Off-the-record information cannot be used in any form; deep background material can be used but not quoted or attributed in any way to the source. "For background only" information may be attributed using a variety of references other than by name (senior White House officials, Pentagon spokesperson, etc.). The objectivity routine normally dictates that reporters name their sources whenever possible, but they accept these ground rules when their alternative is not to get the information at all. Sources find many advantages to giving out not-for-attribution information, foremost among them the ability to avoid accountability for their statements.

Some officials may go beyond these briefings and pass information to reporters anonymously, in what are often called *leaks*. Presidents complain regularly about leaks in their administration. As the flip side of the carefully coordinated "line of the day," leaks threaten unified control of information. Although less common than other channels, leaks are more routine than exceptional and serve many valuable functions for government officials. Hedrick Smith (1988) suggests that because background briefings are so common, they sanction officials to go on background with leaks. While briefings are done on purpose as a part of overall official strategy, often at the request of reporters, leaks are generally initiated by officials acting on their own as a tactic in intraorganization infighting, and they are directed at a single reporter at a time, often on an exclusive basis. Hess (1984, pp. 77–78) lists several potential functions of leaks: to float a trial balloon, to blow the whistle on waste or dishonesty, to promote or sabotage policy, to curry favor with reporters, to carry out a grudge against bureaucratic rivals, and to enhance the leaker's ego by promoting an "insider" image.

Reporters rely on official sources for many reasons. The government provides a convenient and regular flow of authoritative information, which reporters find efficient compared with more labor-intensive research. Reliance on sources reduces the need for expensive specialists and extensive research. Furthermore, Daniel Hallin (1989) argues that professionalization has strengthened the connection between press and state. Given an objective and disinterested stance on the part of the journalist, government officials provide authoritative validation of the news product.

Paradoxically, Sigal (1973) observes that the competitive requirements of journalism often make them reliant on official sources. Reporters can obtain exclusives the hard way through their own legwork and research, or the easy way through inside tips, interviews, and leaks handed to them by officials. Finding the latter far more efficient, they are forced into a bargain that, in exchange for the occasional competitive bone, requires them to accept the far more common news delivered through routine channels (p. 53). Other professional "perks" perpetuate this dependence. Political candidates, for example, use the journalistic reward system as leverage to get what they want in the press. In the 1988 presidential campaign, Joan Didion (1988, p. 21) observed how political journalists reported clearly "set up" campaign events as though they were not. Because reporters like covering campaigns—it leads to prestige and advancement, gets them out on the road—they "are willing, in exchange for 'access,' to transmit the images their sources wish transmitted. They are willing, in exchange for certain colorful details around which a 'reconstruction' can be built, . . . to present these images not as a story the campaign wants told but as fact."

Reagan Era Routines

In recent years, sources have become more sophisticated in dealing with the press, and in making routines work in their favor. Many of these routines have become particularly visible at the presidential level, with the rise of the Reagan era public relations model of information management, although many other sources in government and elsewhere have adopted similar strategies. These routines involve controlling information for government agencies by regulating and shaping the flow of information. Although they may have originated in earlier administrations, they became fully developed under Reagan. He continued Nixon's practice of hiring public relations experts and using the techniques of mass marketing as part of overall political strategy.

Simple distancing of the press constituted an important new routine technique. This included providing visual opportunities of Reagan leaving for Camp David, but using the waiting helicopter to drown out reporters' questions; restricting questions during White House photo opportunities, and drastically reducing the number of press conferences and other unscripted encounters. One of the most radical restrictions in press access came during the 1983 invasion of Grenada. The administration, breaking a long tradition of military-press cooperation, barred all reporters during the early days of the operation.

> When American newsmen tried to get to Grenada on commercial boats, American military planes threatened to fire on them. Four American reporters were held on a Navy ship for several days, forbidden to transmit stories, while the Pentagon set up its own news service, distributing reports with serious omissions and inaccuracies. The administration seemed to want a news monopoly until it could shape public attitudes. (Smith, 1988, p. 435)

Restricted access increased the media appetite for those messages that did flow from the White House, which then had to be carefully coordinated. Behind the daily activities of the president, for example, lies extensive planning. Hedrick Smith notes that the notion of "scripted spontaneity" originated with Nixon, as explained by David Gergen, who later became Reagan's White House communication director:

> We had a rule in the Nixon operation, that before any public event was put on his schedule, you had to know what the headline out of that event was going to be, what the picture was going to be, and what the lead paragraph would be. . . . One of Nixon's rules about television was that it was very important that the White House determine what the line coming out from the president was and not let the networks determine that, not let New York edit you. You had to learn how to do the editing yourself. (Smith, 1988, pp. 405–406)

In one effort to minimize press editing, the Reagan administration in 1983 began letting news organizations tap into a White House computer for electronic press releases compiled by the communication office. A similar strategy involved beaming unedited presidential appearances to local television stations via satellite, thus bypassing the network filter.

If unable to dictate the news itself, administration sources try to put the most favorable light on events through follow-up contacts with reporters. It has become customary, for example, for party spokespersons (administration officials, senators, etc.) to make themselves available to reporters during party conventions and after presidential debates and other campaign events. By presenting a coordinated response, they aim to frame the event in the most desirable manner. Elsewhere, officials may engage in damage control by calling reporters shortly before deadline. David Gergen made a practice of calling network correspondents at the last minute with the White House view, knowing they would be obliged to at least acknowledge it in their closing "stand ups." "The reporters respond to that," Gergen said in defense of the practice. "They like it. They need it. And you could get them to change their feed" (Smith, 1988, p. 410).

One of the most skillful crafters of Reagan's media image was Michael Deaver, who developed what he called a "visual press release," an event crafted to make a visual message: Reagan visiting a job training center during the 1982–1983 recession; Reagan visiting a Fort Worth housing construction site to announce a rise in housing starts. According to Hedrick Smith, "Deep down, Deaver's goal was to become the de facto executive producer of the television network news shows by crafting the administration's story for the networks" (p. 416). He strove to reach this goal by providing the network with irresistible events and, in the process, developed a new set of "symbolic routines."

Adapting to Source Bureaucracy

These routines are the more visible ways sources influence the news product. A more far reaching impact results from the adaptation by news organizations to the entire bureaucratic structure of source institutions. Indeed, news can be considered a product of one bureaucracy gathered from other bureaucracies. In the case of government, Sigal calls it the "coupling of two information processing machines" (1973, p. 4).

Thus, in addition to just having their news regulated by sources, journalists have information structured for them by other bureaucracies. Out of direct audience and often newsroom contact, journalists adopt through these routines the perspectives of the bureaucracies they cover. This highlights some occurrences, while rendering others invisible. In his study of local newsgathering, Mark Fishman (1980) found that the newspaper he studied even depended on the Forestry Service for nature news: "When it turned out that even rocks, trees and squirrels are made available to the newspaper through official agencies, then it is no exaggeration to say that *the world is bureaucratically organized for journalists*" (p. 51) [emphasis ours].

Fishman concentrated on this bureaucratic organization of newswork, observing, among other routines, how reporters made their "rounds." By systematically organizing their stops during the day (courts, sheriff, police), reporters avoided wasting time. Fishman's reporters, for example, made most efficient use of their time by checking with the courts after the sheriff and police. The court office would not know in advance when cases would be coming up, while police and sheriff offices could be monitored at any time for recent developments. Indeed, reporters who failed to follow this routine would be likely to get in trouble with their superiors. As Fishman observes, "The round has a day-in day-out repetitive character, a stability over time. It consists of a series of locations that the reporter moves through in an orderly, scheduled sequence" (1980, p. 43).

Fishman argues that the beat routine is constructed around the structure of bureaucracies and directs reporters to certain features of institutions, those points in the system that yield the most efficient concentrations of information. Fishman identifies two kinds of institutional centers, in particular, that journalists depend on: the "media contact," or press representative; and the "meeting." Reporters value meetings for concentrating lots of information into a short period of time.

The bureaucratic routine renders some occurrences nonevents. Fishman (1980, pp. 78–80) observed a meeting of the county board of supervisors about the following year's sheriff's department budget, during which a woman stepped up to the public podium. Rather than speak for or against a proposal to add new deputy sheriff positions, she related a story about how two deputies had stopped her on the street as she sold wares from a pushcart. The deputies, she said, handcuffed her, pulled her into their car, verbally abused her, and left her at the sheriff's station for several hours bound hand and foot, before eventually releasing her with no explanation. During this time, the chairman tried to dismiss the woman, ultimately threatening to have her removed. All the while, reporters in the room stopped taking notes, doodled, talked among themselves, and generally acted put out with the interruption of the normal bureaucratic flow. Needless to say, the "nonevent" went unreported in the newspaper. Although a potentially newsworthy story about deputies unjustly arresting a citizen, it did not fit the officials' and reporters' bureaucratic perspective on the purpose at hand. As far as the reporters were concerned, the woman was wasting their time.

SUMMARY

Routines have an important impact on the production of symbolic content. They form the immediate environment within which individual media workers carry out their jobs. If these highly interconnected routines constrain the individual, they are themselves functions of constraints. The audience has limited time and attention, the media organization has limited resources, and sources limit and structure the material they provide. Yet those routines cannot be completely separated. The event focus of news, for example, is helpful to the organization in scheduling news, but also helps the audience in providing a concrete focus for the message. Many of the same bureaucratic routines that are functional for the media organization are also used by external sources for their advantage. Routines of newswork provide levers that power centers on the outside can grasp to influence content. Some metaphors, in fact, describe the press as straitjacketed or handcuffed by its own routines. The more powerful sources can lead the press to adapt to their own bureaucratic structure and rhythms. Less advantaged sources must conform to the media routines, if they are to have a chance of getting into the news.

REFERENCES

Altheide, David L. (1976). *Creating reality: How TV news distorts events*. Beverly Hills, CA: Sage.

Atwater, T., & Fico, F. (1986). Source reliance and use in reporting state government: A study of print and broadcast practices. *Newspaper Research Journal, 8*(1), 53–61.

Bantz, C. R., McCorkle, S., & Baade, R. C. (1981). The news factory. In G. C. Wilhoit & H. De Bock (Eds.), *Mass communication review yearbook*, Vol. 2, (pp. 336–390). Beverly Hills, CA: Sage.

Baskette, F. K., Sissors, J. Z., & Brooks, B. S. (1982). *The art of editing*. New York: Macmillan.

Becker, L. (1982). Print or broadcast: How the medium influences the reporter. In J. Ettema and D. C. Whitney (Eds.), *Individuals in mass media organizations: Creativity and constraint*. Beverly Hills, CA: Sage.

Bennett, W. L., Gressett, L., & Haltom, W. (1985). Repairing the news. *Journal of Communication, 35*(2), 50–68.

Breed, W. (1980). *The newspaperman, news and society*. New York: Arno Press.

Brown, J., Bybee, C., Wearden, S., & Straughan, D. (1987). Invisible power: Newspaper news sources and the limits of diversity. *Journalism Quarterly, 64*, 45–54.

Crouse, T. (1972). *The boys on the bus: Riding with the campaign press corps*. New York: Random House.

Dennis, E. E., & Ismach, A. H. (1981). *Reporting processes and practices*. Belmont, CA: Wadsworth.

Didion, J. (1988, October 27). Insider baseball. *New York Review of Books*, pp. 19–31.

Drew, D. (1972). Roles and decisions of three television beat reporters. *Journal of Broadcasting, 16*, 165–173.

Dunwoody, S. (1978). Science journalists: A study of factors affecting selection of news of a scientific meeting. Unpublished Ph.D. dissertation, Indiana University.

Epstein, E. (1974). *News from nowhere*. New York: Vintage Books.
Fico, F. (1984). A comparison of legislative sources in newspaper and wire service stories. *Newspaper Research Journal, 5*(3), 35–43.
Fishman, M. (1980). *Manufacturing the news*. Austin: University of Texas Press.
Gans, H. (1979). *Deciding what's news*. New York: Random House.
Gieber, W. (1960). Two communicators of the news: A study of the roles of sources and reporters. *Social Forces, 39,* 76–83.
Grey, D. L. (1966). Decision-making by a reporter under deadline pressure. *Journalism Quarterly, 43,* 419–428.
Hallin, D. (1989). *The uncensored war*. Berkeley: University of California Press.
Hansen, K., Ward, J., & McLeod, D. (1987). Role of the newspaper library in the production of news. *Journalism Quarterly, 64,* 714–720.
Hertsgaard, M. (1988). *On bended knee: The press and the Reagan presidency*. New York: Farrar, Straus & Giroux.
Hess, S. (1981). *The Washington reporters*. Washington, DC: Brookings Institution.
Hess, S. (1984). *The government/press connection: Press officers and their offices*. Washington, DC: Brookings Institution.
Hirsch, P. (1977). Occupational, organizational and institutional models in mass media research: Toward an integrated framework. In P. M. Hirsch, P. V. Miller, & F. G. Kline (Eds.), *Strategies for communication research* (pp. 13–40). Beverly Hills, CA: Sage.
Ismach, A., & Dennis, E. (1978). A profile of newspaper and television reporters in a metropolitan setting. *Journalism Quarterly, 55,* 739–743.
Lemert, J. B., Mitzman, B. N., Cook, R. H., & Hackett, R. (1977). Journalists and mobilizing information. *Journalism Quarterly, 54,* 721–726.
Mannheim, K. (1936/1964). From ideology and utopia. In Henry S. Kariel (Ed.), *Sources in twentieth-century political thought* (pp. 26–46). New York: Free Press.
Martin, W. P., & Singletary, M. (1981). Newspaper treatment of state government releases. *Journalism Quarterly, 58,* 93–96.
Martindale, C. (1984). Newspaper and wire-service leads in coverage of the 1980 campaign. *Journalism Quarterly, 61,* 339–345.
McCombs, M., & Shaw, D. (1977). Structuring the unseen environment. *Journal of Communication, 27,* 18–22.
Miller, S. (1978). Reporters and congressmen: Living in symbiosis. *Journalism Monographs, 53.*
Molotch, H., & Lester, M. (1974). News as purposive behavior: On the strategic use of routine events, accidents and scandals. *American Sociological Review, 39,* 101–112.
Nimmo, D., & Combs, J. E. (1983). *Mediated political realities*. New York: Longman.
Reese, S., & Danielian, L. (1989). Intermedia influence and the drug issue: Converging on cocaine. In P. J. Shoemaker (Ed.), *Communication campaigns about drugs: Government, media and the public* (pp. 29–46). Hillsdale, NJ: Lawrence Erlbaum.
Sachsman, D. (1976). Public relations influence on coverage of the environment in San Francisco area. *Journalism Quarterly, 53,* 54–60.
Schlesinger, P. (1978). *Putting 'reality' together: BBC news*. London: Constable.
Schudson, M. (1978). *Discovering the news*. New York: Basic Books.
Schudson, M. (1986). *What time means in a news story*. Gannett Occasional Paper No. 4. New York: Gannett Center for Media Studies.
Shaw, D. (1989, August 25). How media gives stories same "spin." *Los Angeles Times* reprint.

Shields, S., & Dunwoody, S. (1986). The social world of the statehouse pressroom. *Newspaper Research Journal, 8*(1), 43–51.

Sigal, L. V. (1973). *Reporters and officials*. Lexington, MA: D. C. Heath.

Smith, H. (1988). *The power game: How Washington works*. New York: Random House.

Stephens, M. (1980). *Broadcast news*. New York: Holt, Rinehart & Winston.

Top 10 censored stories of 1988. (1989, September/October). *Utne Reader*, pp. 59–63.

Tuchman, G. (1973). Making news by doing work: Routinizing the unexpected. *American Journal of Sociology, 79,* 110–131.

Tuchman, G. (1977a). The exception proves the rule: The study of routine news practice. In P. Hirsch, P. Miller, & F. G. Kline (Eds.), *Strategies for communication research* (pp. 43–62). Beverly Hills, CA: Sage.

Tuchman, G. (1977b). Objectivity as strategic ritual: An examination of newsmen's notions of objectivity. *American Journal of Sociology, 77,* 660–679.

Uncounted enemy. (1982, January 22). Advertisement for CBS documentary. *New York Times,* p. a32.

Uncounted enemy: A Vietnam deception (1982, January 23). CBS documentary. Transcript of broadcast.

White, D. M. (1950). The "gatekeeper": A case study in the selection of news. *Journalism Quarterly, 27,* 383–390.

Whitney, D. C., & Becker, L. (1982). "Keeping the gates" for gatekeepers: The effects of wire news. *Journalism Quarterly, 59,* 60–65.

CHAPTER 7

Organizational Influences on Content

In the last chapter we considered how media routines constrain individual media workers, represented by a ring encompassing the individual. Although carried out in different organizations, these routines and their constraints are shared by many different media, giving media workers much in common with others in their profession. These common routines allow, for example, a reporter at the *Baltimore Sun* to work for the *Washington Post* with little retraining, just as broadcast anchors and reporters jump from one network to another. Ultimately, however, routines are carried out within the boundaries of specific organizations, which hire, fire, and promote workers and pay their salaries. In this chapter we add another ring to our "doughnut," another set of constraints as we move up a level to look more closely at the organizational setting.

ORGANIZATION-LEVEL QUESTIONS

Organizations differ in how they solve the problems of production. Here we ask: How are organizations structured, how do they differ, how is authority exercised within them, and what difference does it make to media content? In Hirsch's (1977) terms, this perspective emphasizes differences in organizational roles, internal structure, goals, technology, and markets. It emphasizes the difference made by ownership, goals, and policy. Organizational analysis seeks to explain variations in content that cannot be attributed to differences in routines and individuals. In the last chapter, we reasoned that if two newsworkers behave the same way in spite of individual differences, they are responding to similar work routines. Similarly, if we find that newspaper workers behave the same as broadcasters, in spite of different routines, then we will in turn suspect that organizational similarities make it so. Perhaps both are owned by the same company with the same news policy, overriding the influence of different routines.

Considering an entire organization reveals how role perspectives change depending on an individual's position in the hierarchy. At times the different routines and requirements of media workers, though they may work in the same organization, bring them into conflict. An editor, for example, may need more news bureaus to adequately cover a community, while the publisher may not be able to justify the added expense. Similarly, the routines of editors and reporters, who often have different agendas, must be reconciled. As Gans suggests, editors are more audience related while reporters are more source related. The editor is not tied to a beat, and thus can help reporters avoid being co-opted by their sources. Editors can request that reporters not conform to routine ground rules promoted by sources, or even rotate them to another beat. Ways must be found to mediate such conflicts. When push comes to shove, individual workers and their routines must be subordinated to the larger organization and its goals.

This approach has much in common with the routines perspective introduced in the last chapter. Both stress that media content is produced in an organizational and bureaucratic setting. Both are what Hirsch (1977) calls an "organization" perspective, but the more macro focus shows the points at which routines run counter to organizational logic, and reveals internal tensions not indicated by an emphasis solely on routines or individuals

Macro Nature of Organizational Level

Figure 7.1 visually assigns organizational influence to a more macro level than routines and individual influence levels. Why is this? Here we are dealing with larger, more complicated, more macro structures. The routines of media work form the immediate context for the individual worker, whereas the organization consists of many specialized parts, each having its own routines. Any one person cannot have direct contact with them all. Also, specific policies issued from the top of the organization can overrule lower-level routines. (Although they themselves are individuals and subject to their own routines, organization leaders make and enforce policy on behalf of the organization in the service of organization-level goals.) We question how these internal components fit together to create an organization and allow it to function.

The Organization as Conceptual Model

It may be helpful at this point to return to our familiar news gatekeeper, but to consider it in relation to the organization, a system whose components must work together. The traditional gatekeeping process viewed news selection as a linear process, rather than a complex series of interrelated decisions made at many levels. Rather than treat news as a product of specific, single gatekeepers, bounded though they may be by their routines, let us consider the organization as a whole as the

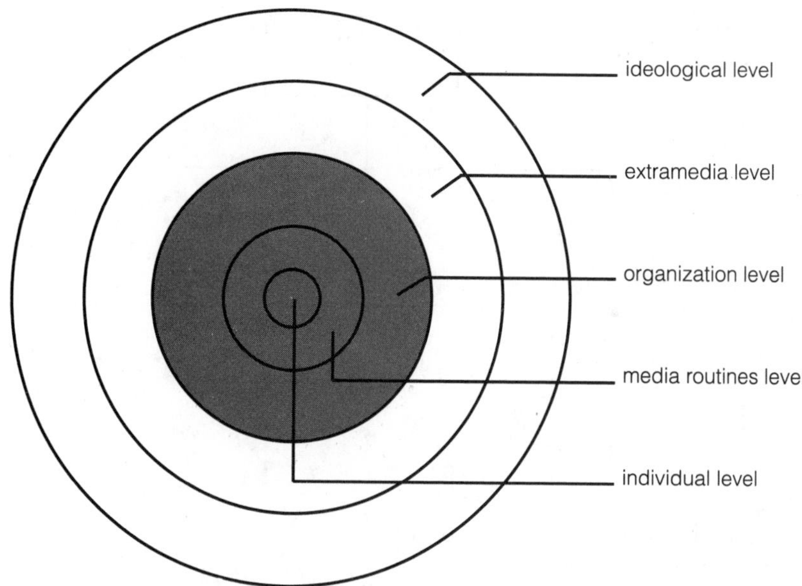

Figure 7.1. Organizational influences on media content in hierarchical model

actual gatekeeper. An example may help to illustrate this. George Bailey and Larry Lichty (1972) examined how NBC News decided to air a dramatic film story during the Vietnam War. The researchers' "cybernetic" approach to gatekeeping likened the news organization to a central nervous control system with many interdependent parts.

During the 1968 Vietnam Tet offensive, an NBC camera crew was covering the skirmishes around Saigon. On Thursday, February 2, correspondent Howard Tuckner and his Vietnamese crew were filming when a group of South Vietnamese marines presented a prisoner to Brigadier General Nguyen Ngoc Loan. Associated Press photographer Eddie Adams was also there and won a Pulitzer Prize for his famous shot of what happened next, as General Loan calmly pulled out his gun and blew the prisoner's brains out.

That afternoon the NBC crew met with the Saigon bureau chief and discussed the best way to package the execution and other events of the day. A telex was sent to New York giving information about the available stories. When the executive producer of the Huntley-Brinkley report, Robert Northshield, arrived for work the next day, the message from Saigon was waiting, notifying him that film of the now widely publicized execution was available. He called the Tokyo bureau, where the film had been sent for satellite transmission, and expressed reservations about whether the film would be in "bad taste," but was assured by the Tokyo producer that the film was "quite remarkable." Only after authorizing the satellite transmission was Northshield able to view the film in New York. He chose to cut the film at the point where the prisoner fell to the ground, rather than show the corpse with blood spurting out of its head, a scene he thought was "awful rough."

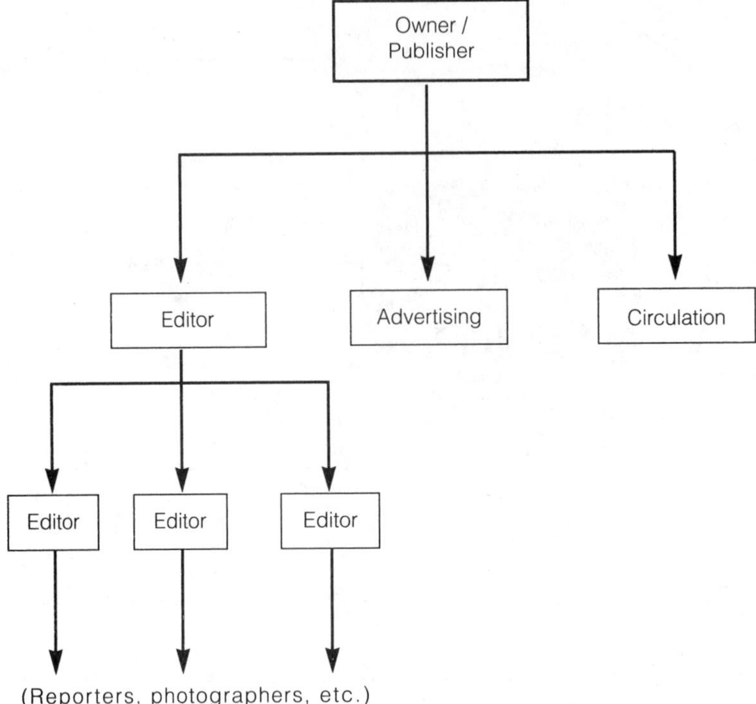

Figure 7.2. Newspaper organization chart

When the story made it to New York, the time remaining before air was short, requiring a go or no-go decision. However, the authors did not consider this a simple "gate," since New York had been involved in the decision-making process all along: "Reporters, editors, producers, others know which stories are most likely to be broadcast. Each 'gatekeeper' has to estimate how the program's executive producer—and even his superiors—will receive the story" (Bailey & Lichty, 1972, p. 229). In this case the executive producer intervened more than usual because the film was stretching the boundaries of perceived audience taste, yet the story had strong news value, having already been certified by the print media in the form of Adams's still photo, and NBC's was the only network crew that had film of it. Such an exceptional case shows how the decision process engaged the organization at its many levels. The very fact that the story was not routine made the network's control more visible. As Bailey and Lichty observed: "The Loan film story was edited by a group. The organization was the gatekeeper" (p. 229).

Organization Questions: The Organization Chart

Perhaps the most basic and familiar model to help structure our questions at this level is the organization chart. These charts typically show how a company is set up, with boxes and lines to designate roles and lines of authority. Like any good model the organization chart singles out objects and relationships of interest. Although visually simple, the condensed organization chart for a newspaper shown in Figure 7.2 contains a lot of information. The owner/publisher occupies the top box. The news department is one of the three major departments within the organization, headed by an executive editor. The editor oversees other editors who in turn supervise several reporters. This chart helps visualize four important questions.

1. *What are the organizational roles?* The boxes in the chart show who does what. As individuals are hired or promoted into these roles, they take on the duties and authorities associated with them. The number and type of roles represented show how specialized or differentiated are the jobs that constitute the media organization.
2. *How is the organization structured?* The arrangement of these boxes, indicated by the connecting arrows, shows the complexity of the organizational structure. What are the lines of authority between the departments? Is power centralized with strong vertical connections or spread among several departments? How are the different departments combined? Traditionally, for example, news departments are kept deliberately distinct from other parts of the enterprise to preserve journalistic autonomy. In some organizations the owner/publisher may have a direct hand in day-to-day news decisions, while others have several intermediaries built into the structure. Of course, some lines of authority may be more tenuous than others, formal but irrelevant. A star columnist at a major paper, for example, may be below an editor in the organization chart, but for all practical purposes is given little oversight.
3. *What is the policy and how is it implemented?* The arrows in the chart indicate who answers to whom, but they don't say what policies are transmitted. Understanding an organization requires that we know something of the content of those arrows. What priorities are set? What goals are established? (Normally we assume that policy comes from the top, although at times lower-level employees exert pressure upward through employee stock ownership or union activity.)
4. *How are these policies enforced?* Finally, the chart suggests another important question. How are the lines of authority enforced? What control do executives have over workers to ensure that policies are carried out?

Implicit in each of these questions is how organizational factors affect media content. We review several research studies to address these points. Some use the organization as a model, to help conceptualize the production of content (as in the Vietnam film and news factory examples). Others have compared actual content differences between media, such as between family- and group-owned newspapers. These studies may not explicitly say so but they locate the cause of content variation in the differences between media organizations. Many nonacademic writers have contributed important insights as well, by describing the internal workings of major media companies. A host of books has been written about CBS alone, from which we will draw examples (e.g., Boyer, 1988; Friendly, 1967). When former high-ranking employees of media organizations recount their experiences they speak from an important organization-level vantage point (e.g., Ed Joyce, 1988). We use all of these sources to gain an understanding of organization influences.

ORGANIZATIONS AND THEIR GOALS

An *organization* can be defined as the social, formal, usually economic entity that employs the media worker in order to produce media content. It has definite boundaries, such that we can tell who is and who isn't a member. It is goal directed, composed of interdependent parts, and bureaucratically structured—members perform specialized functions, in standardized roles. Organizations compete with other organizations for resources (e.g., Turow, 1984).

Many studies have focused specifically on news operations. Although part of a larger firm, news professionals often regard the business side for all practical purposes as outside their organization. Within the newsrooms proper, organizational analysis reminds us that they have the same bureaucratic characteristics as other organizations. Responsibility is divided, authority is structured, seniority is rewarded. There are factions, power struggles, and overly ambitious climbers.

To fully understand the organizational nature of media, however, we must consider the entire structure, within newsrooms and beyond. Ultimately, all members of an organization must answer to the owners and top management, who must coordinate the entire enterprise. The increasing complexity of the corporate ownership structure makes this coordination process more complex and raises important questions. Media organizations often find themselves controlled by nonmedia owners. Larry Tisch of the Loew's hotel chain, for example, owns CBS, while General Electric owns RCA, of which NBC is part. Thus, the lines of authority at NBC News extend from the lowest-level news employee to the chairman of the board of General Electric. We'll examine the implications of this in greater detail below.

Even if a media firm is not actually owned by another company, it can form important interlocks with it, both through stock ownership and in sharing members on their boards of directors (see Chapter 8). RJR Nabisco, a large media advertiser, owns a 20 percent share in the cable network ESPN, which is controlled by Capital Cities/ABC. GE owns NBC and is also a major defense contractor and nuclear power company. France's Hachette Company's leader chairs it and one of the largest French military defense companies (Bagdikian, 1989). Deciding where organizational boundaries stop in this complex network of interlocking interests can be very hard indeed. Yet, these broad connections have an important impact on content and must be considered.

The Primacy of Economic Goals

For most organizations the primary goal is economic, to make a profit. Other goals are built into this overarching objective, such as to produce a quality product, serve the public, and achieve professional recognition. In unusual cases, the owner of an organization may choose to make the economic goal secondary. The controversial Korean figure, the Reverend Sun Myung Moon, for example, has bankrolled the *Washington Times* for years in spite of its heavy financial losses, presumably in order to provide a conservative voice in public affairs and to garner greater prestige (No. 2, 1989). If professional objectives are to be met, the organization obviously cannot afford to ignore the economic goal indefinitely.

When a company is privately owned, the owners can operate the business as they see fit. But most large media firms are owned by stockholders. This form of ownership intensifies the purely economic objectives of the company. Managers of publicly traded companies can be replaced if they fail their responsibility to the stockholders to maximize profit. The stock market cares little for public service if it means sacrificing profitability.

Other trends have also contributed to enhancing the economic objective. For one, media corporations have gotten larger. These larger firms take fewer risks than smaller ones, which includes exerting their power where possible to obtain economic and political advantage. These corporate goals can permeate the entire firm, as illustrated by a case related by Bagdikian (1987). Corporate giant Gulf + Western owned Simon & Schuster, an editor at which in 1979 proposed to publish a book critical of big corporations. Even though the book did not mention Gulf + Western by name, the president of Simon & Schuster rejected the proposed book because it made all corporations look bad. Indeed, as media firms become more diversified and complex, the economic goal is the one thing the many parts of the corporation have in common. Press scholars have been particularly interested in how these economic goals affect the journalistic product.

Economics as Constraints

Media sociologists, like Herbert Gans and Leon Sigal, typically view economic considerations as constraints on newswork and, thus, as indirect influences on editorial decisions. Newsworkers find it hard to relate audience demand and advertising revenue to the nature and quality of news coverage (Sigal, 1973). Would one story, for example, raise newspaper circulation or television ratings more than another? And, if so, by how much? Most media organizations want to make money, but the organizational structure itself acts as a barrier or filter between the larger organization's economic requirements and the routines of newswork. The *New York Times* and *Washington Post* decentralize their budgets, giving each news desk control over its share of resources, within which news decisions are made, with relatively little concern over cost-effectiveness. Thus, Sigal (1973) concludes that "profit maximization provides no guideposts, only constraints," arguing that these economic constraints establish the parameters within which gatekeepers must contend for scarce resources, an interaction that is bureaucratically structured.

In more profitable times, the network news departments often found themselves going over budget to cover unexpected wars, hostage crises, space shots, and other breaking news events. The professional instincts of news managers, rather than any hope of direct commercial payoff, required them to cover important stories. Former CBS news executive Gordon Manning once told his staff "don't ever let me catch you missing a story because you wanted to save money" (Boyer, 1988, p. 89).

Indeed, Sigal suggests that news organizations are unlike others in their responsiveness to the profit motive:

> So long as revenues are sufficient to ensure organizational survival, professional and social objectives take precedence over profits, particularly for the management of firms like the [Washington] *Post* and [New York] *Times*, where a single family maintains financial control. (1973, p. 8)

Economics as Dictates

In recent years, this view appears less accurate. The national newspapers, newsmagazines, and networks studied by Sigal and Gans were relatively flush with money in the late 1960s and early 1970s. From all accounts the profit motive has become more important since these studies, rendering economic constraints into dictates, and weakening the insulation of the news department from the larger firm. We should ask to what extent these economic "constraints," as they become more severe, affect content. Organizations can do two things in response: sell more of their profit to the right people, and/or reduce the cost of production.

In the rush of daily journalism most stories cannot be weighed on the basis of their economic payoff. Many are clearly evaluated for their audience appeal, which translates into higher circulation and ratings, producing greater advertising revenue. As competition for audience attention grows, newspapers are doing more research to discover readers' wants and needs. Most papers of at least 100,000 circulation have in-house research capability (Veronis, 1989). At profit-hungry local television news stations around the country, a look at coverage during ratings sweeps periods shows that producers are well aware of the economic payoff of sex and violence, which grab attention in news just as they do in prime-time entertainment shows. Prime-time documentaries are now dealing less often with serious issues and more with celebrity interviews. In fact, it would seem that television, given its weaker and briefer tradition of public and community service, is more prone to economic influences than newspapers. The examples below show how economics has affected the television news product.

Television networks and local stations have provided a particularly high-profile example of trimming production costs. In recent years, ABC, CBS, and NBC have all had to slash budgets, close bureaus, lay off correspondents, and miss stories they would have covered in the past. The skyrocketing salaries paid to star anchors and correspondents (designed to increase product appeal) have cut the resources available for newsgathering. News directors argue, of course, that these cuts do not affect news judgment, but clearly economic considerations have reduced the traditional core of local community reporting (Standish, 1989).

Before bringing its cost-cutting skills to its merger with ABC, Capital Cities, Inc., was known as one of the leanest local news operations in the country. It cut the news budget of KGO-TV in San Francisco by 20 percent, after which an assignment editor there concluded:

> I have to laugh when I hear executives say the cutbacks haven't affected quality. A producer doesn't have the time he did in the past to carefully consider a story. There's not sufficient planning—not sufficient time to do stories. Too often people aren't getting that time when they say, "Hey, I have a great story. I need two days to report it and two days to shoot it." (Robins, 1989, p. 46)

Another KGO staffer added, "We could do more documentaries if we added more reporters and producers. We could do more follow-up stories—we could be better at going back to pick up where we left off . . ." (p. 56).

KTVY-TV, in Oklahoma City, had its normal staff and budget reduced after it was sold. To adjust, the station made several changes: (1) began planning coverage farther in advance—a step that favors the prepackaged and promoted "pseudo-event," (2) began using more picture stories that didn't require reporters, (3) purchased a "supplemental program service"—canned packaged stories, cheaper than adding more reporters, (4) began rerunning consumer pieces dressed up as the "Best of," (5) introduced a feature in lieu of a reporter package, in which the meteorologist explained weather. The station news director said that even when profits improve, the "efficiencies" will probably remain (Standish, 1989, p. 23). Few local stations are willing to spend more money on news, even if revenues improve, once they find they can get a show on the air with the new cost-saving measures.

Economic Logic of the Media

For the most part, the commercial mass media make their money by delivering audiences to advertisers. To the extent that they are consumed by desirable target audiences, print and broadcast media are attractive to advertisers. They must also provide messages compatible with the ads. *Ms.* magazine, for example, achieved a wide circulation, but its aggressive social issues content was not attractive to advertisers who preferred the softer content of the more traditional women's magazines ("Stakes Sold," 1989). Print media pages are a function of the amount of advertisements attracted. When ad lineage is down, a newspaper's news hole is reduced accordingly. Economics exerts an equally powerful though different effect on broadcast media. While a newspaper or magazine can print additional pages for additional news, television and radio are restricted to no more than twenty-four hours in a day. Additional time for television news, for example, means less time for higher-rated entertainment programming. Breaking into regularly scheduled programs means lost advertising time, and lost revenue.

The economic logic of television news can also be seen in the fate of other discretionary news programming: the network documentaries. Their small audiences make them unprofitable, in a period when no network can afford to write off a block of time. Regular prime-time news "magazine" shows ("20/20," "Prime Time Live") incorporate the same entertainment elements as other prime-time fare: celebrity interviews, sex and crime stories. They have evolved to meet the economic goals of the network organization.

For several reasons, television displays the influence of economic objectives on content most clearly. Most broadcast organizations make all their revenue from advertising. Unlike most daily newspapers, television stations compete head to head with comparable organizations offering a very similar product. The inflexible time within which to program commercials translates every programming decision into an economic trade-off. One famous dispute at CBS illustrates how strongly economic logic can influence media decisions. When Senator J. William Fulbright's Foreign Relations Committee was holding hearings on the Vietnam War in early 1966, Fred Friendly was the head of CBS News. CBS's morning shows drew the majority of viewers, and preempting those shows to cover the hearings live was economically unfavorable. Nevertheless, Friendly had been given permission to do so for two full days of testimony, although not without resistance from his superiors. When Friendly asked for three additional days of preemption to stay with the hearings, the request was rejected. Friendly replied: "I find this situation untenable. You are making a news judgment but basing it on business criteria, and I can't do this job under these circumstances" (Friendly, 1967, p. 233).

Friendly acknowledged that the decision not to continue televising the hearings was one dictated by "the system" (p. 243). Regardless of the executive in charge, the organization required a decision consistent with its economic logic. In his classic study of network news, Edward Epstein concluded from this incident that Friendly showed that "even the president of a network news division cannot consistently buck the economic logic under which the network operates and survive" (Epstein, 1974, p. 123). The secondary goals of divisions within a media organization must ultimately be compatible with, if not further, the goals of the larger organization.

THE ORGANIZATION: ROLES AND STRUCTURE

To carry out its goals, an organization must assign roles and develop a structure through which its members can work together in optimum fashion.

Media Organization Roles

Within most media organizations there are three general levels. The front line employees, such as writers, reporters, and creative staff, gather and package the raw material. The middle level consists of managers, editors, producers, and others who coordinate the process and mediate communication between the bottom and the top of the organization. Top-level corporate and news executives make organization policy, set budgets, make important personnel decisions, protect commercial and political interests of the firm, and when necessary defend the organization's employees from outside pressures (a frequent requirement in the case of news organizations).

The roles that people fill in organizations largely determine their views. Roles shape their orientation toward organizational issues, by providing a distinct vantage point on and stake in decisions. Recruitment patterns help maintain the views associated with these roles. In television, for example, the path to station management traditionally has been through the sales positions, rather than through the news departments. This career path ensures that television managers think more like businesspersons and less like journalists.

Institutional position greatly determines the power vested in a role, although this power does not stem entirely from one's position in the organization chart. Lower-ranking employees may have special expertise or other means to thwart directives from the top, often making negotiation and compromise necessary.

Media Organization Structure

Given this basic outline, there are any number of variations in the ways these roles can be combined and structured with organizations. The power associated with organization roles and the relationships between them vary both across and within media. Organization structure has a pervasive, if not readily identifiable, effect on media content.

In a typical newspaper organization a publisher runs the entire organization, which comprises the news, editorial, advertising, circulation, and production departments. A glance of the masthead of most papers reveals their top management. At the *New York Times,* for example, Publisher Arthur Ochs Sulzberger oversees the executive editor of the paper and the president, who in turn oversees the vice presidents in charge of operations, production, advertising, finance/human resources, systems, and circulation.

The organization chart of the *Wall Street Journal* is shown in Figure 7.3. The managing editor oversees a number of other editors who are responsible for specific sections of the paper. The level two editors, who oversee specialized reporting staffs, are shown below these first-level editors. The arrangement shown was implemented to streamline the placement of news and features, which all go through the news desk staffed by the three senior editors (Tannenbaum, 1989). The foreign editor, for example, would edit stories originating from the various overseas bureaus before sending them to the news desk. The managing editor reports to the publisher and president (who is also chief operating officer of the parent company, Dow Jones & Company, Inc.). The editor and vice-president of the *Journal* is the editorial director and also reports to the publisher, as do the vice presidents in charge of marketing, circulation, production, and technology. Thus, the editorial page is kept separate from the rest of the paper by having its editor report directly to the publisher.

The major television networks are also complex organizations, with the news divisions kept structurally distinct from the larger enterprise. At ABC, for example, reporters, writers, producers, and camera operators report to the executive producer, who reports to the president of the ABC News division. (See Figure 7.4.) The news head is one of five presidents who report to the president of the Television Network Group. He and the heads of the Broadcast and Publishing Group also hold titles with the larger Capital Cities/ABC, Inc., parent company, which has its own corporate management team, headed by the chair of the board and chief executive officer. ABC manages other news operations at its owned and operated stations. Each of these stations has a general manager, who performs the same functions as a newspaper publisher, overseeing both the editorial and business sides. The news directors at these stations act like the newspaper editor, linking the news division and the rest of the organization, and supervising the producers, who have direct responsibility for specific programs.

Regardless of the medium, the ultimate power lies in ownership. In most companies, stock ownership entitles one to vote for directors on the board that runs the company. Top management is either part of the board or accountable to it. That stock may be broadly owned or controlled by one family or a few large investors. The *New York Times* is a good example of how ownership can be structured to ensure the autonomy and control of a media organization. The *Times* is part of the New York Times Company, a $1.7 billion enterprise, which also owns other newspapers, magazines, and broadcasting companies. The paper has remained in the hands of descendants of Adolph S. Ochs, who purchased the paper in 1891, earning for itself a strong reputation as an independent and leading voice among the news media. Recognizing the importance of ownership, Ochs distributed company stock such that voting rights and control remain within the family (the Sulzbergers), and thus management is not subject to pressures from outside stockholders and threats of corporate takeovers. Furthermore, a stockholders' agreement among the trustees prevents them from selling, merging, or giving up the control of the company. Such a move could be taken only if they unanimously agree that it would best serve the primary objective of the trust: "to maintain the editorial independence and integrity of The *New York Times* and to continue it as an independent newspaper, entirely fearless, free of ulterior influence and unselfishly devoted to the public welfare" (Notice of 1989 Annual Meeting and Proxy Statement, 1989, p. 3).

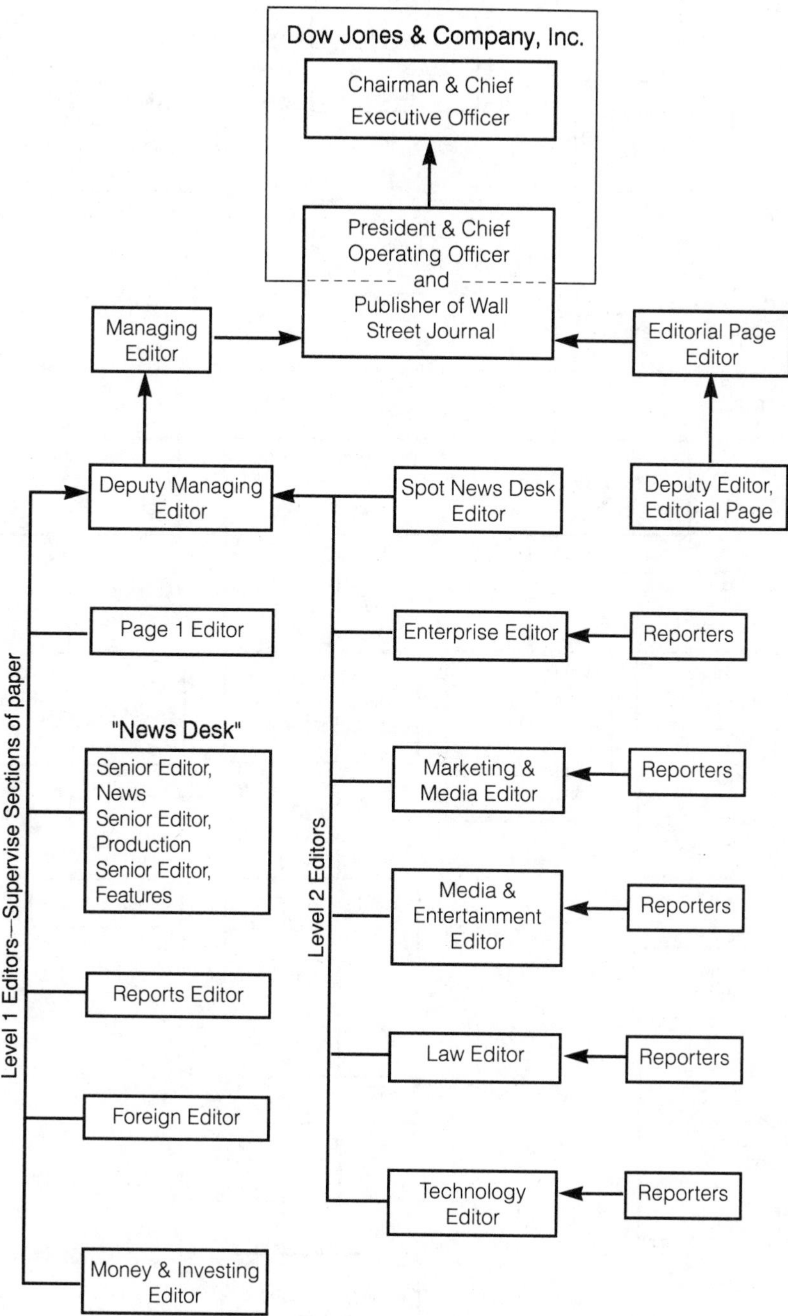

Figure 7.3. Organizational structure of the *Wall Street Journal*

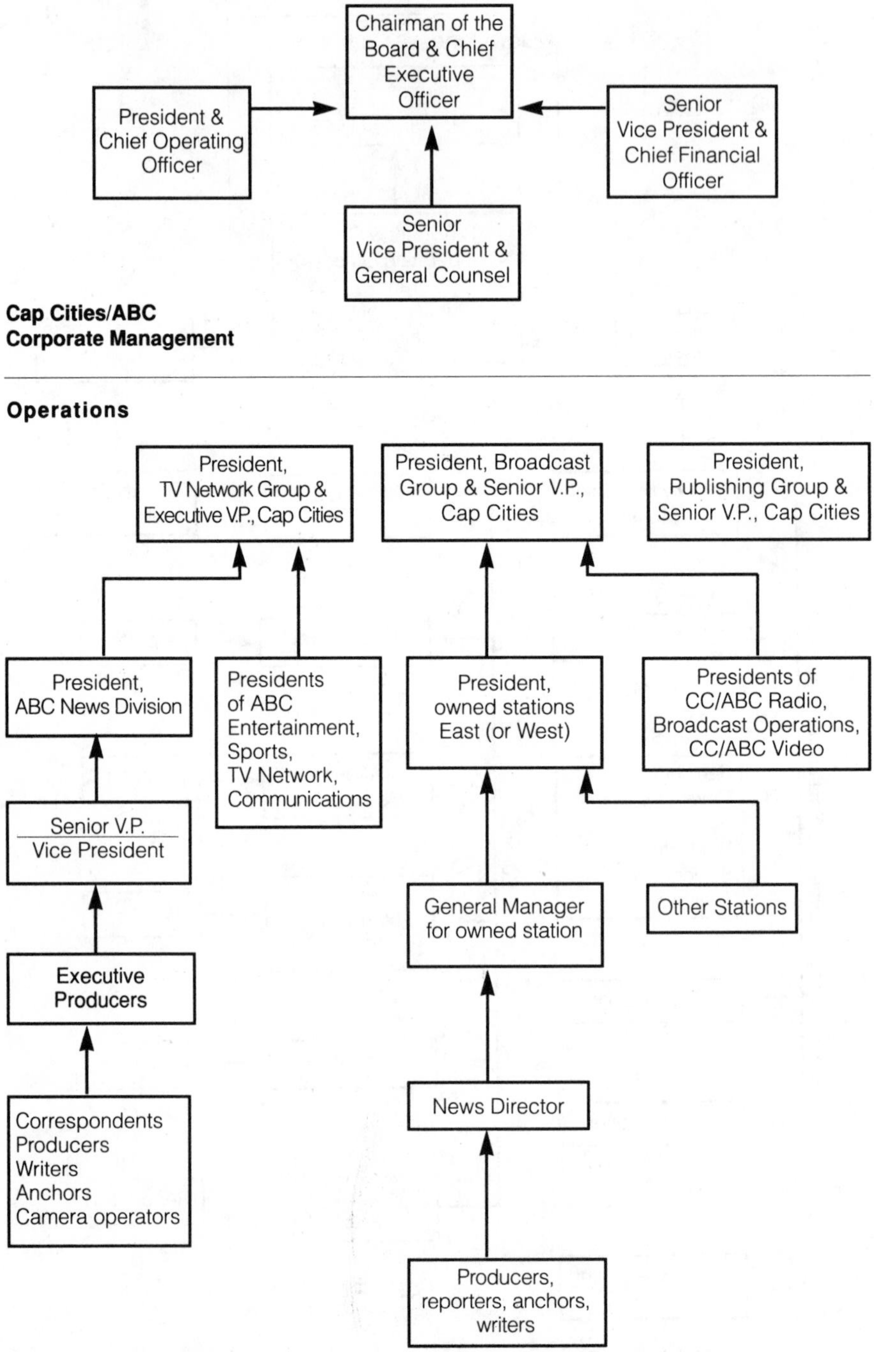

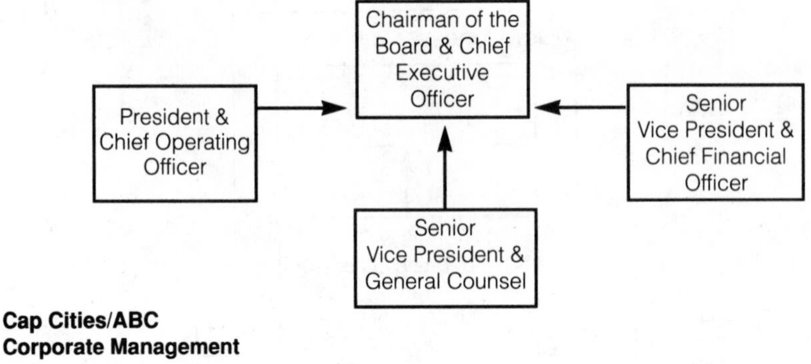

Chairman of the Board & Chief Executive Officer
President & Chief Operating Officer
Senior Vice President & Chief Financial Officer
Senior Vice President & General Counsel
Cap Cities/ABC Corporate Management
Operations
President, TV Network Group & Executive V.P., Cap Cities
President, Broadcast Group & Senior V.P., Cap Cities
President, Publishing Group & Senior V.P., Cap Cities
President, ABC News Division
Presidents of ABC Entertainment, Sports, TV Network, Communications
President, owned stations East (or West)
Presidents of CC/ABC Radio, Broadcast Operations, CC/ABC Video
Senior V.P.
Vice President
General Manager for owned station
Other Stations
Executive Producers
News Director
Correspondents
Producers
Writers
Anchors
Camera operators
Producers, reporters, anchors, writers

Figure 7.4. Organizational structure of Capital Cities/ABC, Inc.

Newsmaking as an Organizational Process

Having established the key components of organizational structure, we ask: How does this structure affect media content? How is the product mediated by the organization? In one sense, the structure simply reflects where an organization chooses to allocate its resources and how it adapts to its environment. A decision to maintain a news bureau in Washington, D.C., ensures that news from the capital has organization value, and clearly affects content. In addition, though, we may ask a more subtle question. What is the effect of the fact that media content is produced in an organizational setting?

In one sense, the organization formalizes conflict, an inevitable part of large, complex media operations, and the structure of these organizations represents the playing field upon which employees contend for scarce resources. For news media, Sigal says the division of labor "forms the lines of cleavage along which organization conflict crystallizes" (Sigal, 1973, p. 21). He argues that the uncertainty of news leaves considerable room for the influence of organizational politics.

Conflicts are built into the system, both vertically and horizontally. Reporters are typically oriented toward their sources, with whom they are in most frequent contact. This brings them into frequent conflict with editors, who are attuned more strongly to audience interest and organization goals (Tunstall, 1971; also Gans, 1979).

Lateral turf conflicts also occur between departments. Within a newspaper, for example, contending departments are represented by editors. They serve as mediators who must balance two constituencies—their reporting staffs and the larger organization. That is, they bargain but ultimately must reach an accommodation with other editors over resources, especially space in the publication. Conflict is seen particularly in turf struggles over stories, particularly those with overlapping jurisdictions (Sigal, 1973, p. 21). When the Watergate story broke, for example, Bob Woodward and Carl Bernstein were assigned the story by the metro desk. Later, of course, it became a major national story, coveted by the more elite national reporting staff (Halberstam, 1979). Similarly, if a Japanese firm buys a U.S. movie company, the business, entertainment, and foreign editors at a paper could conceivably all lay claim to the story.

The newspaper page one makeup process illustrates how organizational politics can affect news content. Editors hold conferences to determine what stories from the various desks (e.g., national, foreign, metropolitan) will make it onto the front page. Each editor advocates the stories being developed by his or her own staff. In his analysis of *New York Times* and *Washington Post* front-page stories, Sigal discovered that out of this bureaucratic conflict emerged a pattern of front-page stories that, over time, balanced the number of stories emanating from the three principal desks. Given that we would not expect actual events to display such a neat balance, it can best be attributed to an organizational structure that requires the three desks to accommodate each other.

Each organizational structure gives rise to distinct occupational cultures. Because of the extra layer of bureaucracy between the *New York Times*'s Washington bureau and its home office, the capital press corps considered it more an editor's paper compared with the *Post,* which they viewed as a reporter's paper (Sigal, 1973).

How the Larger Organization Affects Content

From the organizational perspective, we may ask how the producers of content are affected by other parts of a media organization. How does the business department of a newspaper, for example, affect the editorial side? How do other subsidiaries of a conglomerate affect that firm's media organizations? The wave of media mergers, takeovers, and shakeups in the 1980s has focused attention on the impact of organizational structure on the media product. Particularly in news, the tradition is such that media scholars have been concerned with organizational influences on journalists that may distort their ability to objectively describe the world. An exposé on the dangers of smoking, for example, may endanger a magazine's lucrative advertising, as *Mother Jones* found out in 1980 when tobacco companies pulled their ads following a critical article (Bagdikian, 1987). We can well ask what aspects of organizational structure contribute to or reduce this autonomy, and thus susceptibility to economic pressures.

Traditional studies of newswork paint a picture of a fiercely independent journalistic culture that keeps news departments largely autonomous within the larger organization. Indeed, news organizations are usually structured to ensure journalistic autonomy. However, no law dictates this division, and, in fact, the wall between the editorial and business sides of media organizations has been steadily eroding. Critics have charged the news media with sacrificing journalistic autonomy for greed and arrogance. From an organizational standpoint, it may be a very natural outgrowth of the fact that newspapers and television networks have both been facing declining revenues.

A new breed of budget-cutting market-oriented managers has been installed to oversee many newsrooms. For example, it was no accident that, facing declining profits in the early 1980s, CBS (the traditional leader in broadcast journalism since the days of Edward R. Murrow) turned to Edward Joyce to head the news division. Joyce had been a local television news director, known more for running profitable operations than for his journalistic credentials. Not a part of the strong CBS News journalistic tradition, Joyce was the perfect man to carry out the severe budget cuts mandated by the corporation (e.g., Boyer, 1988). Many at CBS News saw Joyce as less an advocate for the division, and more a hatchet man for the larger corporation. Critics have charged that the decline in traditional news standards can be traced to the closer relationship between CBS News leaders and the higher leaders in the company, weakening the "wall" of independence that had always separated news from entertainment, ratings, networking, and profit (Stone, 1989).

As the corporate organization structure of the media has become more complex, concerns over journalistic autonomy have become greater. In the old days, the primary organizational threat to journalistic objectivity may have been an overeager publisher, anxious to influence news slant. Today, the threat is more abstract. Growing organizational complexity has inserted more hierarchical levels of bureaucracy between front-line media workers and top management. It stands to reason that the more distant these levels become, the less sensitive top management will be to the professional concerns of the workers at the bottom.

Furthermore, greater complexity brings greater interconnections between the top levels and institutions outside the organization. Reporters, for example, are advised not to be politically active for fear it will impede their objectivity. No such restrictions are placed on upper reaches of media management. While publisher of the *Austin American-Statesman,* for example, Roger Kintzel was also chair of the local Chamber of Commerce. The directors of many media firms also sit on the boards of other institutions, including banks, universities, and large corporations that rely heavily on media advertising. Thus, the larger and more complex the firm, the more likely that larger organizational factors will prevail over individual and routine influences.

Network Autonomy: De Facto or De Jure?

At the three major networks, it is understood that the autonomy of the news divisions safeguards their objectivity, and the larger corporation is not to tamper with their news judgment.

News departments may be organizationally buffered, but pressures can still be brought to bear. These influences are often subtle and unspoken, yet help enforce corporate policy. In 1984, an ABC News investigative team had conducted research into scandalous conditions at nursing homes owned by Charles Wick, a close friend of President Reagan and head of the U.S. Information Agency. ABC News brass balked at the proposed script and killed the story. Although theoretically the president of news (Roone Arledge) made the final decisions on news, Wick's lawyer dealt directly with the higher corporate level. He wrote a complaint to the executive vice president of ABC Inc. (before the Capital Cities buyout), saying the story "would hardly appear to be newsworthy." A copy of the letter was routed to the vice president of ABC News, two days before the meeting at which the producers were told the story was not newsworthy and would not air (Dowie, 1985). The connection between these events, although circumstantial, suggests that organizations and their personnel are not immune from pressure.

Three examples follow, all dealing with CBS. As the traditional leader in broadcast journalism, CBS has attracted more than its share of analysis of its internal workings, from scholars and former employees. Network news is a high-profile news medium of wide interest to the public, and the problems at CBS are similar in nature to organizational issues in other media. Furthermore, as a news operation that prides itself on professionalism and independence, CBS represents a conservative test of the likelihood of management interference in news judgment.

Top leaders in media organizations don't often try to influence specific stories, but may do so under pressure from leaders of other powerful institutions. The published presidential files of former president Richard Nixon show that he was obsessed with how the news media treated him, and pressured them accordingly. When his chief media monitor, White House counsel Charles Colson, met with CBS president Frank Stanton on July 15, 1971, Colson goaded Stanton by saying Nixon knew Stanton couldn't get involved with the judgment of the news department. Rising to the bait, Stanton said, "You're damn right I can do something about them and will!" adding that he "would certainly call the President of CBS News and raise hell" (Oudes, 1989, p. 296).

A more specific intervention by top CBS management came the next year. A major and unusually long (fourteen-minute) story on the growing Watergate scandal aired on October 27, 1972, and predictably displeased the Nixon White House, which immediately contacted CBS chairman William Paley. David Halberstam notes that much corporate planning had gone into "setting the limits while at the same time keeping it from looking as if there were any" (Halberstam, 1979, p. 657). This allowed Paley to keep the news division reasonably contained, while preserving the cover story of complete news independence. Paley summoned CBS president Frank Stanton and news division head Richard Salant to criticize the Watergate story and strongly advise against a planned Part II. After much subsequent discussion within the news division, the second piece did air, but with its length much reduced, from fourteen minutes to eight (Halberstam, 1979).

In his analysis of how CBS treated student dissent during the 1960s, Todd Gitlin examined the case of a 1965 CBS documentary, "The Berkeley Rebels." Three weeks before it was to air, CBS chairman Paley and president Stanton intervened to call for substantial modifications, including the addition of comments from the University of California president Clark Kerr, and a deprecating introduction and conclusion to be read by correspondent Harry Reasoner. The documentary's creator said he was told that Kerr had complained forcefully about the upcoming broadcast to Stanton, who in turn ordered the changes. Gitlin argues that the media elite enforce their standards, "even—if necessary—against the normal workings of journalistic routines" (Gitlin, 1980, pp. 63–65).

The Case of Time Inc.

In the print media, the merger of Time Inc. and Warner Communications Inc. in 1989 provides a good example of how the changing structure of media companies affects media content. Time Inc. (publisher of *Time, Life, Fortune, Sports Illustrated,* and *People*) merged with Warner to become the largest U.S. entertainment/communication company. Indeed, one of the primary issues raised by the merger was the impact on "journalistic integrity and editorial independence," that is, the organizational autonomy of Time Inc. magazines. In rejecting Paramount's hostile takeover bid for *Time,* a Delaware judge noted that *Time*'s most important goal was to "maintain an adequate Time Inc." and preserve the "*Time* culture . . . a managerial philosophy and distinctive *structure* that is intended to protect journalistic integrity from pressures from the business side of the enterprise" (Ciabattari, 1989a, p. 27, our emphasis).

Time's original editor-in-chief was the strong-willed founder Henry Luce, whose will stipulated the company be "principally a journalistic enterprise . . . operated in the public interest as well as the interest of the stockholders" (Ciabattari, 1989a, p. 28). Luce made decisions on the basis of his own ideology and personal commitment to anticommunism, procapitalism, and "The American Century," not on business criteria. In fact, he looked down on his business department, often failing to attend business meetings, preferring to spend his time on his duties as "editor" (Halberstam, 1979). After Luce, this power was formalized by making the editor-in-chief a member of the Time Inc. board of directors, editorially equal to the chief executive officer. But the merger with Warner weakened this role, by reducing the earnings contributed by Time publications to the conglomerate.

A more immediate concern of the journalistic community was how *Time* would cover its own story. How impartial would it be? Earlier Jason McManus, editor-in-chief, had decided not to cover the March 4 Time Warner merger announcement, a story big enough for both the *New York Times* and *Newsweek*. McManus later said he didn't want it to appear like part of a big "public relations rollout" (Ciabattari, 1989b, p. 34). Thus, reporting on the larger enterprise is a no-win situation. When Paramount tried to disrupt the merger with a hostile takeover, rival *Newsweek* made it a cover story (June 26). *Time* journalists worried that they were getting scooped on their own story (Ciabattari, 1989b).

Newspapers: The Editor as Manager or Journalist

The same concerns about autonomy are being raised at newspapers as well. Of particular interest are the changing roles of editors, along with their place in the organizational structure. These changes have important implications for content. Newspapers, like television, have faced declining audiences and increasing competition. This has ushered in a greater marketing orientation among media managers to try to maximize productivity.

One indication of the erosion in journalistic autonomy is the way editors relate to the organization. Do they feel allegiance to the news or business side of the enterprise? In an analysis of news management trends in daily newspapers, Underwood (1988) maintains that "as corporations have extended their hold on U.S. newspapers, the editors of these newspapers have begun to behave more and more like the managers of any other corporate entity" (p. 23). For example, upon becoming executive editor at the Gannett-owned *Seattle Times*, Michael R. Fancher outlined his goals in 1986 to his publisher, saying that 40 percent of his time would be devoted to monitoring newsroom budgets and coordinating its marketing role (failing to mention anything about news per se). He would oversee a newsroom management reorganization and be liaison with the circulation department (Underwood, 1988).

Underwood concludes that profit pressures and the corporate MBA mentality are transforming the newspaper business, a traditional haven for the "independent, irreverent, and creative spirits" (p. 24). Here we see the clash between individual and organizational values. While the organization values short stories, to increase audience appeal and revenue, writers obviously like longer pieces that leave more room for creativity. A former *Detroit News* executive editor says modern management techniques (p. 24) are sapping the vitality of creative editors and reporters: "At a managed newspaper it beats you down" (p. 25). These trends lead us to question whether a top-down organization management structure can be carried to such an extreme that the lower-level workers no longer have the freedom traditionally associated with journalists. Clearly, the media workers' opinions of the new management vary depending on their position within the organization.

German sociologist Max Weber wrote of the drive in Western culture toward "rationality," ever-increasing control, predictability, and stability in human relations and organizations (King, 1987, p. 125). This top-down organization structure, which dictates decisions derived from audience marketing, exemplifies the rationalization of the news organization. Bureaucratic structures ensure conformity. Reporters work from lists of stories approved by editors.

USA Today is the modern prototype of the editor- and market-driven paper. Its organization structure can be contrasted with the *San Francisco Examiner,* the managing editor of which is described as identifying with reporters and having little patience with administrative bureaucratic burdens: the paper's executive editor advocates getting good people and giving them a lot of rope (Underwood, 1988, p. 26). The *Examiner*'s structure has the effect of giving relatively more power to the individual at the expense of the organization. Fancher offers an opposing view, arguing:

> Editors must understand dollars and cents today better than ever before. Keeping newsroom operating expenses within budget isn't enough. Editors must understand where their budgets fit with the larger financial picture of their company, and where news priorities fit in the overall strategic plan. (1987, p. 79)

He argues that the editor of a newspaper is responsible for keeping the organism as a whole functioning by coordinating both journalistic and marketing efforts: "Today the editor's job is more a function of 'management' than of editing—managing people, managing systems, and managing resources" (p. 73).

Analyzing these changing roles helps us evaluate the autonomy and relative power of the editorial side of a paper. If the editor controls both the editorial and business sides of the paper, the relative power of the journalistic division is less. The person making decisions primarily on journalistic grounds occupies a place somewhere below the editor in this case. For example, the editor of the *Philadelphia Inquirer* was also placed in charge of circulation and promotion, and made president of Philadelphia Newspapers Inc., an unusual move that broke through the traditional wall between the editorial and business sides of the organization. It was made, according to the publisher, to better coordinate resources (Fancher, 1987). By doing so, the editor is necessarily drawn into a greater marketing posture, responding to audience interests rather than to any autonomous standards internal to the journalistic profession. Ironically, economic pressures have forced news organizations to revise their structure to favor audience-based routines.

As nonjournalistic routines reach further down into the newsroom, the craft values of journalism often collide with "MBA" values. Installing managers in positions formerly filled by newspeople makes a strong impact on content. It changes the entire organizational culture and the extent to which one set of values holds sway over others.

Influence of Corporate Synergy

We have been talking mostly about journalism, but many of the same concerns can be expressed for other media, even those producing entertainment fare. Of special interest in recent years is the "synergy" sought by media organizations, the ability for their products to complement and reinforce one another. Ben Bagdikian offers one model scenario to media synergy:

> Giant Corporation Inc. owns subsidiaries in every medium. One of its magazines buys (or commissions) an article that can be expanded into a book, whose author is widely interviewed in the company magazines and on its broadcast stations. The book is turned into a screenplay for the company movie studios, and the film is automatically booked into the company's chain of theaters. The movie has a sound track that is released on the company record label. The vocalist is turned into an instant celebrity by cover features in the company magazines and interviews on its television stations. The recording is played on the company's chain of Top 40 radio stations. The movie is eventually issued by the firm's videocassette division and shown on company television stations. After that, rerun rights are sold to other television stations around the world. (Bagdikian, 1989, p. 812)

In the case of the Time Warner transaction, for example, critics had speculated that the new synergistic firm would benefit from entertainment shows promoted in the magazines. The same questions have been raised in the case of films produced by large conglomerates. Now it is not uncommon for company products to be featured in company films. When Coca-Cola controlled Columbia Pictures, for example, only its beverages could be featured.

Why should we be concerned with this process? Critics like Mark Crispin Miller have questioned the implications for cinematic narrative, particularly when the needs of CEOs and advertisers predominate over needs (and routines) of filmmakers. We would expect the story to be affirmative and upbeat, avoiding anything that would reflect negatively on the company's products. There is cause for concern when messages are selected not necessarily for their importance to an audience, their newsworthiness, or their artistic significance, but for how they fit into a larger organizational marketing scheme.

Ownership and Policy

At the top command posts of media organizations sit the owners. Their influence has attracted substantial scholarly interest. Ultimately media owners or their appointed top executives have the final say in what the organization does. If the employees don't like it they can quit. Others will be found to take their place, and routines can always be changed. Conservative action groups led by Jesse Helms appreciated the influence of ownership in 1985, when they urged their supporters to buy stock in CBS and "become Dan Rather's boss," ("Conservatives," 1985).

The owner's influence can be for good or ill. The most prolonged debate over ownership has been in the newspaper industry where, early on, Nixon and Jones (1956) concluded that differences in quality appear to hinge on the social responsibility and competence of the owners and operators of a newspaper. The concerns of media scholars have changed with the nature of media ownership, but they continue to question how today's owners have lived up to this responsibility. This responsibility has become greatly diffused, however. Fewer independent owners run their own media organizations, which have become but part of the larger corporate fabric.

We are now less concerned with overt propaganda-style messages, promoted by ideological publishers like Robert McCormack of the *Chicago Tribune,* known for his ultraconservative editorial policy until his death in 1955. The "Colonel's" opposition to change often ran counter to both public opinion and even his own copy editors (Windhauser, Norton, & Rhodes, 1983). Media researchers have in recent years explored questions of news quality, quantity, and emphasis on the local community. If otherwise similar media with different owners vary in their content, we presume an organizational influence that supersedes whatever routines may be held in common.

Changes in Corporate Ownership

Changes in ownership show its influence most clearly. This may come in the form of a corporate takeover, which often brings different values, objectives, culture, and, ultimately, content. Indeed, in recent years the buying and selling of large newspaper and broadcasting companies has become a big story in its own right.

Ownership changes at the big three television networks in the 1980s were widely covered and prominent examples of this phenomenon. In the mid-1980s, declining advertising revenues and rising costs put the networks in a crunch. As media critic Jeff Greenfield observed:

> What all three networks now had in common was a greatly increased debt-to-equity ratio, and new owners with no link to the old tradition that tended to shield network news from the accountants and cost managers. These owners began asking questions about a division that cost more money than it generated, and that was, moreover, under the direct control of the network. (Greenfield, 1987, p. 29)

The new network owners—Tisch/Loew's, Capital Cities, and General Electric—clearly imposed a news policy with far-reaching effects. News was to be treated like their other businesses, expected to support itself—a departure from the traditional view that network news is a loss-leader public service supported by the entertainment side of the enterprise.

These changes have direct implications for content. Media critic Peter Boyer, for example, in decrying the trend toward more sensational, lurid, docudrama-style news, found the root cause in the organization—namely, the "cataclysmic economic change that has jolted the networks in the last five years bringing new managements and with them new philosophies about the missions of the news divisions" (Boyer, 1989, p. 23).

The newspaper industry has had its share of high-profile ownership changes as well. Australian press magnate Rupert Murdoch, perhaps today's most notorious publisher, bought the *Chicago Sun-Times* in 1984 and made it more sensationalistic like his *New York Post* and *Boston Herald*. A large number of *Sun-Times* staffers quit, including the top management, and liberal columnists Ellen Goodman and Garry Wills were dropped ("Roger Simon," 1984). Murdoch used his British papers, the *Sun* and *The Times* of London, to help Prime Minister Margaret Thatcher. Before selling the *New York Post* in 1988, he had used that paper to render similar support to Ronald Reagan (Bagdikian, 1989, p. 806).

The influence of a flamboyant owner like Murdoch can be easily identified and evaluated, but few media buyers today maintain as high a profile as Murdoch. They are not crusaders, preferring to acquire or sell their holdings using economic criteria. Today, there are fewer of the overtly partisan owner/publishers in the mold of *Los Angeles Times* publisher Norman Chandler, who like most newspaper publishers was a strong Republican and helped Richard Nixon throughout his career; William Randolph Hearst (who put his *New York Journal-American* to work on behalf of Senator Joseph McCarthy and his Communist witch-hunt); and *Time* publisher Henry Luce, who also promoted Nixon, a politician eminently compatible with Luce's staunch anticommunism (Halberstam, 1979). Even in the case of Murdoch, his sensationalism is formulaic and calculated to boost circulation, his partisanship designed to curry political advantage for his enterprises. Regardless of motive, by establishing policy for the entire organization, media owners have an unmistakable impact on media content.

Another important feature of ownership patterns today is the sheer size of media conglomerates. The number of publications on the newsstand and radio and television stations, as well as new communication channels, make it appear that ownership is widely distributed. In truth, though, most media are owned by a handful of corporate media giants. Tracing the organizational connections among media reveals greater reasons for concern over the homogenization of content and ownership as an organizational influence. In his 1987 book, *The Media Monopoly,* Ben Bagdikian reports that twenty-nine corporations control most of the media business in this country, down from fifty when the book was first published in 1982. Five mammoth firms that Bagdikian claims now dominate the world's mass media are Time Warner Inc.; Bertelsmann AG (West Germany); News Corporation Ltd. (Murdoch's Australia-based firm); Hachette SA (France); Capital Cities/ABC Inc.

Ownership and Internal Slant: Newspapers

We notice the effects of ownership most when owners try to impose their views on media content. This is of particular concern in the news media, with their tradition of objective news reporting. Unlike broadcasting, newspapers traditionally endorse political candidates. Thus, one may assume that these endorsements provide a direct measure of the owner's or publisher's political attitude or that of the editorial board. To what extent do these attitudes find their way into the more "objective" news pages? Traditionally, newspapers have divided their editorial voice from more objective news reporting, usually placing these opinions on a separate page or pages. Several studies have examined the extent to which a paper slants its news reporting to conform to its editorial voice. Doing so would indicate that decisions at the top levels of the organization had superseded the content dictated by the routines of objective newsgathering. (This distinction between the "objective" news pages and the "subjective" editorial pages seems quaint to Europeans. In London, for example, there are several papers that each occupy a different position in the political spectrum and present their content—front page or editorial page—in accordance with those views.)

Newspapers have shown an overwhelming tendency to endorse Republican candidates. However, newspapers are rarely blatant about systematically favoring in news articles the candidates endorsed in their editorials. There is evidence that newspapers bias their reporting of public opinion campaign polls. Poll coverage favors those candidates that newspapers endorse, unless a nearby competitor has endorsed someone else, in which case coverage is more evenhanded. Interestingly, even papers not making endorsements still show significant bias in the way they report these polls, indicating that not taking an editorial stand does not mean a paper is free of bias (Wilhoit & Auh, 1974).

Of course, at most papers, letting editorial slant influence the news would make a newspaper an easy target for criticism. When one gets away from the traditional election-style endorsements and coverage, there is greater potential for slanting. Donohew (1967) found a direct, positive relationship between a publisher's attitude toward an issue and that publisher's paper's treatment of the issue. More specifically, Mann (1974) found that in reporting anti–Vietnam War demonstrations in the mid-1960s, pro-war papers gave smaller crowd estimates than antiwar papers.

News coverage of the same rally differed dramatically between the *Charlotte Observer,* which called demonstrators "honorable Americans" and the *Atlanta Constitution,* which disparaged marchers as "vile-mouthed anti-American extremists" with the "official blessings of the North Vietnam government" (p. 282). This form of slant, perhaps because it is more difficult to gauge, has been less frequently examined.

Multiple Media Ownership

Media scholars have paid particularly close attention to those companies owning more than one media organization. Absentee owners may be less inclined to adopt a vigorous editorial policy and aggressive news coverage. The greater the physical distance of the owners from the community being served, the more community interests may take a backseat to corporate and economic factors.

Chain v. Independent Ownership

The debate over newspaper chain ownership has increased as the number of independently owned papers has continued to decline. (After World War II, 80 percent of U.S. dailies were independently owned compared with 28 percent by 1986.) Fewer concerns have been raised over broadcast ownership, given the restrictions on the number of stations that can be owned by one company and the weaker public service tradition of local broadcasting. (One study found that group-owned stations broadcast more news than those that are not group owned [Wirth & Wollert, 1976].) Chain ownership usually means absentee ownership, and that raises the question of whether larger organization imperatives may outweigh local community concerns when it comes to news coverage. A group of scholars on press concentration has concluded that "groups [or chains] do not necessarily mean a problem for local autonomy, but the potential exists in many chain ownership situations" (Picard, Winter, McCombs, & Lacy, 1988, p. 204).

Is there a meaningful organizational difference between chain and independent papers? One indication examined by Parsons, Finnegan, and Benham (1988) is the roles in which employees perceive themselves. While the employee of the independent paper is socialized to the single local organization, the chain-paper employee is socialized additionally to the larger chain that transcends the local community. Thus, the organizational role may take precedence over the chain employee's role as a member of the community. These workers form weaker community attachments due to the job mobility necessary to rise within the larger firm. A survey of managing editors shows that the prominence of community role expectations is reduced in chain papers, and conflict resolved in favor of the organization (Parsons et al., 1988).

Bagdikian contends that, when chains take over a paper, they typically increase ad and subscription rates, reduce serious news—which is more expensive to gather—and hire less qualified journalists (Bagdikian, 1987). However, research has found both positive and negative effects of chain ownership (Hale, 1988).

Chains do not necessarily diminish a paper's performance. Indeed, chains can bring acquisitions more in line with industry standards for the proportion of space devoted to news, editorial, and feature selection, and infuse new capital and vigor.

Although broad outlines of the product—such as size of news hole, number of columns, editorials, and so on—do not vary consistently with ownership, other more subtle differences in tone and slant do emerge, however. Clearly, newspapers vary in slant with the ownership. A study of news coverage before and after a takeover of a local paper by Gannett, the country's largest chain, found that the *Knoxville Journal* became more favorable toward the local World's Fair project after the sale (Browning, Grierson, & Howard, 1984). The professional concerns of their news employees limit publishers in the heavy-handed promotion of their views. A closer, more qualitative look at actual content does reveal important differences.

In their analysis of twenty-one Minnesota dailies, Donohue, Olien, and Tichenor (1985) found that locally owned or in-state owned papers devoted three times the space to reporting local community conflict than chain-owned papers with headquarters out of state. Furthermore, during a fourteen-year period from 1965 to 1979, papers remaining under in-state ownership increased coverage of local government conflict by almost a third, while those under out-of-state ownership in 1979 had decreased such reporting by nearly half (p. 498).

Ownership also affects a paper's editorials. Thrift (1977), for example, found that chain newspapers published fewer argumentative editorials, fewer editorials on local matters, and fewer editorials on controversial topics than independent papers.

At least one study has shown substantial partisan differences by ownership. A survey of editorial editors at papers with circulation of 50,000 or greater found that 55 percent of editors at independently owned papers said they had a Republican publisher versus 93 percent of editors at chain-owned papers. And, in fact, 65 percent of chain papers endorsed Reagan in 1984 versus 44 percent of independents; 25 percent of the chain papers endorsed Mondale versus 44 percent of the independents (St. Dizier, 1986).

In general, chain newspapers are more likely to endorse presidential candidates and to endorse the favored candidate of the press overall. Chains are overwhelmingly homogenous in these endorsements, with virtually all members of respective chains endorsing the same candidate (Wackman, Gillmor, Gaziano, & Dennis, 1975). There does not, however, appear to be any overt collusion by editorialists within the chain to stress any particular issue or promote any particular political party (Wagenberg & Soderlund, 1975). Chains may not dictate editorial policy overtly, but there is de facto convergence toward similar views.

Cross-Ownership

Other patterns of ownership that have concerned scholars involve companies that own both newspapers and broadcast organizations, so-called cross-ownership. Of particular interest is how the merging of the two media, with different organizational requirements and structure, affects the news product in both. Cross-ownership has been criticized on grounds of media diversity, because it means one company may own both the television and newspaper outlets in a community.

Cross-owned television stations and newspapers transmit just as much if not more news and public affairs information than media that are not cross-owned (Wirth & Wollert, 1976; Wollert, 1978). Indeed, Wollert argues that a company's newspaper, with its primary orientation toward news, may benefit its television counterpart by infusing its news values into the more entertainment-oriented broadcast organization.

However, as to individual communities, media news is less comprehensive in towns where all the media are owned by one company compared with those towns with multiple media owners (Stempel, 1973).

CONTROL: HOW IS POWER EXERCISED?

How does an organization see to it that its members conform to its policies? How does the organization exert control over its members in the production of content? Editors must control reporters, publishers must control editors, and the owner(s) must control the publishers. Control is essential, given the inherent conflict within an organization. Indeed, Paul Hirsch notes that "organizational analysis reminds us that the issue here is not whether social control exists (for it is a constant), but rather who exercises power and for what reasons" (1977, p. 26). The organization must socialize individual workers to their routines and enforce them, while handling situations not covered by the routines. Most control is straightforward and accomplished through a reward system. Promotions and salary raises go to the workers who perform their jobs well, while those who don't are demoted or fired. Other control is equally powerful because it is subtle and unquestioned.

Control in the News Business

The question of control becomes particularly problematic in the news business, where journalists often assert their own autonomy against what they consider management interference in their professional turf. Nevertheless, as we have seen, organization leaders can dictate content directly with explicit policy guidelines. As a recent example, one paper felt compelled to express an overt policy in response to its coverage of a rally for homosexual rights. A memo urged news staffers to "never forget that we are putting out family newspapers in conservative communities. We must never forget that this should be a prime consideration in story and photo selection, in editing, and in cutline and headline writing" (Document, 1989). However, this kind of influence is less common than other forms of control, which are less direct, but just as powerful.

Studies of newsrooms show that overt conflicts over stories don't come up very often. Beyond the newsroom, both Gans and Sigal agree that publishers do not often exert direct power on a day-to-day basis. Obviously, the multitude of daily news decisions would make closer supervision impossible. Instead, the organization sets the boundaries and guidelines to direct these decisions. Tunstall (1971), for example, argues that most organizational policy is traditional and relatively fixed. Journalists learn these often unwritten policies through experience and by observing what kinds of stories are used by the organization. As demonstrated by the cases of intervention in news decisions by ABC and CBS, top management gets involved when the stakes are high. This intervention itself has the effect of letting newsworkers know that the boundaries have been reached.

The absence of visible attempts at control does not mean that none are being made. Whenever media workers deduce what their supervisors want and give it to them, de facto control has been exercised. The predictable routines of newsgathering prevent many policy conflicts, but these routines are part of and meet larger organizational requirements, which establish the boundaries of acceptability. The relations between reporters and editors cannot be too heavy-handed. Reporters can counterbalance the power of the editor to the extent they have the support of their peers and greater firsthand knowledge of the subject matter than the editor. Each must rely on the other if they are to fulfill the inexorable demands of daily newsgathering.

Gans (1979) notes that the power of top editors and superiors is maintained by organizationwide pressures for conformity. Enhancing this power are the remoteness of these executives, the layers of bureaucracy between them and lower levels, and the fact that they don't have to justify or explain their decisions, "forcing underlings to guess what will please or displease them" (p. 97). Interestingly, reporters often object to an editor changing their stories, but consider it appropriate for editors to kill stories altogether. Writing is considered the reporter's job, while editors properly decide what makes it into a publication. By killing one story, an editor can cause a reporter to self-censor subsequent ones.

Because they strive to be taken seriously, reporters are vulnerable to pressure to conform. If they start saying things that diverge from the common wisdom, they are noticed. Editors may doubt their credibility and wonder if they can be trusted—it's safer to hew to the common wisdom. These pressures to conform may be subtle, as indicated by *Boston Globe* editorial writer Randolph Ryan, who reports that he is known in the newsroom as "Sandino" because he has written critically about Reagan's policy toward Nicaragua (Personal communication, 1989, October 23). (And the editorial page of the *Globe* is considered to be among the most liberal in the country!)

Breed's Social Control in the Newsroom

In one of the early classic studies in media sociology, Warren Breed asked how news organizations enforce "policy." By policy he meant not a firm's printed rules, but the covert and "consistent orientation" of a paper's news and editorials toward issues and events, revolving primarily around partisan, class, and racial divisions (Breed, 1955, p. 327).

Breed asked: "How is policy maintained, despite the fact that it often contravenes journalistic norms, that staffers often personally disagree with it, and that executives cannot legitimately command that it be followed?" (p. 330). Breed notes that if the job of the organization were to report the news as objectively as possible, "control" would not be as important, but this is not the organization's only goal. Breed concludes that the primary news organization objective "to get the news" can override individual disagreements over, for example, professional concerns with objectivity. As Breed put it: "News comes first, and there is always news to get" (p. 342).

Other means of control include editorial blue-penciling, striking out parts of a story. Reporters soon learn what objectionable phrases or facts to leave out. In addition, executives give rare reprimands or make explicit policy decisions (as in the case of the homosexual rally mentioned above), thus further enforcing the boundaries. Internal house organ papers also help tell reporters what is acceptable. Breed says that "in the infrequent case that an anti-policy story reaches the city desk, the story is changed; extraneous reasons, such as the pressure of time and space, are given for the change. . . . Thus the policy remains not only covert but undiscussed and therefore unchanged" (p. 339).

In a more recent application of Breed's concepts, Wilson and Gutierrez (1985) focused on minorities in the newsroom. Black, Hispanic, and other ethnic media workers have many reasons for not comforming to organization policy. They often feel isolated and dissatisfied with media coverage of minority issues and portrayal of minorities in general. Like Breed, Wilson and Gutierrez note that such unwritten policies are stronger than formal ones, which usually come with procedures for changing them. They note that minority reporters may be told their stories lack newsworthiness, or were dropped due to space or time limitations. Given the reporters' primary task to get work in the paper or on the air, failing to do so reflects on professional competence.

Indeed, the persistence of stereotypical coverage of minorities indicates how resistant organization policies are to change. Thus, in view of organizational policy, even minority employees may not be able to change the way media portray minority issues. Policy perpetuates the majority culture viewpoint, as institutionalized in the views of the organization.

SUMMARY

Although less frequently studied than the influence of routines, organization-level factors have a critical impact on media content. When we look at a media organization, we question the roles performed, the way they are structured, the policies flowing through that structure, and the methods used to enforce those policies. The primary goal sought by most media organizations is economic profit. News organizations, in particular, have faced growing economic pressures that now play a greater role in dictating journalistic decisions. The way organizations are structured influences content by affecting occupational culture and by determining the degree of independence media organizations have from the larger corporate enterprises, of which so many are now a part. The growing complexity of media conglomerates means that the organizations composing them must now be more mindful of their effect on each other, and news organizations encounter many more potential conflicts of interest.

Of course, the ultimate organization-level power lies with owners, who set policy and enforce it. The influence of ownership on content has been an important concern in the news media. Although news departments may be organizationally buffered from the larger firm, content is still controlled indirectly through hiring and promotion practices and through self-censorship.

This organizational perspective reveals the context within which the routines of media work are carried out. Of course, these organizations themselves are subject to their own limits imposed by their environment. It is to these extramedia influences that we turn next.

REFERENCES

Bagdikian, B. (1987). *The media monopoly*. Boston: Beacon Press.

Bagdikian, B. (1989, June 12). The lords of the global village. *The Nation*, pp. 805–820.

Bailey, G., & Lichty, L. (1972). Rough justice on a Saigon street. *Journalism Quarterly, 72*, pp. 221–229.

Bantz, C. R., McCorkle, S., & Baade, R. C. (1981). The news factory. In G. C. Wilhoit & H. De Bock (Eds.), *Mass communication review yearbook* (Vol. 2, pp. 336–390). Beverly Hills, CA: Sage.

Becker, L. (1982). Print or broadcast: How the medium influences the reporter. In J. Ettema & D. C. Whitney (Eds.), *Individuals in mass media organizations: Creativity and constraint*. Beverly Hills, CA: Sage.

Boyer, P. J. (1988). *Who killed CBS? The undoing of America's number one news network*. New York: Random House.

Boyer, P. (1989, October 2). When news must pay its way, expect trivia. *New York Times*, p. 19.

Breed, W. (1955). Social control in the newsroom: A functional analysis. *Social Forces, 33*, 326–335.

Browning, N., Grierson, D., & Howard, H. (1984). Effects of conglomerate takeover on a newspaper's coverage of the Knoxville World's Fair: A case study. *Newspaper Research Journal, 6*, 30–38.

Ciabattari, J. (1989a, September/October). Of Time & integrity. *Columbia Journalism Review*, pp. 27–32.

Ciabattari, J. (1989b, September/October). Jason McManus: The man in the hot seat (interview). *Columbia Journalism Review*, pp. 33–34.

Conservatives seeking stock of CBS to alter "liberal bias." *New York Times*, p. B4.

Document (1989, September/October). *Columbia Journalism Review*, p. 25.

Donohew, L. (1967). Newspaper gatekeepers and forces in the news channel. *Public Opinion Quarterly, 31,* 61–68.

Donohue, G., Olien, C., & Tichenor, P. (1985). Reporting conflict by pluralism, newspaper type and ownership. *Journalism Quarterly, 62,* 489–499, 507.

Dowie, M. (1985, November/December). How ABC spikes the news: Three Reagan administration scandals that never appeared on World News Tonight. *Mother Jones,* pp. 33–53.

Drew, D. (1972). Roles and decision making of three television beat reporters. *Journal of Broadcasting, 16,* 165–173.

Dunwoody, S. (1978). *Science journalists: A study of factors affecting selection of news of a scientific meeting.* Unpublished Ph.D. dissertation, Indiana University.

Epstein, E. (1974). *News from nowhere.* New York: Vintage Books.

Fancher, M. (1987). The metamorphosis of the newspaper editor. *Gannett Center Journal, 1*(1), pp. 69–80.

Friendly, F. (1967). *Due to circumstances beyond our control.* New York: Random House.

Gans, H. (1979). *Deciding what's news.* New York: Random House.

Gitlin, T. (1980). *The whole world is watching.* Berkeley: University of California Press.

Greenfield, J. (1987). Making TV news pay. *Gannett Center Journal, 1*(1), pp. 21–39.

Halberstam, D. (1979). *The powers that be.* New York: Alfred A. Knopf.

Hale, F. D. (1988). Editorial diversity and concentration. In R. Picard, J. Winter, M. McCombs, & S. Lacy (Eds.), *Press concentration and monopoly: New perspectives on newspaper ownership and operation* (pp. 161–178). Norwood, NJ: Ablex.

Hess, S. (1981). *The Washington reporters.* Washington, DC: Brookings Institution.

Hirsch, P. (1977). Occupational, organizational and institutional models in mass media research: Toward an integrated framework. In P. M. Hirsch, P. V. Miller, & F. G. Kline (Eds.), *Strategies for communication research* (pp. 13–40). Beverly Hills, CA: Sage.

Ismach, A., & Dennis, E. (1978). A profile of newspaper and television reporters in a metropolitan setting. *Journalism Quarterly, 55,* 739–743.

Joyce, E. (1988). *Prime times, bad times: A personal drama of network television.* New York: Doubleday.

King, A. (1987). *Power and communication.* Prospect Heights, IL: Waveland.

Mann, L. (1974). Counting the crowd: Effects of editorial policy on estimates. *Journalism Quarterly, 51,* 251–257, 294.

Martin, W. P., & Singletary, M. (1981). Newspaper treatment of state government releases. *Journalism Quarterly, 58,* 93–96.

McCombs, M. (1988). Concentration, monopoly and content. In R. Picard, J. Winter, M. McCombs, & S. Lacy (Eds.), *Press concentration and monopoly: New perspectives on newspaper ownership and operation* (pp. 129–138). Norwood, NJ: Ablex.

Nixon, R., & Jones, R. (1956). The content of non-competitive vs. competitive newspapers. *Journalism Quarterly, 33,* 299–314.

No. 2 and trying harder: The *Washington Times* bags a politician, but can it win respect? (1989, November 6). *Time,* p. 74.

Notice of 1989 Annual Meeting and Proxy Statement. (1989). The New York Times Company.

Oudes, B. (Ed.). (1989). *From: The president: Richard Nixon's secret files.* New York: Harper & Row.

Parsons, P., Finnegan, J., Jr., & Benham, W. (1988). Editors and their roles. In R. Picard, J. Winter, M. McCombs, & S. Lacy (Eds.), *Press concentration and monopoly: New perspectives on newspaper ownership and operation* (pp. 91–104). Norwood, NJ: Ablex.

Picard, R., Winter, J., McCombs, M., & Lacy, S. (Eds.). (1988). *Press concentration and monopoly: New perspectives on newspaper ownership and operation.* Norwood, NJ: Ablex.
Robins, J. M. (1989, September). News in the '90s: Stretched to the limit. *Channels,* pp. 42–54.
Roger Simon to depart Sun-Times. (1984, September 15). *Editor & Publisher,* p. 38.
Shields, S., & Dunwoody, S. (1986). The social world of the statehouse pressroom. *Newspaper Research Journal, 8,* 43–51.
Sigal, L. V. (1973). *Reporters and officials.* Lexington, MA: D. C. Heath.
St. Dizier, B. (1986). *Republican endorsements, democratic positions: An editorial page contradiction* (unpublished manuscript).
Stakes sold in magazines. (1989, October 17). *New York Times,* p. D25 (by the Associated Press).
Standish, K. (1989, April). Lean times continue: Painless ways to economize. *RTNDA Communicator,* pp. 18–23.
Stempel, G. (1973). Effects on performance of a cross-media monopoly. *Journalism Monographs, 29.*
Stone, E. (1989, April). News practices (column). *RTNDA Communicator,* pp. 24–25.
Tannenbaum, A. (1989, June). WSJ hopes fortified news desk will cut costs and improve efficiency. *TJFR: The Journalist and Financial Reporting, 3.*
Thrift, R. R., Jr. (1977). How chain ownership affects editorial vigor of newspapers. *Journalism Quarterly, 54,* 327–331.
Tunstall, J. (1971). *Journalists at work.* London: Constable.
Turow, J. (1984). *Mass media industries.* New York: Longman.
Underwood, D. (1988, March/April). When MBAs rule the newsroom. *Columbia Journalism Review,* pp. 23–32.
Veronis, C. R. (1989, November 11). Research moves to center stage. *Presstime,* pp. 20–26.
Wackman, D. B., Gillmor, D. M., Gaziano, C., & Dennis, E. E. (1975). Chain newspaper autonomy as reflected in presidential campaign endorsements. *Journalism Quarterly, 52,* pp. 411–420.
Wagenberg, R. H., & Soderlund, W. C. (1975). The influence of chain-ownership on editorial comment in Canada. *Journalism Quarterly, 52,* pp. 93–98.
Wilhoit, G. C., & Auh, T. S. (1974). Newspaper endorsement and coverage of public opinion. *Journalism Quarterly, 51,* pp. 654–658.
Wilson, C. C., & Gutierrez, F. (1985). *Minorities and media.* Beverly Hills, CA: Sage.
Windhauser, J. W., Norton, W., Jr., & Rhodes, S. (1983). Editorial patterns of Tribune under three editors. *Journalism Quarterly, 60,* 524–528.
Wirth, M. O., & Wollert, J. A. (1976). Public interest program performances of multimedia-owned TV stations. *Journalism Quarterly, 53,* 223–230.
Wollert, J. A. (1978). Programming evidence relative to the issues of the NCCB decision. *Journalism Quarterly, 55,* 319–324.

CHAPTER 8

Influences on Content from Outside of Media Organizations

Are media workers and organizations all-powerful in determining the nature of media content? In Box 8.1, newspaper columnist Mike Kelley (1988) illustrates how journalists, who often enter their profession with optimism and idealism, are eventually accused of being pawns for just about everyone. As the messengers who deliver—and shape—the news, the journalists' job is understood by few and criticized by many. As Fred Barnes has put it, "The New Right and the New Left, the pro-nukes and the anti-nukes, the National Conservative Political Action Committee and the National Abortion Rights Action League have found a common enemy. It is us—the press" (1983, p. 48). And the critics, many of whom have institutionalized methods of communicating their displeasure to the media, are vociferous in their criticism of and advice about media content. Audience members write letters, advertisers withhold economic support, interest groups organize boycotts, and news sources release information so as to reward or punish journalists based on their past cooperation with the sources.

But just how important is all of this? In the last three chapters, we've shown how media content is affected by both media workers' and the media organizations' characteristics. In this chapter, we shift our attention to factors extrinsic to (outside of) the media organizations. They include the *sources of the information* that becomes media content, such as special interest groups, public relations campaigns, and even the news organizations themselves; *revenue sources,* such as advertisers and audiences; *other social institutions,* such as business and government; the *economic environment;* and *technology* (see Figure 8.1).

A Profession of Perceptions

From time to time people ask, "What is it all about, this newspaper business?" I set down the answer to that, as best I knew how, a few years ago and offer it again now.

The young man was thinking of taking up journalism. "I should like to journal," he said.

"Offhand," I said, "I would advise against it. But what sort of journaling do you have in mind?"

"Well," he said, "I would like to make my contribution to our republican democracy by delving into the thoughts and actions of our elected leaders, by divining their sentiments on a variety of the great issues and reporting those concerns so as to inform the very whiz-bang out of the electorate."

"In other words, you are already throwing in with the political elite," I said. "You intend to be a craven conduit for the political power structure."

"Pity no," he said. "I would encourage the dissemination of divergent points of view, no matter how scorned might be their purveyors."

"So you are willing to give a forum to any radical, lunatic fringe group that comes along; you are prepared to betray your great trust and allow yourself to be a virtual publicity factory for any loon who would publicly laminate a gopher to get attention."

"You don't understand at all. I want to tell the world the plight of the powerless. I want to be the voice for those who are not heard."

"Pandering to the minorities and homeless, then, is it? A constant whining and carping about people who could improve themselves if only they would get an honest job and pull themselves up, as countless millions before them have done. You want the hard-working, taxpaying citizens to bankrupt themselves to support a bunch of deadbeats. Just another bleeding-heart liberal."

"Well, of course not," he said with some exasperation. "I have the greatest admiration and respect for people who have succeeded financially. I would lend an eager ear to their opinions, for they have demonstrated their soundness, industry and prudence."

"A shameless hack mouthpiece for the business establishment. A puppet for the three-piece-suited money barons who bend the necks of the working man to their lucre-stained yoke."

"I'm no one's pawn," he protested. "I'm a thinking, perceptive, analytical fellow who simply wishes to employ those attributes to educate my fellow citizens as to the meaning of events."

"A petty propagandist and nothing more. Cringing behind your veil of purported objectivity, you yearn to impose your own warped prejudices on a defenseless readership. Slant the news to line up with your squalid bias, you pitiable tract writer."

"Fairness and objectivity are my very hallmarks." he sputtered. "I swear that my reports would be rigorous in exactitude and literal in every way."

"Then you aspire to be nothing more than a loudspeaker," I said, "repeating precisely the platitudes and self-serving pronouncements of whomsoever might dally with you to indulge his whims. A spineless, mindless siphon sucking up every passing word and spewing it out with no form, no context, no meaning."

"I want only to be a humble messenger," he said.

"A messenger: A messenger of wars and rumors of wars, a messenger of daily tidings so sordid and base, so disheartening and dispiriting, so threatening, tumultuous and unsettling that your fellows will come to doubt there is any hope at all left for themselves or for the world."

"Enough!" he cried. "You have won. I shall never come within a continent's breadth of the wretched practice. But tell me this: How can you ply so sorry a trade?"

"Why," I explained, "it is the only endeavor I know in which you may enjoy such a rich variety of perceptions while remaining droningly consistent."

Mike Kelley, columnist, *Austin* (Texas) *American-Statesman,* September 30, 1988.

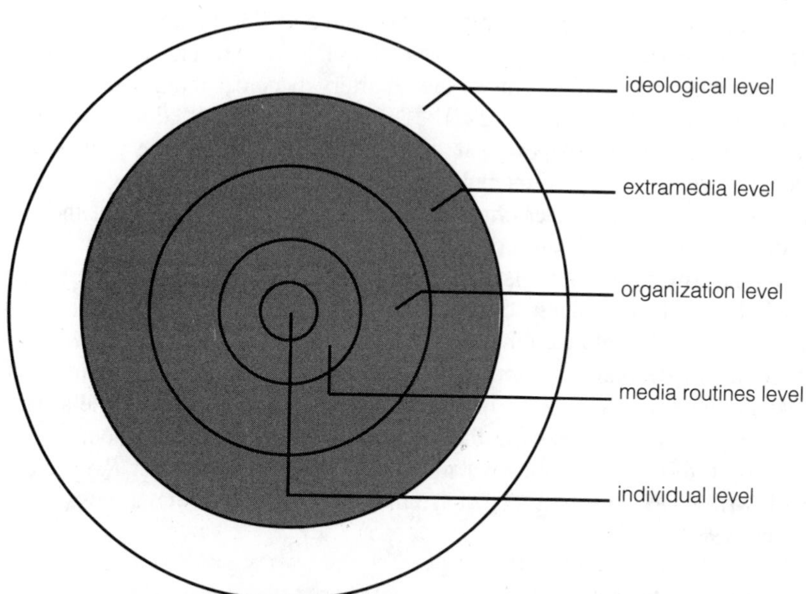

Figure 8.1. Extramedia influences on media content in hierarchical model

SOURCES

Journalists almost never witness airplane crashes. They learn about crashes from other journalists (via news services or media), from people who were on the scene, from government officials and the police, from airline or airport representatives, and from consumer safety advocates, and each individual has a unique point of view about what happened. Each source provides journalists with different information. It is the journalists' job to sift through all of the information they are given—which is often conflicting—and to come up with news reports that are accurate and complete. Gans (1979, p. 80) defines *sources* as "the actors whom journalists observe or interview, including interviewees who appear on the air or who are quoted in . . . articles, and those who only supply background information or story suggestions."

The Journalist-Source Relationship

Sources have a tremendous effect on mass media content, because journalists can't include in their news reports what they don't know. The most obvious influence occurs when sources withhold information or lie, but they may also influence the news in more subtle ways, by providing the context within which all other information is evaluated, by providing usable information that is easier and cheaper to use than that from other sources (what Gandy [1982] calls "information subsidies"), and by monopolizing the journalists' time so that they don't have an opportunity to seek out sources with alternative views.

As Sanford Sherizen (1978) points out in his study of crime news, the police—who are by far the most often used source of information about crimes—"supply reporters with a constant stream of usable crime, and this information, fitting into the work requirements of the reporters, becomes the raw material from which crime news is written" (p. 222). "The police have a vested interest in crime news appearing in newspapers and other media. . . . The more crimes which become known, the more aid the police may be able to gain in seeking increases in departmental budgets. Further crime news results in a strengthening of the police view of the causes and solutions of the crime problem" (p. 212).

But the power imbalance between writers and sources may not always be in the sources' favor. In her highly critical 1989 *New Yorker* series about author Joe McGinniss's relationship with the subject of his nonfiction best-seller *Fatal Vision,* Janet Malcolm denounces journalism as inherently "morally indefensible." The journalist, she says, is "a kind of confidence man, preying on people's vanity, ignorance, or loneliness, gaining their trust and betraying them without remorse" (Malcolm, 1989). In the following months, *Columbia Journalism Review* asked several writers to comment on Malcolm's charges. Here are a few excerpts (Gottlieb, 1989):

- Ken Auletta, columnist for the *New York Daily News:* "It is natural for a source or subject to feel betrayed when the story comes out and the subject doesn't like everything in it. But that doesn't mean the accusation of betrayal is justified. In journalism your loyalty is to the truth as you perceive it, not necessarily to your subject" (p. 22).

- Nora Ephron, screenwriter and novelist: "The world is full of people who honestly don't know that journalists are not their friends. They honestly have no idea how awful it is to be misquoted or to be quoted out of context or to have what they said quoted but used to make a point they never intended—all of which, I'm sorrry to say, is standard operating procedure among the majority of journalists" (p. 22).
- J. Anthony Lukas, author and winner of two Pulitzer Prizes: "I am certainly not denying that reporters do their share of manipulation. Of course they do. But the relationship is *mutually* manipulative. And that's because human relationships are mutually manipulative" (p. 23).
- Joseph Wambaugh, novelist: "If anything, I think many of the people I have interviewed as a policeman and as a journalist were trying to con *me* all the time. I never felt that I was conning anybody" (p. 24).
- Barry Michael Cooper, staff writer for the *Village Voice:* "There is a bit of the con man in the journalist. You have to console, you have to empathize, you have to plead, to get to the truth. And if you don't, if you are just blunt, you can say something that totally turns your subject off and he won't talk to you again. It's happened to me. But I don't consider that malicious lying. I'd call it slanted empathy—empathy with a purpose. And that purpose is that you are trying to get to a larger truth" (p. 30).
- A. M. Rosenthal, columnist for the *New York Times:* "Malcolm is absolutely right when she says that the relationship between subject and reporter can very easily lead to shading the truth, even to falsehood, in order to draw people out. But when she says that this is *inevitable,* I just dismiss that. I don't think it is true" (p. 32).

The Selection of Sources

There are a lot of possible sources of information about an issue or event, because journalists not only talk with those who are directly involved (such as airline officials who announce a plane crash), but they may also get information from sources only indirectly associated with the event (such as consumer safety advocates) or reactions and opinions from "people on the street."

But not all sources are equally likely to be contacted by journalists—those with economic or political power are more likely to influence news reports than those who lack power (Gans, 1979). Big businesses don't hesitate to use that power to get their side of the story out. Returning to our airline crash example, the airlines (and all big businesses) hire people specifically to gather information and make it available to the mass media—if the media don't come to them, they go to the media. They understand the rhythms of media coverage and can time the release of information just before a media deadline, in order to facilitate that coverage. Airline personnel also have easily reachable offices, with secretaries who can refer journalists' calls to the proper person.

Contrast this with the poorly funded and politically inexperienced citizens group that lobbies for better air safety standards. The citizens group may operate out of somebody's home, with a telephone answering machine taking journalists' calls instead of a full-time staff member, and the group probably can't afford to hire anyone to do press relations. Many journalists may not know that the group exists, and those who do know of the group probably have trouble reaching a representative. The result is that the journalists end up writing stories dominated by information provided by the airline.

These same access problems may make it easier for journalists to use information from organizational sources (such as the airline) than from individuals (such as a passenger or mechanic). Organizations' regular office hours and full-time staff members make it easy for journalists to access information. Private individuals, on the other hand, may be reachable for only a short time each day—whatever time is left over from work, sleep, and other obligations.

We might conclude from this that journalists favor organizational sources over individual ones—that is, presented with information from both types of sources, journalists would be more likely to use the organization's information. But that doesn't seem to be the case. In her study of sources used by journalists at a medium-sized daily newspaper, Seo (1988) traced all sources that journalists had contact with during one week and noted which ones were used in subsequent news reports. She found that, although three-fourths of the sources actually covered in the newspaper were from organizations and only one-fourth were individuals, this did not necessarily represent a bias toward organizational sources. Of all sources the journalists had contact with, 96 percent of individual sources were covered, compared with only 71 percent of organizational sources. Seo concluded that journalists will cover individual sources when they are available. The problem is, of course, that organizations often go out of their way to be available, whereas individuals rarely have sufficient time or resources to compete effectively for the journalists' attention.

The nature of the news event may also affect whether individual or organizational sources are used. Atwater and Green (1988) found that individual sources were most likely to be used in the ABC, CBS, and NBC coverage of the June 1985 TWA hijacking—more than half of the sound bites used by the three networks included interviews with either the hostages or their friends and relatives. Such stories about the plight of people—such as a kidnapping—have strong human interest and therefore individual sources may seem more appropriate to the journalist. Because such events often are played out over several days, journalists also have more time than usual to locate and interview individuals.

Official sources, such as government officials or police, are often preferred by journalists, not only because they are more easily available for an interview, but also because journalists and their editors believe that official sources have important things to say (Paletz & Entman, 1981) and tend to accept the things official sources say as being factual (Gandy, 1982). Therefore, interviewing an official source makes the journalists' job efficient by concentrating on individuals with important things to say and by eliminating the need to double- and triple-check "facts" (Hackett, 1985).

For example, Frederick Fico (1984a) has shown that reporters covering the part-time Indiana legislature rely on only a few official sources for their stories. Wire service reporters, under the most stringent time constraints, are most likely to rely on official activities and on the governor. Reliance on a narrow range of sources may be at least partially a function of the fact that the Indiana legislature is part time. When Fico (1984b) studied the full-time Michigan legislature, he found that reporters used more sources and dealt with more topics.

The location of the media organization may also be a factor. Martin (1988) shows that news organizations farthest from the city in which an event occurs will rely primarily on official sources. We also suspect that there is an interaction between the type of event being covered and whether official or nonofficial sources are used. In stories about issues (as is often the case in covering legislation), official sources may be most common because of their vested interest in the debate's outcome. For example, when Congress debates the merits of the proposed budget, you can be sure that officials will be poised to praise the expansion or decry the slashing of their own departmental funds. When the story is about an event, however, especially one involving human interest, we may find that unofficial sources get more play. For example, officials accounted for only 30 percent of the sources in network sound bites about the 1985 TWA hijacking (Atwater & Green, 1988).

Some official sources provide information to journalists but do not want to be personally identified ("a high government source"). The individual may want to let the public know something, provide the journalist with background information (Gassaway, 1988, p. 72), or just test the viability of an idea with a "trial balloon." Many confidential sources provide information because they derive "some satisfaction or benefit from giving information to reporters" (p. 76).

U.S. presidents are notoriously good at influencing what the news media cover, as Bernard Cohen points out in his discussion of how U.S. presidents can control the mass media (Gannett Center for Media Studies, 1989, pp. 2–3): "The president has a natural advantage over the media, giving him a commanding lead in setting the terms of public-political discourse. The president is invariably news and especially so when he's new. . . . The White House can therefore create the news necessary to give the president's agenda wide publicity and even dominance in the political marketplace. . . . All administration can, to one degree or another, work the system, and the media system is particularly subject to being worked because it is so open and so predictable.

But few recent U.S. presidents have worked the media as effectively as Ronald Reagan. In evaluating the Reagan presidency, former president Jimmy Carter says: "President Reagan has handled the press—and I use the word 'handled' advisedly—superbly. Based on his analysis and his advisers' analysis of what is popular and unpopular, President Reagan has been effective in emphasizing those popular items

Presidents and the Press

U.S. presidents and the mass media have always enjoyed a love-hate relationship. The presidents try to control the media, and the media try to find out more from the president than he wants to tell.

Franklin D. Roosevelt (in office 1933–1945) began the now institutionalized custom of presidential press conferences. Although he met with journalists very frequently—nearly seven times a month—he usually didn't permit photographs to be taken.

Franklin D. Roosevelt

John F. Kennedy (1961–1963) was the first U.S. president to have his press conferences televised live, and he used the medium superbly. Kennedy reportedly read the *New York Times* every morning, because he could get information about world events more quickly from the *Times* than from the State Department.

Lyndon B. Johnson (1963–1969) held informal meetings with journalists in addition to about two formal press conferences per month. Johnson ultimately felt that the media undermined his administration.

John F. Kennedy

Lyndon B. Johnson

Ronald Reagan

Richard M. Nixon (1969–1974) had the worst relationship with the media of any modern president, holding press conferences on the average of only every other month. Constant media attention to the Watergate scandal ultimately led to Nixon's resignation.

Jimmy Carter (1977–1981) was the first to hire a media consultant, whose job was to ensure that Carter's image in the media would be favorable. He often held press conferences in small towns, so as to enjoy the attention of local media and audiences.

Ronald Reagan (1981–1989), the "great communicator," was a master at managing the media, even though he held a news conference on average only once every two months. His Saturday afternoon radio broadcasts were targeted at setting the agenda for Sunday newspapers.

Compiled from the following sources: (1) "News? Confrontation? Entertainment? Accountability? Take your pick at the presidential press conference." (1989). In *The press, the presidency and the first hundred days,* pp. 29–31. New York: Gannett Center for Media Studies at Columbia University. (2) Doris A. Graber (1984). *Mass media and American politics,* 2nd ed. Washington, D.C.: Congressional Quarterly Press, pp. 221–237. (Photos courtesy Smithsonian Institution, John Fitzgerald Kennedy Library, Lyndon Baines Johnson Library, and Ronald Reagan Library.)

in dealing with the press. . . . [He] has dealt with the press through very carefully orchestrated encounters and through the passing from the White House to the helicopter, back and forth, and responding to whichever questions he wanted. . . . His ability to emphasize or to orchestrate the daily news item has been remarkably successful" (Gannett Center for Media Studies, 1989, p. 7).

What else affects which sources are selected? Streitmatter (1985) suggests that the source's personality may affect coverage. In his study, extroverted U.S. presidents got two to three times the front-page coverage of their introverted peers. Stempel and Culbertson (1984) suggest that a source's assertiveness, credibility (as determined by the journalist), accessibility, and quotability can affect both a source's *prominence* (frequency of mention) and *dominance* (tendency to be quoted rather than reported about) in news coverage. However, Weaver and Wilhoit's (1980) study of how U.S. senators are covered showed no relationship between visibility of senators and their seniority, committee assignments, state population, conservativism, or success in their last election.

Interest Groups

An *interest group* is composed of individuals who want to communicate their stance on one or more issues to the public. Interest groups often try to influence legislation, as well as public opinion and behaviors. For example, the National Rifle Association lobbies the U.S. Congress against gun control, and the National Organization for Women advocates an Equal Rights Amendment to the U.S. Constitution. Mothers Against Drunk Drivers works to elevate Americans' consciousness about the dangers of driving while intoxicated, and the American Dental Association tries to persuade everyone to have regular dental checkups.

Some interest groups seek to influence media content by providing "guidelines" for covering topics of interest to the group. For example, in 1968 the American Bar Association adopted its "fair trial–free press" guidelines; by 1976 twenty-three states had adopted voluntary press-bar guidelines that specified how the media should cover crime and trials. In their study of compliance with the ABA guidelines, Tankard, Middleton, and Rimmer (1979) found that newspapers operating under a voluntary press-bar agreement were no more likely to follow the ABA guidelines than were those that had no such agreement.

Sometimes one interest group will lobby another, to persuade the mass media on the first group's behalf. For example, in August 1989, a representative of the Austin Society to Oppose Pseudoscience (unsuccessfully) asked members of the Association for Education in Journalism and Mass Communication for the organization to pass a resolution urging newspapers and magazines to stop publishing horoscopes and other astrological features.

Interest groups may also criticize the media and/or individual journalists. In some instances, changing media content *is* the interest group's goal, and criticism *of* the media *through* the media exerts a double influence on content. Not only do the criticisms get on the news agenda (thereby replacing something else that would otherwise have been publicized), but they may cause revisions of media practices or policies.

One organization highly critical of the media is the American Family Association, which describes itself as "a Christian organization promoting the Biblical ethic of decency in American society with primary emphasis on TV and other media" (*Journal of the American Family Association,* 1989, March, p. 2). AFA's executive director, Donald Wildmon, sends frequent form letters to AFA members, to request support in the form of boycotting the advertisers of offending television programs and sending money to AFA. Two such letters sent in early 1989 illustrate the AFA's goals and tactics. The first letter included a transcript of a musical skit aired December 31, 1988, on the NBC television program "Saturday Night Live" (D. E. Wildmon, letter to supporters of the American Family Association, no date [estimated as January or February 1989]), in which four men talked and sang about their penises.

Wildmon's accompanying four-page letter detailed the interest group's objections to specific network television programs, outlined their plan for boycotting those programs' sponsors, and asked readers to take immediate action. Wildmon stated in his letter that he had included the "Saturday Night Live" script only to awaken his supporters' anger and goad them into action. He urged them to:

- Mail signed postcards of protest to the chairman of General Electric, owner of NBC.
- Mail signed postcards of protest to the chairman of Ralston-Purina and Nissan USA, sponsors of "Saturday Night Live."
- Sign up to form the foundation upon which a boycott of "anti-Christian and anti-family" TV shows would be built.

In addition to providing the "Saturday Night Live" script as evidence for a change in television content, Wildmon said that in the previous year CBS had shown three cartoon episodes in which Mighty Mouse sniffed cocaine; that three prime-time series have gay characters; and that "on the 12/01/88 episode of 'L.A. Law'—for the first time on a non-news or non-documentary prime-time TV show—a character said G—— d—— on the air" (D. E. Wildmon, letter to supporters of the American Family Association, early 1989).

A month or so later, Wildmon sent another letter to AFA supporters (D. E. Wildmon, letter to supporters of the American Family Association, no date [estimated as March 1989]). In a postscript on the last page, Wildmon wrote:

> I can give you a recent example of the success we can have. General Mills was a sponsor of "Saturday Night Live." On December 31, 1988 "SNL" aired a skit that was truly vulgar and obscene. I contacted General Mills and asked them why they sponsored this show. After receiving my letter, General Mills cancelled close to a million dollars of advertising they had planned to spend sponsoring "SNL." That's what our boycott can achieve.

How much influence do organizations such as the AFA actually have on television content? In his book *Inside Prime Time,* Todd Gitlin (1985) points out several ways in which interest groups have influenced television content. Hollywood writer Larry Gelbart told Gitlin that "the far righteous" have proven to be very successful at getting the media's attention, both as the subject of news and feature reports and as a force that can affect program choice by applying pressure to program advertisers (p. 250). NBC's research vice president, Gerald M. Jaffe, points out that television has two markets to satisfy—the people at home and the advertisers—whereas movies have to satisfy only the theater audience (pp. 252–253). Although most network programming executives told Gitlin that they are not influenced by advertisers' attitudes—because there are more potential advertisers than there are advertising slots on television—CBS's Herman Keld replied differently: "I would say they are always taken into account. Always taken into account" (p. 254).

Public Relations Campaigns

Interest groups also conduct public relations campaigns that use the media to focus public attention. To the extent that these campaigns are successful, media content is affected directly (through the publication of press releases) and indirectly (through calling the media's attention to the problem). Sometimes journalists themselves are the target of the public relations campaign. For example, Eastman Kodak Company took out a full-page advertisement in *Columbia Journalism Review* to persuade journalists that manufacturing is still an important component of the U.S. economy and to call for a "national debate on the direction of economic policy and how it affects manufacturing" ("America won't work without manufacturing," 1989, p. 13).

Not every organization can afford to buy advertising, however, but getting coverage in the mass media can be an especially cost-effective method of reaching the public for resource-poor interest groups. One way they get their message across is by designing and holding events that the news media will cover, such as demonstrations and protests (Wolfsfeld, 1984). Boorstin (1971, p. 120) calls these *pseudoevents:*

> **1.** It is not spontaneous, but comes about because someone has planned, planted or incited it. . . .
> **2.** It is planted primarily (not always exclusively) for the immediate purpose of being reported or reproduced. Therefore, its occurrence is arranged for the convenience of the reporting or reproducing media. . . .
> **3.** Its relation to the underlying reality of the situation is ambiguous. Its interest arises largely from this very ambiguity. While the news interest in a train wreck is in *what* happened and in the real consequences, the interest in an interview is always, in a sense, in

whether it really happened and in which might have been the motives. . . .

4. Usually it is intended to be a self-fulfilling prophecy. The hotel's thirtieth-anniversary celebration, by saying that the hotel is a distinguished institution, actually makes it one.

The pseudoevent fulfills the interest group's need to get media coverage in order to reach the public, but it also fulfills the media's need for news. In the print media, the amount of editorial content (i.e., news, columns, and features) is determined largely by the amount of advertising content—the more ads a newspaper sells, the more editorial content it needs to put around the ads. In the electronic media, the amount of editorial content is fixed by the amount of time available (minus the time devoted to advertising), but, because the audience tends to expect "new" news at each broadcast, the demand for more and more news continues throughout each day. Interest groups play to the media's need for new content by providing interest group–created events for the media to cover, which are more likely to be covered than real events.

How influential are public relations campaigns in affecting media coverage? The evidence is mixed. In her study of government public information officers in Louisiana, Turk (1986) found that not only was half of the PI0-provided information used by daily newspapers, but the newspapers also gave issues the same emphasis that the PI0s did. On the other hand, she also found that, of all stories about the state agencies being studied, fewer than half included PI0-provided information. Whereas Albritton and Manheim (1983) found that a public relations campaign improved Rhodesia's image in the U.S. press, Stocking (1985) says that public relations activities may have no effect on media content beyond the news value of the organizations being promoted.

Interestingly enough, the news judgments of journalists and public relations practitioners are remarkably similar (Kopenhaver, Martinson, & Ryan, 1984). Journalists incorrectly perceive a large gap between their own news values and those of PR practitioners, who don't perceive the same gap, possibly because some were once journalists. There is a tendency for those outside the public relations industry to conceptualize public relations efforts as very powerful. For example, Turow (1989) suggests that "public relations is a driving force behind what gets on television and into print." He cites evidence that many news stories begin from press releases, thereby showing the "overwhelming importance of PR materials for the contemporary press" (p. 206). Turow also implies that public relations activities have inherently antisocial motivations: Public relations practitioners "insinuate their ideas into hard news stories with the aim of attracting lawmakers' attention (p. 208) and try to disguise their own political agenda from both media and public."

A large proportion of negative attitudes toward public relations is based on the assumption that all public relations efforts involve solely persuasive communication, failing to acknowledge that public relations messages may also have cognitive goals (Shoemaker, 1989). For example, a government agency may create a public relations message intended to warn the public about an environmental hazard, or it might plan a public information program designed both to teach people about the health risks of cocaine use and to ultimately reduce cocaine's consumption (a combination of cognitive and behavioral goals).

Other Media Organizations

To a certain extent, each news organization acts as a source for the others. Journalists read, watch, and listen to news from their own and from competing organizations, and when a story breaks first in one medium, it may quickly be picked up by other media. Some media seem particularly good at setting the agenda for other media. For example, the weekly *New England Journal of Medicine* is an often-quoted source of medical news (Caudill & Ashdown, 1989). Although the *Journal* does not send out press releases about its contents prior to its Thursday publication date, it does provide advance copies of the publication to the news media on Monday. North Americans can generally learn about the *Journal*'s latest research in their Thursday newspapers or from Wednesday evening television and radio broadcasts. "From an editor's point of view, the *Journal* may be an ideal source of medical news because the publication often reflects the conflict and controversy within the medical profession" (Caudill & Ashdown, 1989, p. 458).

For general news, however, the final arbiter of quality and professionalism is the *New York Times*. "If the *Times* did not exist, it would probably have to be invented" (Gans, 1979, p. 181). In their study of the enormous amount of media coverage devoted to cocaine in 1986, Reese and Danielian (1989, p. 40) say that the *New York Times* "took the lead in covering the cocaine issue" in early 1986, with the other newspapers following soon. The television networks picked up the story somewhat later (see also Danielian & Reese, 1989).

The wire services are also influential in passing stories from medium to medium, as a story is transmitted by a wire service and picked up from town to town. Some people have suggested that the wire services act as a powerful "agenda setter" for daily newspapers. Although Whitney and Becker (1982) show that newspaper editors publish the same kind of content in the same proportions that the wire services transmit, this may not be a causal connection. That is, there may be another explanation for the similarities in content, such as similar ideas about what is newsworthy. There is support for this idea in a study by Todd (1983), who found that nonsubscribing newspapers give stories the same play as do wire service subscribers.

ADVERTISERS AND AUDIENCES

"One of the most profitable commodities in the modern world is human attention. Whoever can harvest it in wholesale quantities can make money in kind. . . . One percentage point for a network in prime-time audience share represents more than $30 million in added revenues each year" (Bagdikian, 1989, p. 819).

In the United States, whose mass media companies are by and large privately or corporately owned, the media audience is up for sale anew on every day and for every second. The buyers are advertisers, and they pay a substantial portion of what it costs to run each medium.[1] As Altschull (1984, p. 254) reminds us, "The content of the press is directly correlated with the interests of those who finance the press. The press is the piper, and the tune the piper plays is composed by those who pay the piper." There is substantial evidence that media content is affected—both directly and indirectly—by both advertisers and audiences.

It wasn't always so, however. Advertising played only a minor role in the financing of newspapers and magazines prior to the late 1800s (Peterson, 1981). The trend toward industrialization of the United States in the nineteenth century brought with it a need to sell the new products being produced. Manufacturers approached newspapers and magazines about advertising their products, but nineteenth-century publishers often did not have a strong marketing orientation: Publishers tolerated advertising, but did not treat advertising "with the reverence they do today. One nineteenth-century advertising agent had to importune a publisher to reveal the circulation of his magazine. Reluctantly, furtively, the publisher scribbled a number on a scrap of paper and handed it to the agent" (Peterson, 1981, p. 19).

Magazines became the first national advertising medium, following the "reinvention" of the magazine by S. McClure, Frank Munsey, and Cyrus Curtis in the early 1890s as a medium for the middle class, which was (not coincidentally) also the target for the consumer goods advertisers wanted to promote (Peterson, 1981, pp. 19–20). These magazine entrepreneurs found that, by refocusing magazine content on stories popular with the middle class and by selling subscriptions at a price below the cost of producing and distributing a subscription, the size of the magazine could be dramatically increased, making magazines a desirable advertising medium.

This pattern was quickly repeated in newspapers; when the broadcast media came along, they took this to its extreme—giving away their content to anyone with the equipment to receive the signal. The mass medium became an "adjunct of the marketing system" and "the only industry that normally gives away its wares [to its consumers, the audience] or sells them for less than production costs" (p. 20).

The subscription charge for print media and ultimately for cable and pay-TV channels "became essentially a fee to qualify the reader [or viewer] for the advertiser's interest (Peterson, 1981, p. 20). Today, it costs so much to sell, maintain, and renew subscriptions that, in many cases, it would cost less to distribute a magazine for free. "At the same time, magazine circulation audit rules restrict the number of issues that can be sent free after a subscription expires; otherwise, advertisers could not be sure that the product was being valued by all of the circulation that the publisher claimed" (Rosse, 1981, p. 41).

Because advertising rates are computed according to how many audience members use the medium—what is often called "cost per thousand," having more subscribers means more advertising income for the magazine or newspaper. Up to a point, anyway. Some weekly magazines—such as *Life*—that had built a circulation in the millions during the 1950s and 1960s found that there was a limit to how much advertisers were willing to pay for every additional thousand subscribers. As their circulations climbed (and as the competition for ad dollars from television increased), they soon reached a point at which the additional advertising revenue generated by a thousand new subscribers could not cover the cost of distributing the magazines to them every week. The truly mass circulation magazines went out of business as weeklies, later returning with fewer subscribers and a monthly distribution schedule (Mogel, 1979).

The Target Audience

As a result of these experiences, advertisers recognized that not all audience members are equally important—that segment of the mass audience most likely to buy an advertisers' products is called the *target audience* or market. Target audiences are defined in terms of *demographics* (such as age, gender, income, and education) or *psychographics* (attitudes and life-styles). Advertisers buy space or time from media that have the best target audience for their products.

How does a medium capture the "right" target audience for advertisers? It finds out what target audience members want and then gives it to them. For example, as newspaper circulation has declined over the past twenty years (a 21 percent drop[2] between 1970 and 1980 in the twenty largest U.S. cities, according to Leo Bogart, executive vice president and general manager of the Newspaper Advertising Bureau [1989, p. 49]), publishers have turned their attention more and more toward an "upscale" target audience to ensure a steady stream of advertising income (Fink, 1989, p. 40). Big city newspapers generally reach less than a third of all households in their areas (e.g., 24 percent daily for the *Chicago Tribune* and 32 percent for the *Dallas Morning News*). Newspapers have traded a wide coverage of all types of households for deep penetration in the target audiences most attractive to advertisers—high-income professionals, whom journalism professor Conrad Fink calls the "champagne crowd." The *Wall Street Journal* may have the highest-income readers, with an average subscriber household income in excess of $107,000. The *Boston Globe* "says it reaches, with a single issue, . . . 53 percent of those with $100,000-plus household incomes," even though these wealthy households account for only 9 percent of all those in the area (Fink, 1989, p. 40).

Fink says that newspapers have cultivated high-income readers by "intentionally structuring our news content primarily for [them]. We also market selectively, concentrating circulation drives in the right neighborhoods—those predicted to yield high demographics" (1989, p. 40). Similar results have been found for other media. For example, Cantor and Jones (1983) found that a magazine with a working class target audience published different fiction than a magazine with a middle class audience.

This assumes, of course, that media workers actually do know (or even want to know) what the desired target audience wants, an assumption that is by no means unanimously supported by the research literature. The process through which a journalist is socialized to the norms and routines of an advertiser-funded medium should draw the journalist's attention toward the audience he or she is writing for. In his work on the creation of television news, David Altheide (1976) makes this point by suggesting that low newscast ratings are often blamed on the news staff, who may conclude that the audience is rejecting their work and that they may lose their jobs if they cannot produce content the audience will watch.

The problem is that, even if they want to know what the audience wants, journalists may have little knowledge—or incorrect information—about the audience they communicate with. Minority group members often complain that the media would do a better job of covering the minority community if they hired more minority journalists (Greenberg, Burgoon, Burgoon, & Korzenny, 1983), but as Orlando Taylor, dean of the School of Communication at Howard University, has pointed out, not every black or Hispanic journalist is equally knowledgeable about his or her ethnic group (Taylor, 1989).[3] In some cases, minorities and women may have become acculturated to the predominantly white mass media as a strategy for making themselves attractive as employees. They may need to improve their own "cultural literacy" in order to improve their understanding of what their ethnic audience wants from the media.

Smith (1977, p. 179) says that the circulation and advertising sales departments generally provide journalists with a "picture of the audience for which they are writing," but studies of journalists often show that they do not know their audiences very well (see, for example, Wulfemeyer, 1984; Donsbach, 1983). Although Bell (1982) has shown that radio broadcasters' news style covaried with their perception of their audiences' prestige, Flegel and Chaffee (1971) found that newspaper journalists attribute more influence to their own opinions than to those of their editors or readers.

Advertisers' Muscle

Whereas marketing studies may keep journalists abreast of their audience's general characteristics, only a small portion of the audience will ever communicate directly with a journalist. For better or worse, this is *not* true of advertisers, who are not afraid to "use their financial muscle to protest what they perceive as unfair treatment by the news segment of the mass media" (Jamieson & Campbell, 1983, p. 97).

Because advertising income is crucial to the survival of commercial mass media, the bigger the advertiser, the more muscle it has: Modern multinational manufacturers and advertising agencies therefore have considerable power "to suppress public messages they do not like." Bagdikian reports that in 1988 Saatchi and Saatchi—"the world's biggest advertising conglomerate"—bought a small ad agency that was servicing antismoking ads for the Minnesota Department of Health. To avoid angering the Brown & Williamson Tobacco Company, which was spending $35 million with Saatchi for the Kool cigarette campaign, Saatchi ordered its new acquisition to drop the Minnesota account before Brown & Williamson dropped Saatchi. There was good reason for such fear. Only three months earlier, RJR Reynolds had dropped Saatchi because "it had created a Northwest Airlines television commercial showing passengers applauding the airline's No Smoking policy." RJ Reynolds, one of the world's largest advertisers, markets Camel, Winston, and Salem cigarettes (Bagdikian, 1989, pp. 819–820).

Tobacco companies may have made the most attempts to control mass media content, although some of the controls may be self-imposed by the media themselves in an attempt to ward off censure by tobacco companies.[4] For example, Kessler (1989) investigated the editorial and advertising content of six major women's magazines (e.g., *Cosmopolitan* and *Good Housekeeping*) to see whether the presence or absence of tobacco advertising would be related to the amount of editorial content about the health hazards of smoking—"the number one cancer killer of women" (p. 319). Although women's health was a major topic in the magazines, there was almost no editorial content about any health hazards of smoking, even in *Good Housekeeping,* which does not accept tobacco advertising. The *GH* health editor told Kessler that plans to do a major story on the health hazards of smoking have been "cut down time and time again by people who make the big decisions," because the link between lung cancer and smoking is "not very appealing" and "too controversial" (p. 322). As Kessler points out, even though *GH* can't lose tobacco advertising income, it might lose advertising revenue from nontobacco subsidiaries of the tobacco conglomerates.[5] Elizabeth Whelan, the executive director of the American Council on Science and Health, has noted: "I frequently wrote on health topics for women's magazines, and have been told repeatedly by editors to stay away from the subject of tobacco (Whelan, as cited in Weis & Burke, 1986, p. 61).

Tobacco companies have a long history of influencing media content, as Weis and Burke point out in their review: In 1957, *Reader's Digest* published an article about the health effects of smoking; ads were subsequently withdrawn by the American Tobacco Company (Bagdikian, as cited in Weis & Burke, 1986). In 1959, the Tobacco Institute threatened to withdraw ads from publications that advertised a competing product, "tobaccoless smoke." The institute also "convinced the New York Transit System not to place rail commuter ads promoting an upcoming story on lung cancer in *Reader's Digest*" (Whelan, as cited in Weis & Burke, 1986, p. 60).

Other media are just as vulnerable to pressure from tobacco companies. The billboard industry is even more dependent on tobacco advertising than magazines are, getting "up to half its revenue from tobacco advertising and tobacco industry–owned advertisers (soft drink and alcoholic beverage distributors)." Even movies are affected. "Film producers are often paid to display smoking as an appropriate, desirable behavior among socially active adults. Tobacco companies offer to help underwrite filmmaking costs; in return, the filmmaker agrees to portray the key characters in the film as smokers" (Weis & Burke, 1986, pp. 63–64). And although tobacco ads are no longer permitted on television, the tobacco companies spend millions of dollars advertising nontobacco products on television.

The tobacco companies are not alone in their attempts to influence media content, however. Network television, in the early days at least, was totally dependent on advertising revenues, and advertisers didn't hesitate to give feedback to the young networks. In what is frequently referred to as "the golden age"—the 1950s—"advertisers and their agencies . . . regularly read scripts a day or two in advance of shooting. . . . Sponsors who bought whole shows, or major portions, didn't shrink from direct censorship. . . . At the behest of an ad agency for a gas company sponsor, CBS took out half a dozen instances of the word 'gas' referring to gas chambers in a 'Playhouse 90' drama on the Nuremberg trials." After the quiz show scandals of 1958, CBS president Frank Stanton "set down an explicit rule: Advertisers would no longer be permitted to read scripts in advance and intervene if they thought their corporate images at risk. Instead, they would be permitted to screen the filmed episodes, and, if they wanted to beg off a particular one, the network would excuse them" (Gitlin, 1985, pp. 255–256). Because there are more potential advertisers than there is network advertising time to sell, Todd Gitlin says that "no single advertiser can truly wield a veto power over the network" (1985, p. 254).

Nonetheless, the "bulk of major advertisers" *do* have the power to affect television content, because network executives "take into account whether they think major advertisers in the aggregate . . . are going to consider a show a hospitable setting for their commercials. . . . To advertisers, the programs amount to packaging for commercials" (Gitlin, 1985, pp. 253–254). The television networks react to their *perceptions* of what advertisers will tolerate.

Sometimes the media run content that is specifically designed to draw advertisers. *Vanity Fair*'s editor Tina Brown turned around the revived magazine after a 1984 economic slump by running stories on the magazine's major advertisers, people like Bill Blass, Giorgio Armani, Ralph Lauren, Calvin Klein, and Yves Saint Laurent. The April 1989 issue carried thirty-seven pages of ads from people who had previously been given favorable editorial coverage in the magazine (Lazare, 1989).

Advertiser-Created Television Programming

The 1980s saw an important change in children's television programming—the advent of advertiser-created shows. Popular characters from children's television shows have for a long time been turned into toys, along with a mountain of accompanying paraphernalia, "each sold separately." In the late 1980s, however, the deregulatory climate at the Federal Communications Commission and aggressive marketing by the toy industry "have together created a favorable environment for children's 'program-length commercials,' whose primary purpose is to sell toys through the shows' heroes" (Kunkel, 1988, p. 90). Instead of being conceived of and sold to the networks based on its entertainment value, a program-length commercial is "originally conceived of as a vehicle to provide product exposure to the child audience, in the hopes of stimulating product sales that in turn may help to sustain program popularity. Moreover, creative control for the program content is typically relinquished to the manufacturer of the product upon which the program is based. The product manufacturers specify how the characters must look, what they can or cannot say or do, and what environments they live in" (pp. 90–91).

Ben Bagdikian (1989) refers to American television networks' children's programming as "that enduring national scandal. . . . Despite the harm done by this mindless menu of violent cartoons and blatant commercialism—harm that has been confirmed by the Surgeon General's office and others—decades of parents' and educators' complaints have been ignored" (p. 819).

Advertiser-created programming represents a "new stage in the long relation between advertising and the mass media," and it is not limited to children's programming. "Videocassettes, discs, and cable channels are increasingly being filled with content *entirely* produced by advertisers." For example, J. C. Penney might produce a video on home decorating, complete with decorating advice, examples of different styles, and prices of the J. C. Penney merchandise used in the examples. "To prevent viewers from erasing or skipping over advertising messages in these 'advertiser-created programs' programming is being developed with commercials so skillfully intertwined with other information that they cannot be removed or avoided" (Janus, 1984, pp. 66–67).

Sometimes ads are so interesting that they cross the line from advertising to editorial content. Roger Ailes, who orchestrated George Bush's 1988 media campaign, says that the news media are much more interested in political advertising than they were in previous campaigns. "What's amazing to me is that the network news leads in the evening with the new ads. In the old days you had to buy advertising time. Now you could theoretically run a race and just produce it for the news, get a run, and get a lot of points" (McCarthy, 1988, p. 70).

GOVERNMENT CONTROLS

There is little doubt that governments of all countries exert controls over the mass media. In countries where the media are largely privately owned, controls are exerted through laws, regulations, licenses, and taxes. In countries where the media are primarily government owned, government control is exerted through media financing (Janus, 1984).

In his review of fifty-eight governments' relationships with their mass media, John Merrill (1988) found that the United States, Canada, and Greece have the least inclination toward press control. At the time of the study, those that most controlled their press included East Germany, the People's Republic of China, Iraq, Syria, Tunisia, Cuba, and Peru. Merrill grouped countries into geographic regions and ranked them, with the most inclination to control the press listed first:

- Middle East
- Latin America

- Eastern Europe
- Africa
- Asia
- Western Europe and North America

Peter Galliner, director of the International Press Institute, says that there is "a growing trend toward government interference in democratic countries. . . . This is the most worrying aspect today, because the hopes of nations that are on their way toward more freedom must not be crushed by governments in the free world that should be guardians of press freedom and should not introduce legislation restricting fundamental human rights" (1989, p. 52).

In May 1989, Algerian television and newspaper journalists published information about government manipulation of media content; all Algerian media are government owned. One journalist said: "There are 1,001 methods of repression. Some journalists were forbidden to write, some to sign their articles, some to travel, some to have passports" ("Algerian journalists rebel," 1989, p. 58).

Since 1984, the South African government "has clamped increasingly stringent censorship on news media, both domestic and foreign" (Giffard & Cohen, 1989, p. 3). Control of domestic media is aimed at restoring a sense of normalcy, whereas control of foreign media "is intended to force news of the conflict off the front pages of the world's newspapers and from its television screens" (p. 3). The latter effect did not occur. In fact, the censorship backfired: Foreign coverage of South Africa increased, with the news of the attempted censorship being most heavily covered.

In India, "Doordarshan, the nation's only television channel, is run by the government; politicians and civil servants make all editorial and programming decisions" (Pink, 1989, p. 12). As Prime Minister Rajiv Gandhi ran for election in 1989, television coverage only rarely included opposition candidates.[6] Gandhi is on television so much, says journalist Madhu Trehan, that "you wonder when the guy works" (p. 12). Trehan produces an alternative source of television news called "Newstrack," a videotaped ninety-minute news show available for rental in video stores that was started in 1988 by the company that owns "the country's most respected news magazine, *India Today*" (p. 12). Although viewers must pay a rental charge for the videotape, most revenue comes from about seven minutes of advertising in each ninety-minute segment.

In France, although "the press is largely unfettered" (Goldstein, 1989), the government can ban any book or periodical of foreign origin or inspiration. This provision, added to the French press code just prior to World War II, has been used by the government to "harrass" a monthly magazine, *El-Badil*, which is published by émigrés who oppose the one-party government in Algiers. It was banned by the French government seven times between 1986 and 1989.

In 1988 a senior foreign affairs journalist for the *Sydney Morning Herald*, in Australia, was ordered by the High Court to reveal his sources for a story so that the subject of the story could sue them for defamation (Galliner, 1989).

In Great Britain, one of the most severe cases of peacetime censorship occurred in 1988 when the home secretary banned the BBC and independent radio and television broadcasts of statements by representatives of eleven Irish organizations, including the Irish Republican Army, Sinn Féin, the Ulster Freedom Fighters, and the Ulster Defense Force. "The order also bars statements by any person supporting or inviting support for the organizations named" (Galliner, 1989, p. 53).

In Israel, the government can censor mass media content if they determine that it could incite violence. In 1988, the Palestinian media were banned and shut down several times. "The most far-reaching sanction was the shutdown of the Palestine Press Service, a prime source of information for the foreign press." In addition, two American reporters from NBC and the *Washington Post* "had their press credentials revoked for several weeks after they filed material about the killing of a PLO leader in Tunis by Israeli commandos without submitting it first to military censorship" (Galliner, 1989, p. 54).

A 1988 free trade agreement signed by the United States and Canada included a provision that Canadian journalists who want to work in the United States must have a college degree and three years of experience. Peter Galliner, of the International Press Institute, says that "all attempts to define qualifications for journalists—attempts frequently resorted to by the authorities in Third World countries—pose a serious threat and are particularly disheartening when they involve a country proudly boasting a First Amendment to its constitution that guarantees its citizens freedom of expression" (1989, p. 52).

First Amendment Freedoms

In the United States, the First Amendment to the Constitution declares:

> Congress shall make no law respecting an establishment of religion, or prohibiting the free exercise thereof; or abridging the freedom of speech, or of the press; or the right of the people peaceably to assemble, and to petition the Government for a redress of grievances.

It was a reaction to two aspects of English law: "the wholesale system of licensing and censorship of all publications and the draconian criminal law of seditious libel, the theory of which was that virtually any criticism of government was deemed to contain the seeds of disorder and, indeed, of incipient rebellion" (Schmidt, 1981, p. 61).

But the constitutional protections for the print media did not carry over to television and radio. The First Amendment makes the government a laissez-faire reviewer of the print media: "The First Amendment has erected an all but irrebuttable presumption that, as Learned Hand put it, 'right conclusions are more likely to be gathered out of a multitude of tongues, than through any kind of authoritative selection'" (Schmidt, 1981, p. 60). For the broadcast media, the situation is very different. Anyone wishing to broadcast must get a license, and the "government licenses only those broadcasters it believes will serve the public interest" (p. 60). "Broadcasting is not a second-class citizen, when it comes to First Amendment rights. It is a ninth-class citizen," says Michael G. Gartner, president of NBC News (1988, p. 4).

Not only are the broadcast media licensed, says Gartner, they are also regularly pressured—far more than the print media—by politicians and government officials who want to influence news content. "The networks have been conditioned," says Gartner, "like Pavlov's dogs, to react when a Congressman calls. Indeed, just the threat of a call—the rumor from an aide that his boss will soon be calling—or a statement or, God forbid, a hearing can sometimes force the broadcast industry into submission on a question of policy, programming, or scheduling. Broadcasting today is essentially a public-policy laboratory in which the Congress feels it can play with impunity. For lovers of the First Amendment, it is a nightmare" (pp. 7–8).

Regulations and Laws in the United States

Regulation of the broadcast industry in the United States dates back to 1927, when Congress created the Federal Radio Commission, later to become the Federal Communications Commission in 1934 (Killory & Bozzelli, 1988). Three early decisions directly affected the ownership of broadcast media: that the media would be privately rather than government owned, that limited-term rather than indefinite-length licenses would be granted, and that there would be both public and commercial stations (Dyk & Wilkins, 1989).

To protect public interests against media companies' profit-making interests, however, the FCC in 1949 adopted the Fairness Doctrine, to ensure that broadcasters "behaved as 'fiduciaries' of a public 'trust' " (Killory & Bozzelli, 1988, p. 65). As Diane S. Killory and Richard J. Bozzelli, FCC general counsel and special assistant for mass media affairs, put it, the FCC "turned the First Amendment's right of free speech into a right of the listening public instead of the right of the speaker" (pp. 67–68). Broadcasters were required to provide time for opposing views, but in 1959 Congress amended the 1934 Communications Act to exempt equal-time regulations for political candidates appearing in regular newscasts.

Over the first fifty years of its existence, the FCC introduced more and more controls on the broadcast media, but the result was not more controversy and diversity in content—rather less. An FCC study showed that the Fairness Doctrine's "net effect was to chill free speech" (Killory & Bozzelli, 1988, p. 65). Some broadcasters even adopted policies to avoid controversial issues, for fear that interest groups would complain to the FCC and therefore put the station's license renewal at risk.

As a result, the FCC entered a period of deregulation in the 1980s, and the Fairness Doctrine and other regulations were repealed. Killory and Bozzelli (1988, p. 71) argue that less government interference in broadcasting will "give far greater assurance to the people of this country, who are the ultimate beneficiaries of a free press, that the liberties and protections guaranteed by the Constitution will be passed on to the next generation of speakers." This "absence" of regulation has had a strong indirect influence on media content:

- *Tabloid TV*. Independently produced television shows that emphasize murders, celebrities' personal lives, and sex scandals—such as "A Current Affair," "This Evening," "The Reporters," and "Inside Edition"—lack the journalistic "gatekeeper of news standards" that had previously monitored television programs. Philip Weis, a contributing editor of the *Columbia Journalism Review,* says that "trash TV . . . would never have caught on were it not for this bold, new, deregulated marketplace" (1989, p. 38).
- *No trafficking rule*. The repeal of the no trafficking rule—which required that a broadcast license be held for at least three years—"turned broadcast properties into much more liquid assets" (Rattner, 1988, p. 6). As a result, between 1984 and 1986, 115 television stations were sold less than three years after the previous sale. This compares with only 10 stations sold after less than three years during the 1981–1983 period. It is yet to be seen whether frequent shifts in ownership will reduce stations' commitment to public service programming.
- *Public TV editorials*. In 1984 public television stations were given the right to editorialize, but this apparently has not had much effect on content. Lack of editorializing may be the result of "a journalistic timorousness" (Kleiman, 1987, p. 713).
- *Children's programming*. The deregulatory "climate" has created a favorable environment for advertiser-created children's shows, "whose primary purpose is to sell toys through the shows' heroes" (Kunkel, 1988, p. 90).

Government Policies and Actions

Sometimes government influence on the mass media operates outside of formal laws and regulations. There are more than 3,000 U.S. government workers who primarily produce public information that is designed to give an impression of governmental competence and efficiency. "At every level of government, in every agency, there are information specialists whose responsibility it is to ensure that the nation's public media carry the desired message forward" (Gandy, 1982, p. 74). A less overt influence on media content comes in the form of news leaks, backgrounders, or off-the-record interviews, and these can be used very effectively to set the agenda for the news media—something that U.S. presidents do not fail to attempt. Gandy (1982) says that the executive branch spends more money on publicity than the legislative and judicial branches combined. The late journalist and press critic I. F. Stone commented in 1965 that President Lyndon Johnson "sometimes seems to think the Constitution made him not only commander-in-chief of the nation's armed forces but editor-in-chief of its newspapers" (Boylan, 1989, p. 47). About off-the-record briefings during the Vietnam War, Stone wrote: "The process of brain-washing the public starts with off-the-record briefings for newspapermen in which all sorts of far-fetched theories are suggested to explain why the tiny North Vietnamese navy would be mad enough to venture an attack on the Seventh Fleet [in the Gulf of Tonkin]. . . . *Everything is discussed except the possibility that the attack might have been provoked*" (p. 47).

Paletz and Entman (1981, p. 217) report that hundreds of journalists have had secret relationships with the Central Intelligence Agency, from occasionally trading favors with CIA agents to being paid intelligence officers. In this way, the CIA has been able to slip things into the American media, either through tips or by influencing the content of foreign-based English-language publications read by American correspondents. In addition, American media sometimes provided cover for CIA agents (by allowing them to pose as journalists) and gave outtakes of newsfilms to the agency (Paletz and Entman, 1981, p. 218).

Even general U.S. policy can apparently affect U.S. media content. Chang (1989) found in his study of U.S. policy and coverage of China in the *New York Times* and *Washington Post* between 1950 and 1984 that "the more the government favored U.S.-China relations, the more the newspapers preferred better relations between the two countries" (p. 504). His analysis suggested that newspaper coverage changed in response to government policy shifts.

Government policies have also been used to deny some foreign news sources entry into the United States. For example, the American Society of Newspaper Editors in 1989 wanted to invite presidents Castro of Cuba and Ortega of Nicaragua to address their Washington, D.C., conference. The U.S. State Department refused to allow the two heads of state into the country. When asked about the ruling, Secretary of State James Baker said that the decision was based on policies about diplomatic relations with Cuba and Nicaragua, not censorship: "It would be harmful to our diplomatic efforts to bring those two countries into the community of nations" (Cranberg, 1989, p. 12). Some of those in the audience concluded that Baker "was outlining a relationship in which the government decides what is beneficial for the press, recommends news coverage, and compels the press to shun speakers who happen to be in the administration's doghouse" (p. 12).

THE MARKETPLACE

In the United States, the mass media operate primarily in a commercial marketplace, where each medium must compete with the others for audience and advertiser attention. In this section we will show how characteristics of the marketplace in which a medium operates can influence its content.

Competition

From the newspaper publisher's point of view, the key feature of the marketplace is whether there is another newspaper in town. A competing newspaper requires that the market—readers' and advertisers' dollars—be split between the newspapers; in a monopoly market, the publisher has the only (newspaper) game in town. Would the competitive publisher produce a different newspaper than his or her monopoly counterpart? With the number of daily newspapers declining rapidly in recent years, more and more communities are left with newspaper monopolies, causing a number of researchers to turn their attention to this problem.

A common assumption underlying such research is that two newspapers will cover the news in different ways,[7] but this is not always supported. A study by Weaver and Mullins (1975) showed that there were virtually no differences in the kind of editorial content published by newspapers that compete in the same community, a conclusion that was supported by McCombs in 1987. Utt and Pasternack (1985) looked at ten pairs of competing newspapers to determine whether differences existed in the newspapers' use of graphic devices. Newspapers with similar circulation sizes showed no difference in their graphics. If, however, one newspaper was substantially smaller than its competitor, the smaller tended to be more modern in design. Lacy (1988) suggests that an increase in *intercity* competition—such as when a metropolitan city newspaper encroaches on a suburban newspaper's market—can cause the suburban newspaper to increase its coverage of local news.

Many studies have looked at *diversity*—the variety in the content that is offered the audience—because competition is assumed to create a "marketplace of ideas" that facilitates the free discussion of important issues. When one of the two or more newspapers in a city goes out of business, is the audience left with poorer coverage of the diverse concerns in the community? Apparently not. A number of studies have shown little or no support for such a hypothesis. Entman (1985) compared the content of ninety-one newspapers from communities with either two competing newspapers, two papers with a single owner, or only one newspaper. He found little evidence to suggest that competition encourages diversity. In another study, of four Canadian newspapers, Maxwell McCombs (1988) found that the surviving newspaper may have actually improved its content following the death of its competitor. In a similar study in Cleveland, McCombs (1987) found only random differences between the surviving *Plain Dealer*'s content before and after the *Press* folded.

Unlike newspapers, television stations and networks rarely operate in a monopoly environment—three or four competing local newcasts are not uncommon within one community. To be economically successful, a television station must find its own part of the mass audience and prepare content that will draw viewers. Atwater (1984) says that broadcast editors create diversity in their attempt to position their station's newscasts differently from their competitors', and therefore that each station in the market does increase the diversity of information available to the audience. Almost half of the local news stories in the nine television stations Atwater studied were unique to one station.

The same thing may not be true of nonnews content, however. Gitlin (1985) says that the advent of cable and the expansion of television channels from three or four to fifty or more in many communities has not increased the diversity of content offered the audience. Most programs on the new channels are supplied by only a few distribution companies—those that already have adopted the typical Hollywood conventions. A large part of cable content consists of reruns of movies or old television series.

Market Characteristics

The kind of community from which a medium operates also affects content. The community is the environment in which the medium must operate, and therefore the community's economy and culture as well as its physical and social layout will affect both the kind of media that set up business there and how successful they are (Phillips, Boylan, & Yu, 1982).

Even the size of the community can have an effect, as Carroll (1989) shows in his analysis of fifty-seven television stations' newcasts. The larger the market size, the more the television station covered spontaneous news events; smaller-market stations relied more on features and other stories that could be preplanned (see also Carroll, 1985). Smaller-market stations also ran less local news than did bigger stations. Carroll speculates that the differences may be due to the lower budgets and small staffs of the smaller-market stations. Essentially the same result came from a study of 114 daily newspapers by Lacy and Bernstein (1988): Larger newspapers were more likely to generate their own content, whereas smaller papers relied more on wire service copy and editorials. Stone and Morrison (1976) say the goal of the smaller newspapers is to be the community's voice, which explains their reliance on grass roots copy and legal advertising. The evidence is far from conclusive, however. Becker, Beam, and Russial (1978) found that community size was not related to newspaper performance. Hynds (1980) found that changes in circulation size were not associated with changes in coverage, such as the number of pictures used or the amount of business news. Hynds did find, however, that larger newspapers are more likely to run exposés.

McCombs (1972) carries market influence beyond the community level to the social system as a whole, arguing that the amount of economic support available in the United States is a major constraint on the growth of the mass media. He uses Scripps' Constancy Hypothesis—"that the amount of money spent on mass communication is relatively constant"—to hypothesize "that a relatively constant *proportion* of the available wealth—Gross National Product, for example—will be devoted to mass media." Consumers and advertisers will spend more or less on mass media, depending on how much money they have. In other words, "the media will grow and expand at a rate dictated by the general economy" (pp. 5–6). McCombs shows that over time, spending in new media comes at the expense of the old, such that the proportion devoted to all media remains the same.

In other studies, however, nationwide economic changes are treated as stimuli that cause the media to change their assessment of how newsworthy something is. For example, Erfle and McMillan (1989, p. 127) show that "network news coverage of the oil industry is strongly affected by the market conditions within the oil industry." As the price of oil goes up, the amount of coverage of the oil industry in general increases—not just for the price changes. Apparently when oil is in short supply and therefore costs more, journalists find oil issues to be more newsworthy. Sparkes (1978) found that the coverage of the United States and Canada in each other's press is related to the percentage of foreign trade accounted for by the other country and to the country's gross national product (GNP).

Institutional Affiliations

Although research shows that individual journalists are unlikely to be active in community organizations (Johnstone, Slawski, & Bowman, 1972), the same cannot be said for the directors of large media corporations. Directors of the twenty-four largest newspaper-owning companies in the United States share a "web of affiliations" with those in the U.S. power structure (Dreier, 1983). Such institutional affiliations are accomplished through membership in business and trade associations, activities in nonprofit groups and social clubs, and through corporate directorships. Dreier argues that large and influential newspapers—such as the *New York Times, Washington Post, Wall Street Journal,* and *Los Angeles Times*—have a common ideology with other large corporations. This ideology—corporate liberalism—is used by those in the capitalist power structure to "forestall changes from below and stabilize the long-term foundations of capitalism by implementing strategic reforms to co-opt dissent" (p. 447). Large corporation leaders differ from those in small and medium-sized companies in their interest in the welfare of the system as a whole. The leaders of small and medium-sized companies have a greater parochial outlook and concern with a single company's short-term interests. The corporate ideological outlook supports unions, social welfare, foreign aid, and government regulations, and Dreier implies that newspapers owned by such corporations tend to reflect a more liberal ideology in their content. Some, such as the *Chicago Tribune* and *Los Angeles Times,* changed from extreme conservativism to a liberal outlook (Dreier, 1983, p. 447). Another effect of the increasing number of corporate affiliations between media and other organizations is an increase in the proportion of newspapers that do *not* make presidential endorsements: from 13.4 percent in 1940 to 25.6 percent in 1976 (Emery & Emery, 1978, p. 483, cited in Dreier, 1983, p. 447).

In his study of fifty publicly held media corporations, Han (1988) found that media corporations' boards of directors are *interlocked* with boards of directors from nonmedia corporations; that is, the boards of directors share members. Most of the 300 directors of the twenty-five largest newspapers also serve as directors of leading businesses, banks, and law firms (Dreier & Weinberg, 1979, as cited in Han, 1988).

Media corporations are most often interlocked with financial institutions, and this may have serious consequences for media corporations that are bought out with the cooperation of financial institutions. By varying their stock ownership, financial institutions can control the basic decisions in media corporations. "Interlocking directorate ties with major advertisers, financial houses, law firms, competing firms, and other elite social institutions thus can raise a question of the autonomy of media firms" (Han, 1988, p. 182). Large media organizations may themselves be dependent on resources controlled by these elite social institutions, putting the media potentially under the control of giant corporations. "The greater the dependency of a media firm on the elite institutions, the greater the chance for their control over mass media" (p. 183).

TECHNOLOGY

Media content may be affected by the adoption of technological advances. As Theodore Peterson (1981) points out, the technological revolution that occurred during the 1880s and 1890s revolutionized the mass media. Instead of being primarily local, the new mass-produced newspapers and magazines could cover a wider geographic area. But to appeal to people from a wider area, the newspapers had to standardize their product. Today newspapers across the United States are largely alike, and journalists can move easily from one to another. "One issue of a given magazine is much like every other, for once an editor has hit upon the editorial balance that pleases his readers, he changes it gradually or not at all. And the spin-off of television series is testimony to the inherent sameness of broadcast fare" (p. 26).

Have technological advances in broadcasting changed broadcast news? There is little research to answer this question, but Ostroff and Sandell (1989) suggest that it has not in any important way. They studied election campaigns for Ohio's governor in 1978, 1982, and 1986 to see how changes in technology at three television stations would affect coverage of the elections. The changes included switching from film to ENG, which allows live coverage of events; use of satellites for newsgathering; and enhanced graphics, which help news staff present complicated information more effectively. Although there was an increase in the number of live stories between 1982 and 1986, coverage remained sporadic and gave audience members little information about the election.

Two studies have looked at the effects of computer technology on newspaper content. Randall (1979) found that newspapers that use full electronic editing have fewer errors in spelling, punctuation, sentence construction, hyphenation, and typography. Shipley and Gentry (1981) found that video display terminal (VDT) editing is more accurate than hard copy editing. The *New York Times,* the *Wall Street Journal,* and *USA Today* are using satellite technology to transmit national editions of their newspapers to regional centers for printing and distribution (Cranberg, 1988). The technology made a standardized national edition feasible.

Janus (1984) suggests that the creation of a transnational communication infrastructure will facilitate the growth of global advertising campaigns—"one standard message designed at company headquarters and transmitted to all the countries where the product is made or distributed." Television commercials can be based "around internationally recognized visual symbols to overcome the major obstacles posed by language diversity and illiteracy" (p. 59).

SUMMARY: INFLUENCES OF EXTRAMEDIA FORCES ON MEDIA CONTENT

In this chapter, we have shown that there is a wide variety of influences on media content that operate outside of the media organization. Sources can stimulate or constrain the diffusion of information according to their own interests, and journalists' choice of which source to interview can color the stories they write. Although interest groups make organized efforts to influence media content (for example, through press guidelines), their success in influencing content is mixed. Interest groups that can retaliate economically (such as with a consumer boycott of advertisers' products) do apparently affect content. There is anecdotal evidence to suggest that some media organizations may self-censor the content they produce in order to prevent even the threat of economic retaliation. The creation of pseudoevents is one way in which public relations practitioners can control media content.

Do the mass media give the audience what it wants? Although most journalists are uninformed about their audiences' characteristics and preferences, the marketing departments of some newspapers have provided publishers with enough information to "position" the newspaper so as to draw the desired target audience.

But for most commercial media, audiences are important only because their attention can be sold to advertisers, who provide the bulk of revenues. And advertisers often tell the media what they think and how they believe content should be altered. With new technologies, advertisers are taking the offensive in the battle over media content, with advertiser-created programming for children and videocassette offerings of programming with commercials integrated so they cannot be "zapped" out.

Another frequent influence on media content comes from government. Although some countries have fewer press controls than others, all governments control the mass media to some extent. In the United States, this control takes the form of laws (such as those designed to punish libel) and regulations that determine both who can own a broadcast medium and what kinds of content will be permitted.

Each commercial mass medium operates within a marketplace, and the nature of the marketplace can sometimes affect content. For example, the size of the market and its opportunities for profits affect content, as does the general health of the economy. On the other hand, numerous studies of the effects of competition on newspaper content show that competition does not ensure increased diversity within a market.

NOTES

1. For example, advertising accounts for nearly 100 percent of television and radio broadcasting, 75 percent of newspaper, and 50 percent of magazine revenues (Dunn & Barban, as reported in Weis & Burke, 1986).
2. Population size in these cities also fell during the same period, but by only 6 percent, according to Bogart (1989).
3. The same could be said for women. Those who say that women or minorities will bring something different to media content assume that journalists' individual characteristics will override forces due to job socialization and organizational imperatives. Interestingly enough, these are often the same people who say that journalists' personal attitudes don't affect content.

4. Not only tobacco advertising seems to affect magazine content. In 1982, Tankard and Peirce showed that magazines that accepted alcohol advertising had more favorable editorial coverage of alcoholic beverages.
5. For example, Phillip Morris owns General Foods Corporation, RJR Reynolds owns Nabisco Brands, Inc., and Del Monte Foods (Kessler, 1989).
6. Gandhi became prime minister following the assassination of his mother in 1984.
7. The assumption is almost always that competition will have beneficial effects on content, but Entman (1985, p. 163) suggests that rivalry may have negative effects, such as sabotage, creating bogus scandals, and attacking public officials for minor offenses. "The competitive energies may be spent in childish one-upmanship, with each paper determined to mine the ultimate nugget of trivia so as not to be 'beat' by its rival."

REFERENCES

Albritton, R. B., & Manheim, J. B. (1983). News of Rhodesia: The impact of a public relations campaign. *Journalism Quarterly, 60,* pp. 622–628.

Algerian journalists rebel. (1989, August). *World Press Review,* p. 58.

Altheide, D. L. (1976). *Creating reality*. Beverly Hills, CA: Sage.

Altschull, H. J. (1984). *Agents of power*. New York: Longman.

America won't work without manufacturing. (1989, January/February). *Columbia Journalism Review,* p. 13.

American Family Association. (1989, March). *Journal of the American Family Association,* p. 2.

Atwater, T. (1984). Product differentiation in local TV news. *Journalism Quarterly, 61,* 757–762.

Atwater, T., & Green, N. F. (1988). News sources in network coverage of international terrorism. *Journalism Quarterly, 65,* 967–971.

Bagdikian, B. H. (1983). *The media monopoly*. Boston: Beacon Press.

Bagdikian, B. H. (1989, June 12). The lords of the global village. *The Nation,* pp. 805–820.

Barnes, F. (1983, January/February). The view from the fringe: Left and right ideologues take issue with the press. *Washington Journalism Review,* pp. 48–51.

Becker, L. B., Beam, R., & Russial, J. (1978). Correlates of daily newspaper performance in New England. *Journalism Quarterly, 55,* 100–108.

Bell, A. (1982). Radio: The style of news language. *Journal of Communication, 32,* pp. 150–164.

Bogart, L. (1989). Newspapers in transition. In P. S. Cook, D. Gomery, & L. Lichty (Eds.), *American media* (pp. 47–48). Washington, DC: Wilson Center Press.

Boorstin, D. J. (1971). From news-gathering to news-making: A flood of pseudo-events. In W. Schramm & D. F. Roberts (Eds.), *The process and effects of mass communication* (pp. 116–150). Urbana: University of Illinois Press.

Boylan, J. (1989, September/October). Reconstructing I. F. Stone. *Columbia Journalism Review,* pp. 46–47.

Cantor, M. G., & Jones, E. (1983). Creating fiction for women. *Communication Research, 10,* 111–137.

Carroll, R. L. (1985). Content values in TV news programs in small and large markets. *Journalism Quarterly, 62,* 877–882, 938.

Carroll, R. L. (1989). Market size and TV news values. *Journalism Quarterly, 66,* 49–56.

Caudill, E., & Ashdown, P. (1989). The *New England Journal of Medicine* as news source. *Journalism Quarterly, 66,* 458–462.

Chang, T. K. (1989). The impact of presidential statements on press editorials regarding U.S. China policy, 1950–1984. *Communication Research, 16,* 486–509.

Cranberg, L. (1989, September/October). What Baker and Quayle told ASNE. *Columbia Journalism Review,* pp. 12, 14.

Cranberg, L. (1988, September 8). Satellite technology making major papers obese with power. *New York City Tribune.*

Danielian, L. H., & Reese, S. D. (1989). A closer look at intermediate influences on agenda setting: The cocaine issue of 1986. In P. J. Shoemaker (Ed.), *Communication campaigns about drugs: Government, media, public* (pp. 47–66). Hillsdale, NJ: Lawrence Erlbaum Associates.

Donsbach, W. (1983). Journalists' conceptions of their audience. Comparative indicators of the way British and German journalists define their relations to the public. *Gazette, 32,* 19–36.

Dreier, P. (1983). The position of the press in the U.S. power structure. In E. Wartella, D. C. Whitney, & S. Windahl (Eds.), *Mass communication review yearbook* (Vol. 4, pp. 439–451). Beverly Hills, CA: Sage.

Dreier, P., & Weinberg, S. (1979). The ties that bind: Interlocking directorates. *Columbia Journalism Review,* pp. 51–68.

Dunn, S. W., & Barban, A. (1986). *Advertising: Its role in modern marketing* (6th edition). Hinsdale, IL: Dryden Press.

Dyk, T. B., & Wilkins, W. J. (1989). Regulation and ownership: Washington's influence on who owns the press. *Gannett Center Journal, 3,* 74–91.

Emery, E., & Emery, M. (1978). *The press and America.* Englewood Cliffs, NJ: Prentice-Hall.

Entman, R. M. (1985). Newspaper competition and First Amendment ideals: Does monopoly matter? *Journal of Communication, 35,* 147–165.

Erfle, S., & McMillan, H. (1989). Determinants of network news coverage of the oil industry during the late 1970s. *Journalism Quarterly, 66,* 121–128.

Fico, F. (1984a). The ultimate spokesman revisited: Media visibility of state lawmakers. *Journalism Quarterly, 61,* 383–391.

Fico, F. (1984b). News coverage of part-time and full-time legislatures. *Newspaper Research Journal, 6,* 49–57.

Fink, C. C. (1989, March). How newspapers should handle upscale/downscale conundrum. *Presstime,* pp. 40–41.

Flegel, R. C., & Chaffee, S. H. (1971). Influences of editors, readers, and personal opinions on reporters. *Journalism Quarterly, 48,* 645–651.

Galliner, P. (1989, February). New threats in the democracies. *World Press Review,* pp. 52–57.

Gandy, O. H. (1982). *Beyond agenda setting: Information subsidies and public policy.* Norwood, NJ: Ablex.

Gannett Center for Media Studies. (1989). *The press, the presidency and the first hundred days.* New York: Gannett Center for Media Studies at Columbia University.

Gans, H. J. (1979). *Deciding what's news: A study of CBS Evening News, NBC Nightly News, Newsweek and Time.* New York: Pantheon Books.

Gartner, M. G. (1988, November 10). *Buncombe, broadcasters & the first amendment.* Speech given before the Practising Law Institute, New York City.

Gassaway, B. M. (1988). Are secret sources in the news media really necessary? *Newspaper Research Journal, 9,* 69–77.

Giffard, C. A., & Cohen, L. (1989). South African TV and censorship: Does it reduce negative coverage? *Journalism Quarterly, 66,* 3–10.

Gitlin, T. (1985). *Inside prime time*. New York: Pantheon Books.

Goldstein, E. (1989, July/August). The magazine that wouldn't die. *Columbia Journalism Review*, pp. 8, 10.

Gottlieb, M. (1989, July/August). Dangerous liaisons: Journalists and their sources. *Columbia Journalism Review*, pp. 21–35.

Greenberg, B. S., Burgoon, M., Burgoon, J. K., & Korzenny, F. (1983). *Mexican Americans and the mass media*. Norwood, NJ: Ablex.

Hackett, R. A. (1985). A hierarchy of access: Aspects of source bias on Canadian TV news. *Journalism Quarterly, 62*, 256–265, 277.

Han, K. (1988). *Interlocking directorates of major media corporations: The main determinants*. Unpublished Ph.D. dissertation, The University of Texas at Austin.

Hynds, E. C. (1980). Business coverage is getting better. *Journalism Quarterly, 57*, 297–304, 368.

Jamieson, K. H., & Campbell, K. K. (1983). *The interplay of influence: Mass media and their publics in news, advertising, politics*. Belmont, CA: Wadsworth.

Janus, N. (1984). Advertising and the creation of global markets: The role of the new communication technologies. In V. Mosco & J. Wasko (Eds.), *The critical communications review, Volume 3. Changing patterns of communications control* (pp. 57–70). Norwood, NJ: Ablex.

Johnstone, J. W. C., Slawski, E. J., & Bowman, W. W. (1972). The professional values of American newsmen. *Public Opinion Quarterly, 36*, 522–540.

Kelley, M. (1988, September 30). A profession of perceptions. *Austin* (TX) *American-Statesman*, p. B1.

Kessler, L. (1989). Women's magazines' coverage of smoking related health hazards. *Journalism Quarterly, 66*, 316–322, 445.

Killory, D. S., & Bozzelli, R. J. (1988). "Fairness," the First Amendment and the public interest. *Gannett Center Journal, 2*, 62–72.

Kleiman, H. M. (1987). Unshackled but unwilling: Public broadcasting and editorializing. *Journalism Quarterly, 64*, 707–713.

Kopenhaver, L. L., Martinson, D. L., & Ryan, M. (1984). How public relations practitioners and editors in Florida view each other. *Journalism Quarterly, 61*, 860–865, 884.

Kunkel, D. (1988). From a raised eyebrow to a turned back: The FCC and children's product-related programming. *Journal of Communication, 38*, 90–108.

Lacy, S. (1988). The impact of intercity competition on daily newspaper content. *Journalism Quarterly, 65*, 399–406.

Lacy, S., & Bernstein, J. M. (1988). Daily newspaper content's relationship to publication cycle and circulation size. *Newspaper Research Journal, 9*, 49–58.

Lazare, D. (1989, May/June). Vanity fare. *Columbia Journalism Review*, pp. 6, 8.

Malcolm, J. (1989, March 13). Reflections: The journalist and the murderer, I—the journalist. *New Yorker*, pp. 38–73.

Malcolm, J. (1989, March 20). Reflections: The journalist and the murderer, II—the murderer. *New Yorker*, pp. 49–82.

Martin, S. R. (1988). Proximity of event as factor in selection of news sources. *Journalism Quarterly, 65*, 986–989, 1043.

McCarthy, L. (1988). The selling of the president: An interview with Roger Ailes. *Gannett Center Journal, 2*, 66–72.

McCombs, M. E. (1972). Mass media in the marketplace. *Journalism Monographs, 24*.

McCombs, M. E. (1987). Effect of monopoly in Cleveland on diversity of newspaper content. *Journalism Quarterly, 64,* 740–745.

McCombs, M. E. (1988). Comparison of newspaper content under competitive and monopoly conditions. In R. Picard, J. Winter, M. McCombs, & S. Lacy (Eds.), *Press concentration and monopoly: New perspectives on newspaper ownership and operations.* Norwood, NJ: Ablex.

Merrill, J. C. (1988). Inclination of nations to control press and attitudes on professionalization. *Journalism Quarterly, 65,* 839–844.

Mogel, L. (1979). *The magazine.* Englewood Cliffs, NJ: Prentice-Hall.

Ostroff, D. H., & Sandell, K. L. (1989). Campaign coverage by local TV news in Columbus, Ohio, 1978–1986. *Journalism Quarterly, 66,* 114–120.

Paletz, D. L., & Entman, R. M. (1981). *Media, power, politics.* New York: Free Press.

Peterson, T. (1981). Mass media and their environments: A journey into the past. In E. Abel (Ed.), *What's news* (pp. 13–32). San Francisco: Institute for Contemporary Studies.

Pink, D. (1989, May/June). India: VCR enlightenment. *Columbia Journalism Review,* pp. 12, 14.

Phillips, W., Boylan, J., & Yu, F. T. C. (1982). *Mass media.* New York: Holt, Rinehart & Winston.

Randall, S. D. (1979). Effect of electronic editing on error rate of newspaper. *Journalism Quarterly, 56,* 161–165.

Rattner, S. (1988). Broadcasting deregulation on Wall Street. *Gannett Center Journal, 2,* 1–15.

Reese, S. D., & Danielian, L. H. (1989). Intermedia influence and the drug issue: Converging on cocaine. In P. J. Shoemaker (Ed.), *Communication campaigns about drugs: Government, media, public* (pp. 29–46). Hillsdale, NJ: Lawrence Erlbaum.

Rosse, J. N. (1981). Mass media: The economic setting. In E. Abel (Ed.), *What's news* (pp. 33–53). San Francisco: Institute for Contemporary Studies.

Schmidt, B. C., Jr. (1981). The first amendment and the press. In E. Abel (Ed.), *What's news* (pp. 57–80). San Francisco, CA: Institute for Contemporary Studies.

Seo, S. K. (1988). *Source-press relationship: Major characteristics of sources which influence selection of sources in news coverage.* Paper presented to the Newspaper Division, Association for Education in Journalism and Mass Communication, Portland OR.

Sherizen, S. (1978). Social creation of crime news: All the news fitted to print. In C. Winick (Ed.), *Deviance and mass media* (pp. 203–224). Beverly Hills, CA: Sage.

Shipley, L. J., & Gentry, J. K. (1981). How electronic editing equipment affects editing performance. *Journalism Quarterly, 58,* 371–374, 387.

Shoemaker, P. J. (1989). Public relations versus journalism? Comments on Turow. *American Behavioral Scientist, 33,* 213–215.

Smith, A. (1977). Technology and control: The interactive dimensions of journalism. In J. Curran, M. Gurevitch, & J. Woollacott (Eds.), *Mass communication and society* (pp. 174–194). Beverly Hills, CA: Sage.

Sparkes, V. M. (1978). The flow of news between Canada and the United States. *Journalism Quarterly, 58,* 420–427.

Stempel, G., III, & Culbertson, H. (1984). The prominence and dominance of news sources in newspaper medical coverage. *Journalism Quarterly, 61,* 671–676.

Stocking, S. H. (1985). Effect of public relations efforts on media visibility of organizations. *Journalism Quarterly, 62,* 358–366, 450.

Stone, G. C., & Morrison, J. (1976). Content as a key to the purpose of community newspapers. *Journalism Quarterly, 53*, 494–498.

Streitmatter, R. (1985). The impact of presidential personality on news coverage in major newspapers. *Journalism Quarterly, 61*, 66–73.

Tankard, J. W., Jr., Middleton, K., & Rimmer, T. (1979). Compliance with American Bar Association fair trial–free press guidelines. *Journalism Quarterly, 56*, 464–468.

Tankard, J. W., Jr., & Peirce, K. (1982). Alcohol advertising and magazine editorial content. *Journalism Quarterly, 59*, 302–305.

Taylor, O. (1989). *The education of journalists and mass communication for the 21st century: A cultural perspective*. Speech made to the Association for Education in Journalism and Mass Communication at its annual conference, August 11, Washington, DC.

Todd, R. (1983). *New York Times* advisories and national/international news selection. *Journalism Quarterly, 60*, 705–708, 676.

Turk, J. V. S. (1986). Public relations' influence on the news. *Newspaper Research Journal, 7*, 15–27.

Turow, J. (1989). Public relations and newswork: A neglected relationship. *American Behavioral Scientist, 33*, 206–212.

Utt, S. H., & Pasternack, S. (1985). Use of graphic devices in a competitive situation. A case study of 10 cities. *Newspaper Research Journal, 7*, 7–16.

Weaver, D. H., & Mullins, L. E. (1975). Content and format characteristics of competing daily newspapers. *Journalism Quarterly, 52*, 257–264.

Weaver, D. H., & Wilhoit, G. C. (1980). News media coverage of U.S. senators in four congresses, 1953–1974. *Journalism Monographs, 67*.

Weis, P. (1989, May/June). Bad rap for TV tabs. *Columbia Journalism Review*, pp. 38–42.

Weis, W. L., & Burke, C. (1986). Media content and tobacco advertising: An unhealthy addiction. *Journal of Communication, 36*, 59–69.

Whitney, D. C., & Becker, L. B. (1982). Keeping the gates for gatekeepers: The effects of wire news. *Journalism Quarterly, 59*, 60–65.

Wildmon, D. E. (no date, circa January or February 1989). Letter sent to supporters of the American Family Association.

Wildmon, D. E. (no date, circa March 1989). Letter sent to supporters of the American Family Association.

Wolfsfeld, G. (1984). Collective political action and media strategy. *Journal of Conflict Resolution, 28*, 363–381.

Wulfemeyer, K. T. (1984). Perceptions of viewer interests by local TV journalists. *Journalism Quarterly, 61*, 432, 435.

CHAPTER 9

The Influence of Ideology

In this chapter we consider the ideological influences on media content. By *ideology* we mean a symbolic mechanism that serves as a cohesive and integrating force in society. We want to know the role of the mass media in propagating this ideology, and the forces that dictate the nature of that ideology. Here we want to know how media people, practices, and relations function ideologically. Hall (1989) argues that, having previously ignored ideology, mainstream U.S. communication theory has begun to take it up for two reasons: (1) a greater recognition now of the media's ability to " 'define situations' and label groups and individuals as deviant," and (2) the breakdown of the social consensus following the political unrest in the 1960s and 1970s, creating greater ideological polarization and focusing attention on the media's exercise of ideological control (p. 309). He adds that ideology focuses our attention on the symbolic influence of media on audiences, the "definition" that prevails, and the legitimation and exercise of symbolic power (p. 309).

Definition of Ideology

Raymond Williams defines ideology as a "relatively formal and articulated system of meanings, values and beliefs, of a kind that can be abstracted as a 'world-view' or a 'class outlook' " (Williams, 1977, p. 109). According to Samuel Becker (1984), ideology "governs the way we perceive our world and ourselves; it controls what we see as 'natural' or 'obvious' " (p. 69). "An ideology is an integrated set of frames of reference through which each of us sees the world and to which all of us adjust our actions" (Becker, 1984, p. 69).

Questions of ideology center around how diverse groups with conflicting interests hang together in a society. As Gouldner puts it: "Ideology assumes special importance as a symbolic mechanism through which interests of these diverse social strata may be integrated; through the sharing of it the several dominant strata are enabled to make compatible responses to changing social conditions" (Gouldner, 1976, pp. 230–231).

Ideological Values in Media

What is the basis for ideology in the United States? Fundamental is a belief in the value of the capitalist economic system, private ownership, pursuit of profit by self-interested entrepreneurs, and free markets. This system is intertwined with the Protestant ethic and the value of individual achievement. The companion political ideology centers around liberal democracy, a system in which all people are presumed to have equal worth and a right to share in their own governance, making decisions based on rational self-interest. These values are articulated and reaffirmed through the media (e.g., Exoo, 1987).

Ideological Levels v. Other Levels

In our sense, ideology is not, as U.S. scholars have typically used it, an individual belief system. Rather, ideology represents a societal-level phenomenon. This is in keeping with the European tradition of media studies, in which ideology is considered a total structure, compared with a system of individual attitudes and values. This ideological level subsumes all the others we have been talking about and, therefore, is the most macro of the levels in our hierarchy of influences model (see Figure 9.1). The ideological level differs from the previous levels in that all the processes taking place at lower levels are considered to be working toward an ideologically related pattern of messages and on behalf of the higher power centers in society.

Moving to this level also involves a shift in research tradition and perspective compared with our previous chapters. Scholars concerned with ideology typically have adopted a Marxist approach, a perspective also termed *critical,* or *radical.* Their studies have emphasized more general, abstract theorizing than testing specific hypotheses with empirical data. Indeed, critical scholars typically reject the notion that a traditional behavioral scientific approach, drawn from the natural sciences, is appropriate for the study of society, preferring to take a more qualitative, analytical, and philosophical approach. Becker (1984) notes that, although scholars working within British Marxist studies have an aversion to the positivist tradition, they aren't agreed on the proper data to test their ideas.

Studies in this tradition focus on the larger culture and how it manages to hang together, rather than the operation of any component part. Theories of communication become mixed in with theories of society. In the Marxist tradition, it is an object of faith that no aspect of society can be understood apart from its social and historical context. At this level we ask: In whose interests do routines and organizations ultimately work? As a result, researchers working at this level cannot

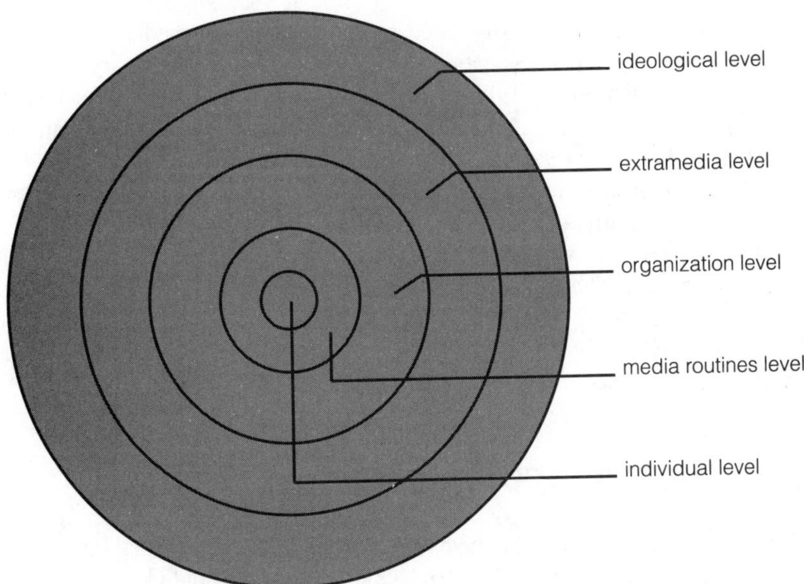

Figure 9.1. Ideological influences on media content in the hierarchical model

avoid questions of value and interests and, ultimately, power. As such, studies discussed here provide an important overarching context for those at the lower levels covered previously.

In Chapter 4 we discussed how media content constitutes a rough mapping of power relations in society. At the ideological level we look more closely at the powerful in society, and expressly how that power is played out through the media. We assume that ideas have links to interests and power and that the power to create symbols is not a neutral force. Not only is news about the powerful, but it structures stories so that events are interpreted from the perspective of powerful interests. The Glasgow University Media Group (1976) has compiled extensive documentation of media content in the book *Bad News*. It shows how labor unions, rather than corporate management, are blamed for industrial disputes. The same is true in the United States, where labor positions are termed "demands," while management positions are called "offers." At the ideological level, we examine specifically how the media function as extensions of powerful interests in society, how the routines, values, and organizational structure combine to maintain a system of control and reproduction of the dominant ideology.

In Chapter 6, for example, we considered how media routines often work to the advantage of powerful sources. At the ideological level we are now in the position of examining how these powerful sources act in their own interest, not as individuals but as a class, transcending any one organization, industry, or place.

From an ideological perspective, advertiser influence, for example, becomes not just the self-interested action of a single firm but a systematic and structural result of a capitalist advertiser-supported media system. One media sponsor made the point directly. When PBS station WNET showed a documentary critical of multinational corporations in 1985, it lost its funding from Gulf + Western. The corporation's chief executive complained that the program was virulently antibusiness if not anti-American (Herman & Chomsky, 1988, p. 17).

At the ideological level we seek to predict when media and political elites will intervene against normal journalistic routines and professionalism. From an ideological perspective, we can interpret many of the interventions in the news process mentioned in Chapter 7. When the story about the Berkeley Rebels (Gitlin, 1980, p. 67) was being produced by CBS News, for example, changes were instituted after the intervention by the Berkeley president, an indication that the story pressed against key ideological boundaries.

MEDIA AND SOCIAL CONTROL

As Stuart Hall indicated, it is the media's ability to "define" the situation that gives them their ideological power. Before we tackle the power behind ideology, we must first appreciate the nature of ideology as a social integration mechanism, and the related social control function of the media. One of the key functions performed by media is to maintain boundaries in a culture. To integrate societal interests, some views and values must be defined as within the bounds of acceptability, while others are read out of legitimacy.

Media and Deviance

Communicating Deviance. The sociology of deviance has been of long-standing interest to social scientists. Their work has given us a start in understanding how the media function in that process. From a symbolic interactionist perspective, we view deviance not as an unchanging condition but as continually being defined and renegotiated as the participants interact with each other symbolically. The media are continually coping with new ideas, reaffirming social norms, and redrawing or defining boundaries. Thus, communication is an essential part of defining deviance. Clearly, the media do not just convey the labels created by others. They make their own decisions about tone, emphasis, placement, and portrayal, based on the routines and organizational logic discussed in earlier chapters.

Deviance in the News

Shoemaker and her colleagues have done extensive analysis of the way the media communicate deviance. She found, for example, that those political groups perceived as deviant by newspaper editors were typically given less favorable treatment. Although not given less prominent attention, their legitimacy was more likely to be questioned. Indeed, journalists accentuated the differences among groups that could not be considered to differ intrinsically in their legitimacy (Shoemaker, 1984).

News selection criteria themselves may be said to be based on dimensions of deviance, including the controversial, sensational, prominent, and unusual. Shoemaker, Chang, and Brendlinger (1987) found that world events covered by the U.S. media were more deviant than those not covered, in the sense that those events threatened the status quo in the country in which they occurred (such as terrorism). Similarly, covered events often conveyed normative deviance. That is, they would have broken American norms had they occurred in the United States (Shoemaker, Chang, & Brendlinger, 1987).

World events presented most prominently in the news were deviant events, and those with economic or political significance to the United States. The next most prominent events were deviant, but with low significance (Shoemaker, Danielian, & Brendlinger, 1988).

Media Techniques of Communicating Deviance. As agents of social control, the media must first identify threats to the status quo. As suggested by the Shoemaker research, the media do not screen out deviant ideas, but rather portray them in a way calculated to underscore their deviance. The ideological status quo is reaffirmed by ridiculing deviant ideas as, in Miliband's words, "irrelevant eccentricities which serious and reasonable people may dismiss as of no consequence" (Miliband, 1969, p. 238).

Earlier, in observing patterns of content, we observed that the powerful receive news coverage routinely while those with less power must break into the news via deviant acts, such as protests, strikes, or crime. Considered in the context of deviance and social change, the media act as a key control mechanism in society. The normal is reaffirmed by being presented routinely and in juxtaposition to the deviant, which competes at the boundaries for attention. Ironically, when many political groups are shut out of the media spotlight, they may become even more shrill and radical, confirming the original deviant label.

In his study of how the media covered the student radical movement in the 1960s, Gitlin (1980) identified a number of specific techniques that were used to make students' actions appear more deviant. These included trivialization; polarization by showing counterdemonstrations; emphasis on internal dissension; disparagement by undercounting the students' numbers and minimizing their effectiveness; reliance on officials; emphasis on the presence of Communists, Vietcong flags, and violence; and considerable attention given to right-wing opposition.

Media and Boundaries

Media scholar Daniel Hallin (1986) introduces a useful model to help understand the ways that the news media maintain ideological boundaries (see Figure 9.2). He divides the journalistic world into three spheres: legitimate controversy, consensus,

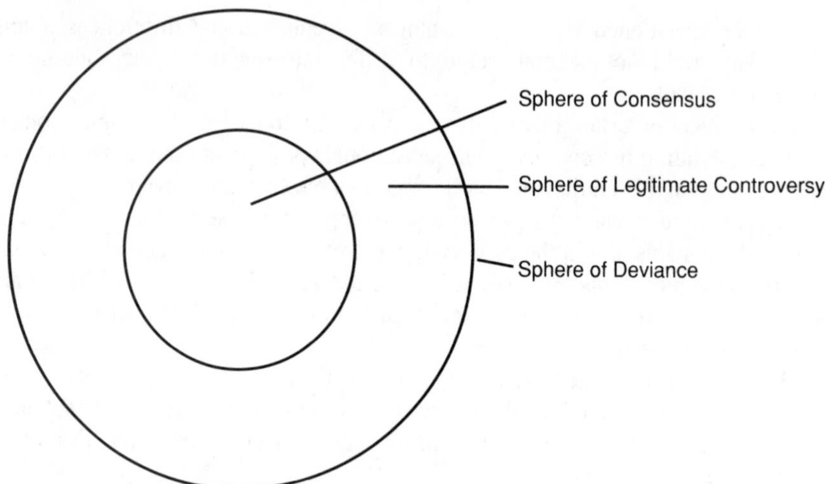

Figure 9.2. Spheres of consensus, controversy, and deviance. (From: *The "Uncensored War,"* Hallin [1986].)

and deviance. The sphere of legitimate controversy is where objectivity and balance are sought: "This is the region of electoral contests and legislative debates, of issues recognized as such by the major established actors of the American political process" (p. 116). At the core is the sphere of consensus, the "motherhood and apple pie" domain: "Within this region journalists do not feel compelled either to present opposing views or to remain disinterested observers. On the contrary, the journalist's role is to serve as an advocate or celebrant of consensus values" (pp. 116–117). Beyond the sphere of legitimate controversy is the sphere of deviance, the realm of those people and ideas outside the mainstream of society. Here, says Hallin, journalism casts off neutrality: "It plays the role of exposing, condemning, or excluding from the public agenda those who violate or challenge the political consensus. It marks out and defends the limits of acceptable conflict" (p. 117).

But who gets to decide what is deviant? It's not that there are limits—there must be—but who gets to set the limits and how are they made to appear "natural"? Here is where we turn to larger forces acting on the media. Who has the power to set boundaries, and how does it work? What are the means through which that power is expressed?

POWER AND IDEOLOGY: THE MARXIST PARADIGM

Power and the Marxist Paradigm

The dominant democratic pluralist model values and assumes diversity in U.S. society. Power is seen as distributed across many competing interests, which act as veto groups as they vie with one another to create a more or less stable, self-maintaining, and balanced political equilibrium. Even the elites are viewed as sufficiently divided so as to make unlikely any undue concentration of power (e.g., Rose, 1967). Thus, questions of power and ideology typically have not been raised, for power is not considered problematic. As McQuail (1986, p. 143) states, the relevant question in media research using a pluralistic model is "whether media offer opportunities for politically diverse audiences and/or audience interests to flourish."

As we mentioned above, however, research at the ideological level typically takes on a more critical, radical view of media. Power is viewed as much more concentrated, whether in elites or propertied classes, and media content is seen as both expressing and furthering the power of these interests. Critical scholars focus on showing how the restriction of voices furthers class dominance, making power a central concern. Individuals are viewed as unable to compete effectively against major power centers in society, which manipulate people in ways contrary to their natural interests. Institutions are not accepted as a given, but must be related to existing power structures (e.g., Parenti, 1978, 1986).

In news content, this perspective draws our attention to the issues that don't make it onto the agenda, the alternatives that are not voiced. Radical critics argue that, by focusing on those issues that do make the press agenda, pluralists overlook the operation of concentrated power. Bachrach and Baratz (1962), for example, suggest examining how the scope of the political process is narrowed to only those issues that are innocuous to the powerful. Molotch and Lester (1974) make a similar point: By taking decisional "events," pluralists have guaranteed diversity by focusing only on those issues on which elites agree. Lukes (1974) argues that the most effective power prevents conflict from arising in the first place.

The major strain of research within this critical perspective may be loosely termed a *Marxist* tradition, which regards society as rooted in conflict along class lines between dominant and subordinate groups. The major effect of the media is considered ideological. The point of departure from the pluralist view is the following famous quote from Marx:

> The ideas of the ruling class are in every epoch the ruling ideas: i.e. the class which is the ruling material force in society is at the same time its ruling intellectual force. The class which has the means of material production at its disposal has control at the same time over the means of mental production, so that thereby, generally speaking, the ideas of those who lack the means of mental production are subject to it. (Marx and Engels, 1970, p. 64)

Here Marx directly links ideology to the ruling class, which derives its power from its control of capital. There are clashes of opinion, however, within the Marxist perspective over how completely economics determines ideology. Political economists take the link between economic conditions and ideology to be fairly direct, regarding media content as ultimately determined in the last instance by the economic relations in society. They do not examine the specific practices or mechanisms through which economic relations manifest themselves in media content. Scholars taking a "cultural studies" approach, on the other hand, do not consider the ruling class ideology to be monolothic and automatically determined. Rather, they see a greater autonomy for media and its messages, which are viewed as containing many contradictory elements, as the ruling ideas struggle to domesticate subversive ideas and retain their privileged status.

Political Economy View

Political economists take the more traditional Marxist approach. Using the Marxist base/superstructure metaphor, ideology is regarded as part of the superstructure, determined by the economic base. As Curran, Gurevitch, and Woollacott (1982) argue, "The role of the media here is that of legitimation through the production of false consciousness, in the interests of the class which owns and controls the media" (p. 26). To do this, the media must disguise and distort class antagonisms that are at the heart of a Marxist view of society.

Ownership is considered the primary means through which the ruling class exerts control over media institutions. Ultimately, a political economy approach leads us to expect that capitalist-owned media decisions and content will tend to favor those with economic power. From a political economy perspective, changes in media ownership do not greatly alter power relations, because each owner acts in a manner consistent with the interests of capital.

Political economists, Murdock and Golding (1979) for example, argue that a proper analysis of news production needs to focus on the economic context, as well as the class base, of control. Capitalism is said to have a generalized, abstracting drive to reduce everything to the equivalence of exchange value (Garnham, 1979). Media content is a cultural commodity of a capitalist system. In recent years, cultural domains from the Statue of Liberty to the Berlin Wall have been colonized by this capitalist drive to commodity. Capital in the culture industry seeks out the most lucrative markets, with the most resources going to lucrative nonnews information-gathering. Dan Schiller (1986) finds that, in the changing structure of the news commodity, the trend is toward ever more sophisticated means of data gathering for large corporations and ever less effective information transmission to the masses.

Another political economist, Nicholas Garnham (1979), observes that the present stage of industrialization of culture is characterized by a sharpening struggle to increase productivity. The high-profile buyouts of media firms by nonmedia corporations (such as CBS and NBC, discussed earlier), the well-publicized layoffs at the network level, and the erosion of the lines between the business and news departments in many newspapers and television stations can be interpreted within this framework.

Variations in Ideology by Funding Source. Altschull has proposed a framework for studying variations within owner control of the media. Like the political economists, Altschull starts with the assumption that media reflect the ideology of those that finance them, or "pay the piper." He outlines four sources of media support: (1) under the "official" pattern, media are controlled by the state (such as in many Communist countries), (2) in the "commercial" pattern, media reflect the ideology of advertisers and their media-owning allies, (3) under the "interest" pattern, media content reflects the ideology of the financing group, such as a political party or religious group, and (4) in the "informal" pattern, content reflects the goals of individual contributors who want to promote their views. The mix of these financing patterns varies from country to country and over time within countries (Altschull, 1984, p. 254).

This framework reminds us that whether the press is called free or state controlled, it reflects the ideology of the paymaster. Of course, in the United States the wealthiest paymasters fund the commercial media. Variations in ideology can be introduced through the "interest" and "informal" funding patterns, but these are relatively insignificant in challenging the ruling ideas. These media make up a small percentage of the available content, and their messages must contend on a playing field structured by the dominant ideology transmitted through the commercial media.

Instrumental Variation of Political Economy. A major variation of the political economy perspective is termed by Mosco and Herman (1981) the *instrumental approach*. Elite analysts like Domhoff (1967, 1970, 1979) give the media little independent power. As in the traditional Marxist view, the media are viewed as organically inseparable from elites and, thus, far from autonomous. Obviously, conflicts among elites are played out through the press, but they are seen as far more instrumental for elites than antagonistic to their interests. Scholars like Domhoff focus on the means by which the ruling class exerts control. In his case, however, Domhoff rejects the economic as the only basis for ruling class power, as traditional Marxists would claim.

These theorists follow the lead of C. Wright Mills in tracing the pervasive control exerted by the ruling class, or "power elite," on the social structure. In *The Power Elite,* Mills (1956) proposes that the convergent interests of business, economic, and military elites form an apex at the top of the social structure. Class cohesion, assisted by connections and exchange of personnel between these sectors, strengthens and maintains this power elite. These interconnections are found by scrutinizing the ways members of the ruling class come in contact with one another (prep schools, clubs, boards of directors, etc.) and influence policy (stock holding, policy groups, funding of institutes and think tanks, political action committees, etc.). The upper class is regarded as having much greater class cohesion than the bottom and can, thus, focus its power more effectively.

Although this form of analysis seldom has been applied to the media elite, the interconnections between media and other institutions present evidence of this same coordination and convergent interests. Top media leaders circulate with other elites. Elite reporters spend time at top think tanks (e.g., *New York Times* reporter Hedrick Smith wrote *The Power Game* [1988] while at the conservative American Enterprise Institute). Mid-career fellowships, like the Niemans at Harvard, allow top journalists to spend time at major universities, rubbing elbows and absorbing elite values. Top journalists, politicians, business leaders, and academicians often appear on panels together, usually without any adversarial exchange. These are all avenues for the media elite to circulate with other elites, developing firsthand contacts, personal bonds, and shared values.

Some have called today's press corps a new social elite, arguing that it makes them hostile to American society and government (a view expressed in the conservative critiques by Corry [1986] and Rusher [1988]). This elite view bears little in common with the C. Wright Mills tradition. Far from making journalists hostile to American values, social elite status should link journalists even more strongly to the power elite. Shared elite schooling provides important links between top journalists and other members of the power structure. A recent informal survey of twenty top young business journalists, for example, found all but five attended Ivy League schools (the others were not much less prestigious: Duke, Northwestern, New York University, Trinity, and Williams) ("Meet tomorrow's editors," 1988).

In another instrumental approach, Dreier (1982a) examined the interlocks between media boards of directors and others, finding that the most prominent elite media companies (publishers of the *New York Times, Wall Street Journal,* and *Washington Post*) were the most strongly interconnected with other power centers (elite universities, Fortune 500 corporations, etc.). This commanding vantage point within the inner circle of the capitalist structure leads these media, according to Dreier, to adopt a corporate liberal philosophy. Thus, they may adopt an adversarial tone on occasion (Pentagon papers, Watergate), but only as a corrective action, in the best long-term interests of preserving the capitalist system.

Under this instrumental approach, media do have a degree of relative autonomy, which allows them to challenge specific people and practices. This adversarial reporting may arouse the displeasure of elites, who seek to reassert their power. Instrumentalists view these reactions as a class or elite versus individuals or specific firms. Dreier (1982b) argues, for example, that the criticisms of big business have developed out of social movements, governmental responses, and the professionalization of journalism, which all increased the specific criticisms directed at business in the media. He notes several ways the business class has mobilized to stave off public opinion and the possible consequences of additional government regulation: funding of think tanks, economic reporting programs, awards and prizes for reporting, conferences and workshops between media and business executives, and advocacy ads, such as those by Mobil Oil. In each case, these strategies take advantage of the professional occupational routines of journalists to further the corporate ideology. These actions represent *ideological* mobilization because they transcend the interests of any single business or industry, addressing instead the needs of the business class in general.

A Propaganda Model. Two of the more widely known scholars of media political economy are Edward Herman and Noam Chomsky. Like other radical media theorists, they start from the assumption that media serve the dominant elite. They argue that this is just as true (although perhaps less obvious) when the media are privately owned without formal censorship, as when they are directly controlled by the state. Carrying out their function is said to require systematic propaganda.

Their propaganda model, combining elements of political economy and instrumental influence, includes five news "filters": "(1) the size, concentrated ownership, owner wealth, and profit orientation of the dominant mass media firms; (2) advertising as the primary income source of the mass media; (3) the reliance of the media on information provided by government, business, and 'experts' funded and approved by these primary sources and agents of power; (4) 'flak' as a means of disciplining the media; and (5) 'anticommunism' as a national religion and control mechanism" (Herman & Chomsky, 1988, p. 2).

The ownership and advertising filters link media to economic power and make it difficult for alternative media to gain a hearing. Source influence and flak are two instrumental links to the media. Media routines cause them to rely on government and corporate sources, both of which have many advantages in gaining coverage for their views, as we've discussed earlier. The government is able to produce great quantities of authoritative news through its vast information staff, while corporations have large budgets for public relations efforts that effectively "subsidize" the cost of information gathering for the media (Gandy, 1982).

In this model, pressure groups (discussed in Chapter 8) also serve an ideological function as an enforcement mechanism. Herman and Chomsky (1988) define *flak* as negative responses to the media, including complaints, threats, petitions, letters, and articles. They view flak originating mostly from the right, which is most apt to have the resources to fund it, through, for example, foundations, think tanks, and media monitors like Accuracy in Media designed to harass, intimidate, discipline, and generally keep the media from straying too far from acceptable elite viewpoints.

The last filter, anticommunism, is considered a political control mechanism. Because communism threatens the very basis of the propertied class, it is firmly fixed in the sphere of deviance. Herman and Chomsky give anticommunism an instrumental value for elites, who use it to justify military action to suppress it and support for fascist governments to oppose it, and to keep domestic left and labor movements off balance and fragmented.

They argue that the operation of these filters allows propaganda campaigns to be mounted with a double standard, against the enemies of the "National Security State" and for its friends; against Nicaragua, for example, but not against human rights abuses in Guatemala and El Salvador.

> In sum, a propaganda approach to media coverage suggests a systematic and highly political dichotomization in news coverage based on serviceability to important domestic power interests. This should be observable

> in dichotomized choices of story and in the volume and quality of coverage. (Herman & Chomsky, 1988, p. 33)

This propaganda model, as in the other political economy approaches, presents a direct control over media by elites. The other major Marxist approach we'll take up makes this control more problematic and examines the more subtle and dynamic means through which it is carried out. Clearly, there are ideological variations within a society, and ruling ideas must respond to challenges. To better understand this dynamic process we must turn to another perspective within the Marxist tradition.

Cultural Studies View: Hegemony

The cultural studies approach combines aspects of political economy and the Marxist structuralist perspective, a more literary approach that concentrates on media "texts." It rejects the simple base/superstructure connection, looks more closely at the connections between society and media, and places them in a broader cultural context.

One of the key theoretical approaches within cultural studies is hegemony. The theory of hegemony, as proposed by Gramsci (1927/1971), examines the link between power and practice and has been a strong current running through critical analyses of the media. Gramsci emphasizes the role of ideology, giving it greater autonomy than traditional Marxists, although still linking it ultimately to the dominant structure. Because media have relative autonomy, the ruling powers cannot directly supervise this important cultural apparatus. Thus, ideology serves as a unifying force. *Hegemony* refers to the means by which the ruling order maintains its dominance. Media institutions serve a hegemonic function by continually producing a cohesive ideology, a set of commonsensical values and norms, that serves to reproduce and legitimate the social structure through which the subordinate classes participate in their own domination (see also Gitlin, 1980).

Gitlin defines hegemony as the "systematic (but not necessarily or even usually deliberate) engineering of mass consent to the established order" (p. 253). Control must be maintained without sacrificing legitimacy, which ruling power seeks in order to maintain authority. Under hegemony, ideology is regarded as an essentially conflicted and dynamic process, which must continually absorb and incorporate disparate values (Gitlin, 1980, p. 51). In Raymond Williams's words, hegemony "does not passively exist as a form of dominance. It has continually to be renewed, recreated, defended, and modified" (1977, pp. 112–113). Existing cultural values are structured and interpreted to best serve the interests of the dominant groups.

Hegemonic values in news are said to be particularly effective in permeating common sense, because they are made to appear natural and are placed there not by coercion, but indirectly through the normal workings of media routines and the interconnections between the media and other power centers. Indeed, the relative autonomy of media gives their messages more legitimacy and credibility than if they were directly controlled.

Thus, by not appearing openly coercive, this control is all the more effective. The media "certify the limits within which all competing definitions of reality will contend" (Gitlin, 1980, p. 254). They do this largely by accepting the frames imposed on events by officials and by marginalizing and delegitimating voices that fall outside the dominant elite circles.

Routines for the Powerful. Thus, within hegemony we look to the ideological implications of media practices and institutional arrangements. Routines develop to meet hegemonic requirements, not just organizational needs.

Returning to Hallin's spheres of deviance, consensus, and legitimate controversy (Figure 9.2), we recall that routines are clearly related to ideology. The objective routine of balancing sources, for example, becomes important only within the sphere of legitimate controversy. In the sphere of consensus, Hallin says journalists act as advocates and celebrants, while in the sphere of deviance they expose, condemn, and exclude those outside the political consensus. Miliband draws a similar connection: "the more radical the dissent, the less impartial and objective the media" (Miliband, 1969, p. 224).

The Vietnam period, an era of great social upheaval, provides many good examples of media treatment of political deviance. In his study of media and the New Left, Gitlin notes that when student leaders were caricatured, they were not balanced, but when treated seriously they were. Thus, a respectful CBS News story on the political evolution of "Chicago Seven" member Rennie Davis was cancelled for not "balancing" its treatment with a spokesperson from the House Un-American Affairs Committee (Gitlin, 1980, p. 174).

The routines of media work may require coverage of stressful events, such as political demonstrations. To retain credibility, the media must, after all, not stray too far from what the public knows is happening. Indeed, the images we remember from this period are often the exceptional, hegemonically: the 1968 Chicago riots, or Morley Safer's story at Cam Ne showing a GI igniting a Vietnamese thatched hut with a Zippo lighter. When these events are ideologically threatening, the upper levels of the system must intervene against the normal workings of routines and organizational policy. Thus, both presidents Johnson and Nixon were active in trying to influence the way the news media covered the student antiwar movement (see Chapter 7).

In some cases, the media and government were not of one mind as to where the boundaries between the spheres should be drawn. Gitlin observes that the Nixon White House wanted the line blurred between the militant protest movement against the war in Vietnam and the moderate alternative, painting the entire group as outside the boundary of legitimate controversy ("radiclib"). The big media, in seeking a moderate alternative, tried to keep the lines distinct, creating a clash in frames (Gitlin, 1980).

Normally, though, routines work to the advantage of the dominant ideology. In his study of news coverage of Vietnam, Hallin observes that reporters shared the cold war consensus prevalent in the early years of the war, a consensus reinforced by their routines. Journalists in Vietnam relied on military officials for information and transportation. They became close to the soldiers as they shared hardships and faced risks together. Defending one unit's search and destroy mission, an NBC reporter said in his story: "There was no discriminating one house from another. There couldn't be and there did not need to be. The whole village had turned on the Americans, so the whole village was being destroyed" (Hallin, 1986, p. 140).

In covering the air war, reporters stationed on aircraft carriers saw little of the enemy and had to rely on Defense Department film and interviews with pilots who, like the journalists themselves, were upwardly mobile professionals. Thus, coverage focused on the technology and professionalism of the pilots and crews. As one television report said: "The smoking target gives impressive evidence of just how effective these and similar raids have been." Said another: "This is the shape of things to come for Communist aggression in Vietnam" (p. 137). Reporting focused on individual heroes, American boys in action. The point of view was typically "inside" American policy. Thus, Hallin argues that routines pushed battle coverage toward the sphere of consensus. The ideological frames included "war as national endeavor," "war as American tradition," "war as manly," and "winning is what counts" (pp. 142–144), effectively purging war of political and moral implications.

Hallin's study shows the news media are not an ideological monolith. He argues that the power of television or its perceived power, for example, makes television more sensitive to staying within the sphere of consensus as it provides ideological guidance and reassurance for the mass public. The need for television to force news into a unified story line, he says, creates a more unified, ideological worldview. Thus, television reporters' role in covering Vietnam was more active than that of the print media, as Hallin shows in the following excerpts:

> NBC, Jan. 21, 1966, David Brinkley: As for the peace campaign, the Communist side has repeatedly called it a sham. If it is, they could come to the bargaining table and expose it. But they haven't.
>
> Chet Huntley: The Communists in Vietnam demonstrated today that they attach no more solemnity to a truce than to their politics.

THE NEWS PARADIGM AND HEGEMONY

Samuel Becker notes that, although little progress has been made, one of the key questions being asked in the British Marxist school of media studies is how the dominant ideology is linked up to the norms and practices, or "occupational ideology," of media workers (1984, p. 73). Murdock and Golding (1977, p. 35) argue that scholars must analyze the "link between the general set of values in that culture and the ruling ideology and occupational ideologies." One way to examine these links is to examine the journalistic "occupational ideology" and consider to what extent it serves a hegemonic function. In the remainder of this chapter, we first explore this link and then examine a specific case in point.

The Concept of Paradigm

One useful concept in considering the journalistic occupational ideology is Thomas Kuhn's (1962, p. 23) notion of *paradigm,* "an accepted model or pattern," that helps to make sense out of the world. The paradigm remains valuable as long as it provides a useful practical guide and practitioners who share its underlying assumptions. Although Kuhn spoke of scientific paradigms, it can be applied to journalism as well. Both science and journalism are empirical information-gathering activities, both have developed learnable routines for their practitioners. Both scientists and journalists are presumed to be dispassionate observers of the world, guided primarily by their observations. The journalistic paradigm, like the others, is validated by consensus.

While focusing attention on some problems, a paradigm necessarily excludes from study other questions that cannot be as easily stated using the tools it supplies. By providing a model, a paradigm exerts a powerful influence on our views of the world, by restricting the range of questions deemed appropriate for study. The naturalness of an accepted paradigm is similar to the way we consider hegemony to work. As Kuhn (1962) notes, paradigms provide examples rather than explicit rules. Thus, one learns the paradigm by engaging in the discipline rather than learning a set of rules. This means that the defining features of paradigms are not necessarily written down and available for study, nor are practitioners necessarily able to articulate complete rationalizations of them. Thus, the routines that practitioners engage in give us valuable clues about the contours of the guiding paradigm, and a violation of routines becomes a threat to the news paradigm itself. Routines may be invoked as a defense of paradigm violation, particularly by those within the profession. The borders of a paradigm can be revealed by *anomalies,* cases that do not fit comfortably into the defining characteristics of the paradigm. These cases threaten the paradigm by calling into question its limitations and biases, and, therefore, must be "repaired." If enough such cases accumulate, the paradigm may have to shift to accommodate them.

Paradigm and Hegemony

The news paradigm must conform to hegemonic requirements. A key paradigm feature in this regard is the notion of objectivity, discussed in earlier chapters. In more recent years, journalists have found it increasingly hard to maintain that they are wholly objective, and have fallen back on more defensible standards, like "accuracy," "balance," and "fairness." Even if the world has become somewhat outdated, media workers act as though it weren't, and the underlying principle of reporter detachment remains firmly entrenched. As Hackett (1984) observes, the opposite of objectivity is bias, and conventional evaluations of news bias assume that the fault lies with the individual reporter or editor.

Assuming the biased communicator to be the chief barrier to wholly objective reporting of the facts, journalists operating within the news paradigm do not find strongly held values to be occupationally useful. Of course, journalists hold many values that aren't obvious because they are safely within the range of core societal values. Left-wing journalists, for example, have found mainstream journalism uncomfortable, and Noam Chomsky has noted that he knows of no socialists in the strikingly uniform media (quoted in MacDougall, 1988a). When *Los Angeles Times* publisher Otis Chandler was asked in 1977 about *Times* staffer Robert Scheer, former editor of the leftist publication *Ramparts,* Chandler said: "A radical? If that were true he wouldn't be here" (MacDougall, 1988b, p. 12).

These assumptions fit hegemonic requirements. Thus, journalists are being objective when they let prominent sources dictate the news, while they are considered biased when they use their own expertise to draw conclusions. The press gave Ronald Reagan largely uncritical treatment during his first term, because no opposing elites were able to mount an effective challenge and thus make themselves available as oppositional media voices (Hertsgaard, 1988). Hallin (1986) shows that the media did not become strongly critical of the war in Vietnam until the Johnson administration's elite council of advisers, the "wisemen," changed their opinions. Giving serious attention to nonofficial sources is discouraged as unnewsworthy. By accepting valueless reporting as the norm, the media accept the boundaries, values, and ideological rules of the game established and interpreted by elite sources.

The editing process is also compatible with hegemonic requirements. Editors rise to their positions only after fully internalizing the norms of the journalistic paradigm (e.g., Breed, 1955). Although reporters are presumably in closer contact with reality, editors are considered less apt to succumb to bias than reporters, who may get wrapped up in a story and be blinded to the big picture. High-ranking editors, particularly at major papers, are also more directly in touch with the values of official and other elite sources, and are reluctant to break from these boundaries. Experiences by reporters during the Vietnam War provide an excellent example of this process. In the early 1960s David Halberstam was a knowledgeable reporter on the scene in Vietnam, yet he often had difficulty getting his stateside editors to accept his pessimistic version of the war. The editors had received a more optimistic version from Pentagon and administration officials and were reluctant to contradict it (Sheehan, 1988).

THE CASE OF A. KENT MACDOUGALL

We conclude this chapter with an actual example of a paradigm violation, which illustrates some of what we've been talking about: a radical who was also a mainstream journalist. The case provides some insight into how hegemony is exercised through the newsroom practices that constitute the journalistic "occupational ideology," or paradigm. Paradigm violations call for repair work, or normalization, particularly when the violations strike at hegemonically sensitive borders of the paradigm.

Background

A. Kent MacDougall, now on the faculty at the Graduate School of Journalism at the University of California at Berkeley, began his award-winning mainstream press career in 1956 at the *Herald News,* Passaic, New Jersey. Between 1961 and 1972 he worked at the *Wall Street Journal,* followed by ten years at the *Los Angeles Times* beginning in 1977. His two-part memoirs, "Boring from within the Bourgeois Press," published in November and December of 1988 in the socialist *Monthly Review,* set off a storm of controversy in journalistic circles. In the article, he said he had written under an alias for radical publications while at the *Wall Street Journal* and had selected story topics based on his radical beliefs. For example, at the *Wall Street Journal* he profiled I. F. Stone and wrote other articles surveying radical economists and historians; at the *Los Angeles Times* he profiled other radical economists and the left-leaning magazine *Mother Jones.* The case generated a strong response, including articles and columns in the mainstream press as well as industry publications.

MacDougall himself acknowledged the ambiguous nature of the paradigm, having used the uneasy relationship between routines and values to his advantage. He learned that "editors would support a reporter against charges by a news source, special interest group, or reader that the reporter's story was biased or had some other major defect as long as the reporter had gotten all the minor facts right" (MacDougall, 1988a, p. 19).

Knowing that reporters must speak through sources, he said, "I made sure to seek out experts whose opinions I knew in advance would support my thesis. . . . Conversely, I sought out mainstream authorities to confer recognition and respectability on radical views I sought to popularize" (MacDougall, 1988a, p. 23). His writing followed enough attributes of the paradigm to be acceptable, although not without the occasional angry audience response: "Are you a communist?" said one reader in reaction to his *Mother Jones* piece (MacDougall, 1988b, p. 14). A forestry industry group, critical of his series for the *Los Angeles Times* on "The Vanishing Forests," suggested he was fostering an "anti-private enterprise view" (Benneth, 1989).

MacDougall said his stories contained enough "significance, controversy, color and surprise to satisfy commercial journalistic standards for relevance and readability," and that his "calm, matter of fact, non-polemical tone fit the formula" (MacDougall, 1988a, p. 24). He said the *Los Angeles Times* permitted wide latitude to reporters, valuing diversity as an attention-getter, as long as the reporter "adheres to the readily assimilated professional code of objectivity and impartiality and doesn't violate canons against being shrill and propagandistic or stating a personal opinion" (MacDougall, 1988b, p. 13).

For example, MacDougall's editor made him introduce a conservative spokesperson to balance a story about inequality: "Even though I knew he was wrong, I quoted Gilder as saying that the growing gap between rich and poor was almost entirely demographic . . . " (MacDougall, 1988b, p. 18). In another example of paradigmatic limits, MacDougall's editor allowed him to mention Marx, but only if introduced in a humorous way. MacDougall agreed, to get the story in print (MacDougall, 1988b, p. 17).

A Paradigm Violation

If the case was problematic for the paradigm, journalists should have had difficulty coming to grips with it. Repair work should be observable as the paradigm undergoes defense and reaffirmation.

The violation was signified in part by the publicity surrounding the case and the way it was characterized. For example, David Shaw, in a nationally distributed *Los Angeles Times* story, said MacDougall's memoirs had "sparked a contretemps in the mainstream journalistic community" (Shaw, 1989a, p. 1). An article in the newspaper trade publication *Editor & Publisher* said MacDougall had "created a media furor with his revelations" (Stein, 1989, p. 10).

The case did present other ample evidence of being problematic, centering on the uneasy relationship between reporter values and objectivity. Journalists who express values threaten the paradigm. A business journalism newsletter called MacDougall's career "exemplary," but questioned his professionalism, particularly the practice of seeking out sources supportive of a thesis and of having preconceived sympathies or antagonisms toward subjects (Rotbart, 1989a; rewritten as 1989b). It said the case strikes at perhaps the most sensitive nerve: journalistic credibility; how vulnerable is a paper to reporters manipulating the news in pursuing their own personal agenda? ("Recent," 1989).

It was said to provide a rare glimpse of the fuzzy lines between right and wrong in journalism, where there is often no rule book or final arbiter ("Recent," 1989, p. 1). The same article noted that journalists like to present a united front to the outside world, while lacking internally that degree of unanimity in beliefs and behavior (p. 1).

Dow Jones & Company, Inc., parent company of the *Wall Street Journal*, issued a strongly worded reaction:

> We are offended and outraged that a former *Wall Street Journal* reporter now claims he tried to pursue a hidden ideological agenda within the pages of the *Journal*. However, this reporter left the *Journal* more than 15 years ago and his importance at the *Journal* or in journalism seems somewhat greater in his own mind these days than it was in fact. We have reviewed articles he wrote while at the *Journal* and we believe our editing process succeeded in making sure that what appeared in print under his byline met *Journal* standards of accuracy, newsworthiness and fairness. Finally, we find it bizarre and troubling that any man who brags of having sought to push a personal political agenda on unsuspecting editors and readers should be teaching journalism at a respected university. (Austin, 1989)

The ambiguity of the case is also revealed through MacDougall's editors' reactions to his work. At the *Los Angeles Times* one editor liked a series on economic inequality enough to write a glowing Pulitzer Prize nomination statement, which noted that MacDougall had backed up his research with "interviews with scores of economists, historians, sociologists, and anthropologists"; the page one feature editor downplayed the series, declining to run it on consecutive days (as was the custom) and to run one of the four stories on page one (MacDougall, 1988b, p. 19).

The notion that MacDougall fell outside the boundaries maintained by the news paradigm is supported by the language used to describe him. Throughout the case, the rhetorical content is filled with terms that set limits. MacDougall himself said, "What I was and wasn't able to report in two of the nation's most enlightened dailies indicates the limits within which socially conscious journalists can practice their craft in mainstream media" (MacDougall, 1988a, p. 14). He admitted that he had been "pushing against the limits set by the *Wall Street Journal*'s standardized news formula" (MacDougall, 1988a, p. 24). Columnists referred to MacDougall's "subterranean antics" (Cheshire, 1989) as a "clandestine Marxist" (Morris, 1989).

The predictable attack from the conservatives—what Herman and Chomsky (1988) would term "flak"—zeroed in on this idea of violated boundaries. Accuracy in Media, for example, started a letter-writing campaign to media heads, asking, for example, if NBC "has adequate safeguards against similar abuses by other media moles" (Kincaid, 1989, p. 7). Elsewhere it was said to have raised concern "about the ability of Marxist agents to penetrate the mainstream media," and that the case makes it harder for the *Wall Street Journal* to defend itself against charges of liberal bias (Kincaid, 1988, p. 4).

Assuming the MacDougall case represented a paradigm violation, then repair work should be observable. Given that the stories themselves written by MacDougall were beyond repair, several post hoc repair strategies appear to have been followed: (1) disengage and distance threatening values from the reporter's work, (2) reassert the ability of journalistic routines to prevent threatening values from distorting the news, and (3) marginalize the man and his message, making both appear ineffective.

Disengaging Values. Here, radical values are asserted to not have affected news judgment. In response to the attack on him, MacDougall mounted some of the repair work himself through a vigorous defense, reaffirming the distinction between values and his professional work. He contended that he was "a journalist first and a radical second throughout my career. . . . I stuck to accepted standards of newsworthiness, accuracy and fairness" (Shaw, 1989a, p. 15).

Others also reaffirmed, although uneasily, the distinction between values and reporting, claiming that reporters should not seek to promote their own agenda. Berkeley Dean Tom Goldstein, a former *Journal* reporter, praised MacDougall's teaching, saying, "We have no ideological litmus test at this school," adding that MacDougall's personal beliefs were his own, "not ours, and he scrupulously keeps ideology out of the classroom" (Shaw, 1989a, p. 16). An unsigned editorial in

Columbia Journalism Review summed up this disengagement repair, asking: Is there a place for socialist reporters in the capitalist media? It contended that a reporter should be "judged not on the basis of his political beliefs but by the integrity of his work," maintaining that his work did have integrity ("Comment," 1989, p. 16).

This disengagement repair work was neither completely successful nor possible. The counterparadigmatic, yet appealing, notion of free expression of diverse opinion kept intruding. *Wall Street Journal* and *Los Angeles Times* editors said they valued diversity. Frederick Taylor, *Journal* managing editor during MacDougall's last two years there, accepted that MacDougall would choose some stories over others because of his views, as would others with more conservative values (Shaw, 1989a, p. 16). A *Seattle Times* ombudsman's column similarly argued that reporters with divergent views "can help broaden and enrich" political discussion, while of course being held to the same "rigorous standards of fairness" MacDougall followed (Wetzel, 1989).

Reasserting Journalistic Routines. The primary defense within the journalistic community was to reaffirm the effectiveness of news routines. The editing routine was said to have worked to perfection, succeeding in wringing any bias out of the news. As the *Columbia Journalism Review* senior editor told a reporter: "The safeguards worked, the editing system is in place" (Vick, 1989). The Dow Jones letter had made the same point: "We believe our editing process succeeded . . . " (Austin, 1989). If that was true, why was Dow Jones so upset? Indeed, journalistic consensus was not perfect.

Los Angeles Times editor at the time, John Lawrence, explicitly stated that he edited out any hints of MacDougall's bias (Shaw, 1989a, p. 16). Elsewhere, Lawrence expressed ambivalent statements about MacDougall's reporting, saying that "being a Marxist doesn't necessarily have to detract from his journalistic integrity. Every reporter comes to a story with some level of bias. The question is: Are they capable of rising above that bias to write a fair story?" Lawrence concluded that MacDougall was capable, and he went on to contend that radicals might make better journalists by being more objective ("Recent," 1989, p. 8). And yet, he said he would not have allowed him to write about a Marxist economist if he knew he was "as strong a proponent . . . as he now claims to have been" (Shaw, 1989a, p. 16).

MacDougall was largely supported by his former editors. Of course, they could hardly do otherwise in reaffirming the editing process. They were the ones, after all, who approved his stories. Michael Gartner, now head of NBC News, edited MacDougall at the *Wall Street Journal*. He said he assumed that MacDougall was liberal but that it didn't affect his reporting: "I judge journalists by one thing, whether they are fair, thorough and accurate" (Shaw, 1989a, p. 15). Gartner agreed that the strict *Wall Street Journal* editing process would have filtered out any bias before it got into print ("Recent," 1989, p. 8). Former editor William F. Thomas, of the *Los Angeles Times*, affirmed the ability of a reporter to keep values separate from professional duties. He said he knew MacDougall was left of center, but praised him, saying he "met every journalistic standard. He was a professional" (Shaw, 1989a, p. 15).

Minimizing Man and Message. The third repair technique was to minimize MacDougall and his message. This included, as in the Dow Jones letter quoted above, questioning his role in carrying on the paradigm by teaching journalism. In the first apparent media mention of the case and official response, the December 15 *New York Post* carried a blurb quoting *Journal* corporate relations spokesperson Charles Stabler: "He said in the story that he spent his weekends writing about CIA dirty tricks and restrictive immigration laws. If he had been doing that for us, he'd have had a more successful career." He added that "no one cared" that MacDougall was using the *Journal* to spread his ideology, concluding that "he wasn't taken that seriously" ("Radical," 1988).

Others continued this theme. Columnist Donald Morris (1989) quoted an anonymous *Los Angeles Times* editor saying, "If he slipped any messages through, they were so oblique that nobody got it," concluding that there are easier ways to get messages across than being a closet Marxist. Others attempted to marginalize MacDougall and deemphasize his contribution, by referring to him in derogatory terms. *Times* editor William Thomas said the name that came to mind was "Walter Mitty" (Gomes, 1989). Paul Steiger, deputy managing editor of the *Journal,* said MacDougall was "more a secret agent in his own mind" (Shaw, 1989a). *Los Angeles Times* editor Tim Rutten explained, "You know, there's something concocted about this. I catch the odor of rationalization for personal dissatisfaction with his life. . . . I don't find any politics in this man's pieces" (quoted in Cockburn, 1989). Frederick Taylor, *Journal* editor, also took this tack (having also supported the diversity value), saying he's "madder than hell. I think it is gutless of him to confess now. He's like a lot of liberals. They want their cake and to eat it too. Why didn't he say so up front if he believes it so strongly?" ("Recent," 1989, p. 8). Taylor said he would not have fired MacDougall for being a socialist but would have had he known of his extracurricular writing. He said he is especially upset about defending him against conservative attack, and then finding he was a leftist after all ("Recent," 1989, p. 9).

Three columns labeled MacDougall a "Marxist" (Cheshire, 1989; McCarthy, 1989; Morris, 1989), a term not used by MacDougall in describing himself and one with more negative connotations than *socialist*. One of these writers said he "insinuated his flaky politics into news stories" (Cheshire, 1989). One article used a loaded term in saying, inaccurately, that MacDougall claimed to have worked to popularize "Marxist dogma" (Vick, 1989). An article in *Time* termed MacDougall's career "shadowy," and featured a picture of Karl Marx with the caption "his favorite newsman" (Zuckerman, 1989). (MacDougall had said Marx was his favorite journalist in his two-piece *Monthly Review* contribution, the only mention in the twenty-seven pages.)

The Paradigm, Repair, and Hegemony

This case helps us understand how the news paradigm upholds hegemonic boundaries. By crossing the lines of hegemonic acceptability, the MacDougall case required repair. Different people within the media engaged in different kinds of repair work. Certainly, MacDougall's immediate editors had less problem with his work than did the *Journal*'s top editor, Taylor, and its corporate office, which issued the denunciatory letter. These higher levels in the media system are more concerned with protecting the paradigm at the institutional level.

The MacDougall case prompted more attack from the right than from the left, not surprising, perhaps, given his value system. One right-wing attack charged that, in addition to MacDougall, the *Journal* sheltered other "left-wing" reporters, including Jonathan Kwitny, a writer often critical of U.S. foreign policy (Kincaid, 1988). An Accuracy in Media report noted that the MacDougall case "explodes the myth that our media have effective safeguards to screen out propaganda hostile to our country and our system" (quoted in "Comment," 1989, p. 16). On the other hand, MacDougall found support in a *Washington Post* column: Coleman McCarthy (1989) criticized writers and reporters for often being glorified dictationists, supporting MacDougall's advocation that journalists improve their vantage point by stepping outside the system.

MacDougall maintained that radical journalists may be even more objective than "bourgeois" journalists, who are often not conscious of the hidden presuppositions that they bring to their reporting on capitalist institutions (MacDougall, 1988b, p. 22). Radical journalists, by taking the system itself as problematic, may be better equipped to address the structural causes for social ills. The *Columbia Journalism Review* article supported this claim that socialist perspectives can contribute to robust journalism, hearkening back to the muckraking socialist journalists at the turn of the century who called the country's attention to the Beef Trust, child labor, and urban poverty ("Comment," 1989).

SUMMARY

Like ideology, a paradigm is not static but is continually being renegotiated. Like ideology, the news paradigm contains self-contradictory oppositional values, such as diversity in the newsroom versus valueless reporting. These values must be managed and adapted to the ideological requirements of the society. The MacDougall case helps us appreciate that neither paradigms nor ideologies are imposed directly, but are constituted by the institutional, occupational, and cultural practices that make up the mass media. In neither the political economy nor cultural studies view are ideological influences considered conspiratorial. Ideology is not directed behind the scenes by a top television anchor, a publisher, or a board of directors. Rather, ideology happens as a natural outgrowth of the way the system operates, making it a true societal macrolevel phenomenon with which to conclude our hierarchy of influences.

REFERENCES

Altschull, J. (1984). Agents of power. New York: Longman.

Austin, D. (1989). *Dow Jones & Company, Inc. corporate relations statement,* January 6.

Bachrach, P., & Baratz, M. (1962). Two faces of power. *American Political Science Review, 56,* 948.

Becker, Samuel. (1984). Marxist approaches to media studies: The British experience. *Critical Studies in Mass Communication, 1,* 66–80.

Benneth, J. E. (1989, March 7). Letter to the editor. *Wall Street Journal,* p. a21.

Breed, W. (1955). Social control in the newsroom: A functional analysis. *Social Forces, 33*(May), 326–335.

Cheshire, W. P. (1989, February 5). Kent MacDougall: The journalist who came in from the cold (column). *The Arizona Republic,* p. c4.

Cockburn, A. (1989, February 9). Secret life of radical journalist pure milquetoast (column). *Wall Street Journal,* p. a19.

Comment: The case of the closet socialist. (1989, March/April). *Columbia Journalism Review,* pp. 16–17.

Corry, J. (1986). TV news and the dominant culture. *Media & Society Monograph Series.* Washington, DC: Media Institute.

Curran, J., Gurevitch, M., & Woollacott, J. (1982). The study of the media: Theoretical approaches. In M. Gurevitch, T. Bennett, J. Curran, & J. Woollacott (Eds.), *Culture, society and the media* (pp. 11–29). London: Methuen.

Domhoff, G. W. (1967). *Who rules America now?* Englewood Cliffs, NJ: Prentice-Hall.

Domhoff, G. W. (1970). *The higher circles: Governing class in America.* New York: Random House.

Domhoff, G. W. (1979). *The powers that be: Processes of ruling class domination in America.* Englewood Cliffs, NJ: Prentice-Hall.

Dreier, P. (1982a). The position of the press in the U.S. power structure. *Social Problems, 29,* 298–310.

Dreier, P. (1982b). Capitalists vs. the media: An analysis of an ideological mobilization among business leaders. *Media, Culture & Society, 4,* 111–132.

Exoo, Calvin. (1987). Cultural hegemony in the United States. In C. Exoo (Ed.), *Democracy upside down: Public opinion and cultural hegemony in the United States* (pp. 1–33). New York: Praeger.

Gandy, O. (1982). *Beyond agenda-setting: Information subsidies and public policy.* Norwood, NJ: Ablex.

Garnham, N. (1979). Contribution to a political economy of mass communication. *Media, Culture and Society, 1,* 123–146.

Gitlin, T. (1980). *The whole world is watching.* Berkeley: University of California Press.

Glasgow University Media Group. (1976). *Bad news.* London: Routledge & Kegan Paul.

Gomes, L. (1989, March 27). When a radical comes out of the closet (business profile). *The Tribune* (Oakland, CA), p. B-8.

Gouldner, Alvin. (1976). *The dialectic of ideology and technology: The origin of grammar, and future of ideology.* New York: Seabury Press.

Gramsci, A. (1971). *Selections from the prison notebooks of Antonio Gramsci.* Q. Hoare & G. Smith (Eds. & Trans.). New York: International Publishers.

Hackett, R. A. (1984). Decline of a paradigm? Bias and objectivity in news media studies. *Critical Studies in Mass Communication, 1*(3), 229–259.

Hall, Stuart. (1989). Ideology. In E. Barnouw (Ed.), *International encyclopedia of communication* (Vol. 2, pp. 307–311). New York: Oxford University Press.

Hallin, Daniel. (1986). *The uncensored war: The media and Vietnam*. Berkeley: University of California Press.

Herman, Edward, & Chomsky, Noam. (1988). *Manufacturing consent: The political economy of the mass media*. New York: Pantheon.

Hertsgaard, M. (1988). *On bended knee: The press and the Reagan presidency*. New York: Farrar, Straus & Giroux.

Kincaid, C. (1988, December 24). The *Wall Street Journal*'s "closet socialist." *Human Events*, pp. 4–6.

Kincaid, C. (1989, March 4). How many media moles are out there? *Human Events*, pp. 6–7.

Kuhn, T. S. (1962). *The structure of scientific revolutions*. Chicago: University of Chicago Press.

Lukes, S. (1974). *Power: A radical view*. London: Macmillan.

MacDougall, A. K. (1988a). Boring from within the bourgeois press. Part one. *Monthly Review, 40*(7), 13–24.

MacDougall, A. K. (1988b). Boring from within the bourgeois press. Part two. *Monthly Review, 40*(8), 10–24.

MacDougall, A. K. (1989, March/April). Memoirs of a radical in the mainstream press. *Columbia Journalism Review*, pp. 36–41.

Marx, K., & Engels, F. (1970). *The German ideology*. London: Lawrence and Wishart.

McCarthy, C. (1989, February 25). Confessions of a Marxist newsman (column). *The Washington Post*, p. a23.

McQuail, D. (1986). Diversity in political communication: Its sources, forms and future. In P. Golding, G. Murdock, & P. Schlesinger (Eds.), *Communicating politics: Mass communications and the political process* (pp. 133–149). New York: Holmes & Meier.

Meet tomorrow's editors today (1988). *TJFR: The journalist & financial reporting, 2* (13), 1, 6–9.

Miliband, R. (1969). The process of legitimation. In R. Miliband (Ed.), *The state in capitalist society* (pp. 179–264). London: Weidenfeld and Nicolson.

Mills, C. W. (1956). *The power elite*. New York: Oxford University Press.

Molotch, H., & Lester, M. (1974). News as purposive behavior: On the strategic use of routine events, accidents and scandals. *American Sociological Review, 39*,101–112.

Morris, D. R. (1989, March 2). Marxist slanted his stories, but few got the message (column). *Houston Post*, p. a29.

Mosco, V., & Herman, A. (1981). Radical social theory and the communication revolution. In E. McAnany, J. Schnitman, & N. Janus (Eds.), *Communication and social structure* (pp. 58–84). New York: Praeger.

Murdock, G., & Golding, P. (1977). Capitalism, communication and class relations. In J. Curran, M. Gurevitch, & J. Woollacott (Eds.), *Mass communication and society* (pp. 12–43). Beverly Hills, CA: Sage.

Parenti, M. (1978). *Power and the powerless*. New York: St. Martin's.

Parenti, M. (1986). *Inventing reality: The politics of the mass media*. New York: St. Martin's.

Radical doings at Wall St. Journal. (1988, December 15). *New York Post*, p. 6.

Recent revelations of a "closet" socialist stir strong emotions among journalists. (1989, January). *TJFR: The journalist & financial reporting, 3*(2), p. 1, 8–9.

Rose, A. (1967). *The power structure*. New York: Oxford University Press.

Rotbart, D. (1989a, January). A socialist in the capitalist press. *TJFR: The journalist & financial reporting, 3*(1), p. 1, 11–14.

Rotbart, D. (1989b, March). A hidden agenda. *Fame*. p. 16, 18, 20.

Rusher, W. (1988). *The coming battle for the media: Curbing the power of the media elite*. New York: William Morrow.

Schiller, D. (1986). Transformations of news in the U.S. information market. In P. Golding, G. Murdock, & P. Schlesinger (Eds.), *Communicating politics: Mass communications and the political process* (pp. 19–36). New York: Holmes & Meier.

Shaw, D. (1989a, January 31). A "closet socialist" stirs furor over news stories: Ex-reporter tells of radical ideas. *Los Angeles Times*, p. 1, 15–16.

Shaw, D. (1989b, February 3). Leftist reporter's boast raises a ruckus (syndicated reprint of Shaw, 1989a). *San Francisco Chronicle*.

Sheehan, N. (1988). *A bright shining lie: John Paul Vann and America in Vietnam*. New York: Random House.

Shoemaker, P. (1984). Media treatment of deviant political groups. *Journalism Quarterly, 61*, 66–75, 82.

Shoemaker, P., Chang, T. K., & Brendlinger, N. (1987). Deviance as a predictor of newsworthiness: Coverage of international events in the U.S. media. In M. McLaughlin (Ed.), *Communication yearbook, 10* (pp. 348–365). Newbury Park, CA: Sage.

Shoemaker, P., Danielian, L., & Brendlinger, N. (1988). *Deviant acts, risky business and U.S. interests*. Paper presented to the International Communications Association, New Orleans, May.

Smith, H. (1988). *The power game: How Washington works*. New York: Random House.

Stein, M. L. (1989, March 18). Radical defends his revelation. *Editor & Publisher*, p. 10–11.

Vick, K. (1989, March 5). Reporter's hidden agenda gives fuel to media critics. *St. Petersburg Times*.

Wetzel, F. (1989, March 12). Journalism needs divergent point of view (ombudsman column). *Seattle Times*.

Williams, Raymond. (1977). *Marxism and literature*. New York: Oxford University Press.

Zuckerman, L. (1989, February 6). Confessions of a closet leftist: A veteran reporter reveals his 24-year undercover career. *Time*, p. 58.

CHAPTER 10

Linking Influences on Content to the Effects of Content

We began this book with a close look at media content, and we return to it now. Content is the common element to two main bodies of research: the *influences* on mass media content and the *effects of* content on people and society. As we pointed out in Chapter 2, research and theory in mass communication have focused *on* media effects or, even more often, the effects of media *use*. In this chapter, we suggest how linking influences on content with the effects of content can help build theory and improve our understanding of the mass communication process.

DOMAINS OF MASS COMMUNICATION RESEARCH

Figure 10.1 identifies five general groups of variables that have been used in mass communication research, each of which can be dealt with singly (just domain B) or in combination (the B-E link), creating eleven other domains of research.[1] We will discuss these twelve domains in three groups—those that involve content, do not involve content, or suggest new ways to integrate studies of content with studies of effects.

Current Research Involving Content

- *Media Sociology*. Domain A covers the material outlined in this book—media sociology studies that look at how mass media content is shaped by the characteristics of the media, media workers, and the environment in which

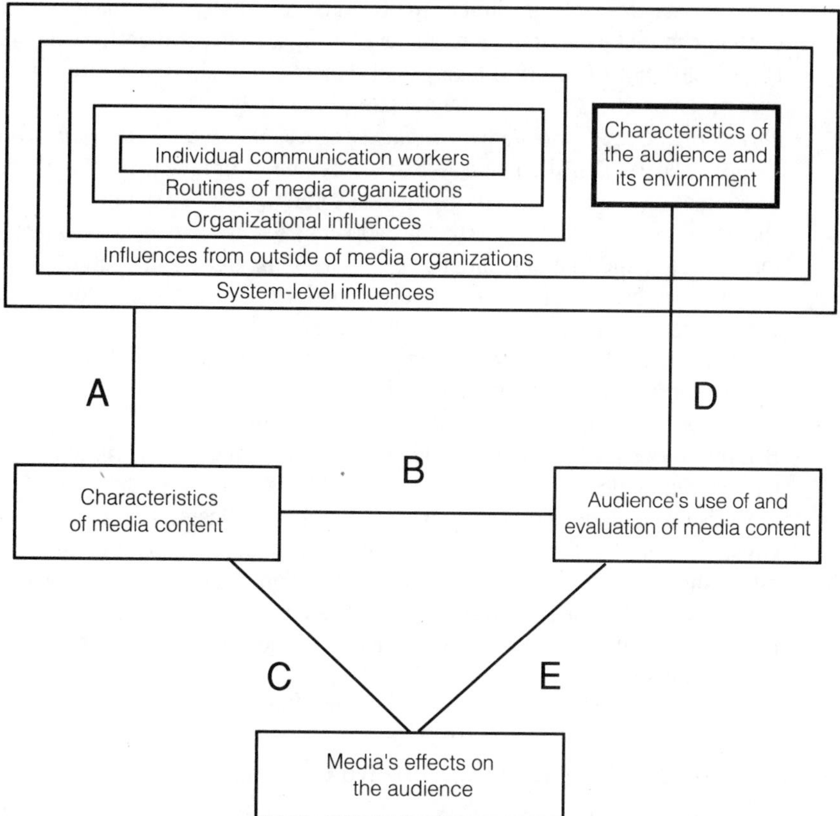

Figure 10.1. Domains of mass communication research

the media exist. These influences on media content are outlined in depth in Chapters 5 through 9 of this book.

- *Marketing Media Content.* Domain B includes studies of how changing the nature of media content can affect the audience's use and evaluation of the content. This is largely a marketing domain, with primarily atheoretical studies of content's effects on newspaper and magazine circulation and discussions of how to improve television program ratings. For example, Smith (1989) studied the extent to which the use of color and graphic design influenced readers' evaluations of a newspaper.
- *Direct Effects of Content.* Domain C involves directly looking for content's effects on the audience without directly examining the audience's use of content. This use may be considered an intervening stage, which the

researchers assume is taking place. Agenda setting (McCombs & Shaw, 1972) is an example of this: The more the media emphasize an issue, the more important people will think the issue is.[2] Domain C also includes experimental research in direct effects, such as whether violent television content can make children more aggressive. In such experiments, media use is generally not *assumed* to take place; rather, it is under the control of the experimenter and is often an integral part of the study.

- *Direct Effects of Content, with Influences on Content as Contingent Conditions*. The combined domain A-C involves studies of how the direct effects of content on the audience (e.g., agenda setting) may be contingent on the characteristics of the media, media workers, and the other environmental forces that shape that content. For example, Palmgreen and Clarke (1977) have shown that the agenda-setting effect on local issues may be more likely with content from newspapers than with local television news, whereas on national issues network television may be more effective than a local newspaper in setting the national agenda.
- *Effects of Content, with Audience Use Intervening*. The combined domain B-E involves studies of how the audience's use of content intervenes between the characteristics of the content and its effects. Although the cultivation analysis research done by George Gerbner and his colleagues (e.g., Gerbner, Gross, Morgan, & Signorielli, 1986) has included content analysis studies to establish the level of violence in television drama, cultivation hypotheses generally involve measures of overall television exposure (for example, how many hours a day do you watch television?) instead of exposure to specific violent content.

Current Research That Does Not Involve Content

The right side of Figure 10.1 (domains D, E, and E-D) describes research areas that are by and large content free—they do not incorporate an important theoretical or empirical role for mass media content.

- *The Active Audience*. Domain D includes those theoretical approaches that look at how and why people use the mass media. This domain represents an enormous body of research, incorporating both the uses and gratifications approach (Rosengren, Wenner, & Palmgreen, 1985) and studies of the diffusion of innovations and messages (Rogers & Shoemaker, 1971). More recent research shows how a family's communication patterns affect parents' and children's media use (Chaffee, McLeod, & Wackman, 1973; Meadowcroft, 1986).
- *Direct Effects of Media Use*. Domain E includes traditional effects studies, such as investigating the role of the media in political socialization of children (Atkin, 1981) or the effects of media reliance on political knowledge

and attitudes (Reese & Miller, 1981; Miller & Reese, 1982). In such studies, media content is generally not addressed; only exposure to the media is measured. This donation is frequently crossed with domain D, as shown below.

- *Direct Effects of Media Use, with Audience Characteristics as Contingent Conditions.* Domain D-E includes media effects studies that commonly control for audience demographic, life-style, and environmental characteristics as alternative explanations for the observed relationship (for example, Clarke & Fredin, 1978). Such studies assume that audience characteristics mitigate the effects of media exposure.

Integrating Content and Effects Studies

The following domains suggest ways in which media content and media effects research can be combined to help our understanding of the role that the mass media play in society.

- *Marketing Media Content, with Media Characteristics as Contingent Conditions.* The combined domain A-B could add to our understanding of the marketability of specific media messages. For example, although a domain B study might tell us that television programs about detectives get better ratings than do westerns, we might be better at predicting ratings if we factor in our understanding of which production company was responsible for creating the shows. Some production companies may do a better job than others of producing westerns (or a worse job of producing detective shows).
- *Effects of Content, with Audience Use Intervening and Media Characteristics as Contingent Conditions.* Domain A-B-E involves studies that look at both (a) how characteristics of the media environment operate as contingent conditions for the relationship between content's characteristics and its effects, *and* (b) how the audience's use of content intervenes in the same relationship. For example, we might add an investigation of the production companies that make violent television shows (see domain A-B above) to cultivation analysis research (see domain B-E above). Perhaps we would find that, although two shows have the same amount of violence according to the Gerbner violence index (Gerbner, Gross, Signorielli, Morgan, & Jackson-Beeck, 1979), the show produced by company #1 had more of an effect on the audience's conceptions of social reality than the show produced by company #2. As a result of a qualitative difference in the type of violence portrayed, one show might make viewers more fearful about being the victim of a crime. Why might the two shows differ? Perhaps because of differences in the values and goals of the producers. By understanding the differences between the production companies, we improve our ability to explain and predict the effects of the content.

- *Effects of Media Use and Media Content, with Media and Audience Characteristics as Contingent Conditions.* Domain A-B-D-E adds to domain A-B-E another set of contingent conditions—characteristics of the audience and its environment. Domain A-B-D-E involves studies that look at (a) how characteristics of the media and their environment operate as contingent conditions for the relationship between content's characteristics and its effects, (b) how characteristics of the audience and its environment operate as contingent conditions for the relationship between the media use and its effects, *and* (c) how the audience's use of content intervenes in the content-effects relationship. For example, we might add to the domain A-B-E example above an investigation of the socioeconomic status of the audience members. Perhaps we would find that, although two shows have the same amount of violence according to the Gerbner violence index (1979), the show produced by company #1 made people more fearful than the show produced by company #2, *and* that the effect is heightened for people of low socioeconomic status.
- *Direct and Inferred Effects of Content, with Influences on Content and Audience Characteristics as Contingent Conditions.* Domain A-B-C-D-E is the fully elaborated model of mass communication research. It adds to domain A-B-D-E the possibility that some content may have an effect on people directly, without media use as an intervening variable. This kind of effect could occur when people talk a lot about what they've seen or heard in the media, thereby causing an effect of the content above and beyond (or instead of) a given individual's media use.

WHY INTEGRATE CONTENT AND EFFECTS STUDIES?

Integrating content and effects studies will facilitate the growth of mass communication theories. Given that most theories used in mass communication studies are derived from other disciplines—psychology, sociology, and political science—the emphasis often is on social and psychological processes, not on the processes through which media content is first formed and then affects people and society. As a result of our reliance on these disciplines, we have in many cases ignored two of the most important elements of the mass communication process—media content and the factors that shape it.

When our media effects studies include only those variables that neatly fit theories developed by other disciplines (and thus ignore media content and media characteristics), we oversimplify the mass communication process and hamper the development of mass communication theories. This may result in conclusions that the media have little effect (as has been the case from time to time), it may minimize the strength of the effects, or it may result in an incomplete understanding of their social significance.

We believe that the development of mass communication theories is stuck on a plateau. We have borrowed theories from other disciplines and created a few of our own (for example, agenda setting, uses and gratifications, cultivation analysis), but we will not see much more theory development specifically dealing with mass communication until we start integrating media content and the factors that shape it into our studies of media effects.

Such an integration will reveal more about the process through which the mass media shape social reality. There is ample evidence to show that media content does not always mirror reality and that different media produce different content. These content differences are a function of a network of influences, ranging from communication workers' personal attitudes and role conceptions, routines of media work, media organizational structure and culture, the relationships between the media and other social institutions, and broad cultural and ideological forces.

The media are not just channels. Information that passes through them is changed in a variety of ways before ultimately offering a specific view of social reality to the audience. We cannot fully understand the effects of that version of social reality if we do not understand the forces that shape it. For example, is the large amount of violence on television the result of hegemonic forces that are striving to control audience members by making them feel afraid and defenseless? Or is it the result of market forces that give the audience what it wants? The effect in either case may be the same—fear—but our response to that fear may differ substantially if we know what created the violent content in the first place.

Another reason for identifying the influence on media content involves our need to develop precise and valid measures of content. The factors that shape media content may result in two messages that appear identical, using our current measures for content, but actually vary in important ways. For example, applying Gerbner's (1979) television violence index to two television shows may result in the same violence score. But does this necessarily mean that the violence in the two shows is identical? Could there be other attributes of these shows that are related to the quantity of violence? Lacking a more sophisticated awareness of content and media environment can prevent us from developing measures that are sensitive enough to detect important differences between content. That is why these domains are so important in understanding the overall mass communication process.

SUMMARY: HOW WE CAN INTEGRATE CONTENT AND EFFECTS STUDIES

First, we need more information in our effects studies about what a person has been exposed *to*. Although mass communication researchers have become adept at identifying, measuring, and statistically controlling for variables that express individual differences between audience members, we have not been as good at doing the same for media content. We must recognize that exposure to a *medium* is not equivalent to exposure to specific *content* within that medium. When Gerbner and his colleagues (1979) ask respondents how many hours a day they watch television, they assume that there is a positive relationship between overall television viewing and the amount of violence seen. Although their content analyses of prime-time television show a stable and substantial amount of violence in most dramatic shows, the amount of violence in prime-time content can vary substantially. In fact, with the multiplicity of channels available to cable customers today, it would be possible for a heavy viewer of television to totally avoid violent content.

Likewise, communication researchers often measure exposure to public affairs content by asking people to report how many days a week they read a newspaper. But a person who says that he or she reads a newspaper every day may be selecting only the comics or sports news and may not be paying any attention at all to public affairs content. When we measure exposure to a medium instead of exposure to specific content, we effectively equate all content within the medium with the kind that is of interest (e.g., that all newspaper stories provide affairs information or that all television shows are equally violent).

The same problem occurs when we assume that media content on one day is equivalent to content on another. Mass communication content occurs in cycles that we can easily identify and control for. For example, the number of pages in a newspaper varies day by day, with midweek issues being larger than those on Saturday. Television news programs also vary day by day. Although the amount of news presented doesn't vary, the amount of news available to be reported does. As Stempel (1989) points out, business and governmental sources account for much of the news, and these sources are least available between noon Friday and noon Monday, cutting the volume of potential news items.

Second, we need to develop content analysis measures that are reliable and valid across many kinds of content.[3] Standardization of content analysis measures lags behind standardization in survey or experimental research. Consequently, content analysis results are often not comparable and the measurement schemes may not be valid in other studies.

Third, along with treating the audience's exposure to the mass media as a variable intervening between content characteristics and media effects, we need to assess the extent to which the audience may be aware (correctly or not) of factors that influence media content. If a newspaper publisher has substantial ties to the business community, readers may interpret everything the newspaper does as being favorable to business. If the newspaper supports a candidate for an election, some may vote against the recommendation precisely because they think the newspaper is influenced by business.

Fourth, we need to assess the relative importance of factors that influence media content and identify those that are crucial contingent conditions for the effects being studied. Not all influences on content will be equally important for the study of media's effects. Media routines or the idiosyncratic behaviors of individual communicators may not be the decisive influence on content in every instance. In many cases influences on media content may best be understood within the context of broad social and institutional forces. These broader forces are thus vital to our understanding of the overall social significance of the effects of media content. By and large, news media workers produce content routinely, according to the professional norms of their employers. When the ideological stakes are high, however, media owners and managers intervene to keep content within appropriate bounds, and they can override normal professionalism and routines. In any case, linking organizational factors to larger power centers in society helps us understand the wider origin of media content. By integrating this "hierarchy of influences," we have shown the variety of perspectives that can be applied to the mass communication process and the relationships between them in hopes of better understanding the media, media content, and society.

NOTES

1. Studies could also be done within each group of variables, such as looking at how ideological or cultural influences affect the nature of social institutions.
2. This is the case with agenda-setting studies at the social system level; studies at the individual level may or may not include exposure as intervening variables. Agenda setting can be studied in four basic ways (McCombs & Gilbert, 1986). The social system level studies, including the original (McCombs & Shaw, 1972), fall within domain C. The individual-level studies would fall within domain E.
3. We are indebted to Dr. Barbara Brown, University of Texas at Austin, for this idea.

REFERENCES

Atkin, C. K. (1981). Communication and political socialization. In D. D. Nimmo & K. R. Sanders (Eds.), *Handbook of political socialization* (pp. 299–328). Beverly Hills, CA: Sage.

Chaffee, S. H., McLeod, J. M., & Wackman, D. B. (1973). Family communication patterns & adolescent political participation. In J. Denniss (Ed.), *Socialization to politics: A reader*. New York: John Wiley.

Clarke, P., & Fredin, E. (1978). Newspapers, television, and political reasoning. *Public Opinion Quarterly, 42,* 143–160.

Gerbner, G., Gross, L., Morgan, M., & Signorielli, N. (1986). Living with television: The dynamics of the cultivation process. In J. Bryant & D. Zillmann (Eds.), *Perspectives on media effects* (pp. 17–40). Hillsdale, NJ: Lawrence Erlbaum.

Gerbner, G., Gross, L, Signorielli, N., Morgan, M., & Jackson-Beeck, M. (1979). The demonstration of power: Violence profile no. 10. *Journal of Communication, 29,* 177–196.

McCombs, M. E., & Gilbert, S. (1986). News influence on our pictures of the world. In J. Bryant & D. Zillmann (Eds.), *Perspectives on media effects* (pp. 1–15). Hillsdale, NJ: Lawrence Erlbaum.

McCombs, M. E., & Shaw, D. L. (1972). The agenda-setting function of mass media. *Public Opinion Quarterly, 36,* 176–187.

Meadowcroft, J. M. (1986). Family communication patterns and political development: The child's role. *Communication Research, 13,* 603–624.

Miller, M., & Reese, S. D. (1982). Media dependency as interaction: The effects of exposure and reliance on political efficacy and activity. *Communication Research, 9,* 227–248.

Palmgreen, P., & Clarke, P. (1977). Agenda-setting with local and national issues. *Communication Research, 4,* 435–452.

Reese, S. D., & Miller, M. (1981). Political attitude holding and structure: The effects of newspaper and television news. *Communication Research, 8,* 167–187.

Rogers, E., & Shoemaker, F. (1971). *Communication of innovations.* New York: Free Press.

Rosengren, K. E., Wenner, L. A., & Palmgreen, P. (Eds.). (1985). *Media gratifications research: Current perspectives.* Beverly Hills, CA: Sage.

Smith, R. F. (1989). How design and color affect reader judgment of newspapers. *Newspaper Research Journal, 10,* 75–85.

Stempel, G. H., III. (1989). Content analysis. In G. H. Stempel, III, & B. H. Westley (Eds.), *Research methods in mass communication* (pp. 124–136). Englewood Cliffs, NJ: Prentice-Hall.

CHAPTER 11

Building a Theory of News Content

A first step toward understanding the many and complex factors that influence media content is identifying those factors. A second step is reviewing studies that examine these factors and that may test related hypotheses. Our book has tried to accomplish these two goals.

But a third step is also needed—synthesizing what is known about influences on media content into a more systematic set of interrelated statements about the relationships between media content and the influences on it—a *theory*. In this final chapter, we will sift through the many studies presented earlier and establish a series of representative hypotheses and assumptions to guide future research in this area. By this process, we hope to improve our ability to describe media content, explain why it takes on the characteristics it does, and predict the direction that media content will take in the future. An *assumption* is something taken for granted. A *hypothesis* is a statement about the relationship between two or more concepts or ideas. We will also provide *propositions*—statements that describe the current state of media content.

Although the majority of the hypotheses are derived from empirical research, we also provide some that have been inferred from our knowledge of the topic. The following list of assumptions, propositions, and hypotheses is not intended to be comprehensive, but it is a beginning for our ongoing search for understanding media content.

ASSUMPTIONS

- *Mass media content is a socially created product, not a reflection of an objective reality.* Although the stimulus for a story might be a real-world event or problem, measurable through other sources of social information, there are many factors that determine what will be transmitted and how it will be treated.
- *Understanding the nature of media content is crucial in understanding the nature and importance of content's effects on people and society.* Knowing what media content is like helps us predict its effects on the audience. When we avoid content-specific measures in our effects studies, we run the risk of ignoring important causal connections between exposure to content and its effects.
- *From media content we can infer many of the factors that shaped it.* For example, the language used may tell us something about the writer's attitudes, and the editor's selection of stories tells us something about his or her priorities.
- *The general forces operating to shape news content also shape entertainment content.* Both types of content are influenced by individual media workers, media routines, media organizations, extramedia factors, and ideology.
- *Influences on media content can be ranked hierarchically, from the ideological and other macrosystem-level factors to the more micro characteristics of individual media workers.* Each level has its own range of influence but is subjected to and has limits set by each hierarchically superior level. What explains the role conceptions of journalists? Their socialization to the routines of the workplace. Why do such routines exist? In order to meet organizational standards and goals. What is the source of these standards and goals? Pressures from advertisers and audiences, sources, the market economy, and so on. Why do these extramedia factors relate to the media in the way they do? Because of ideological and cultural imperatives on the role that the mass media should play in society.
- *Not everything "eligible" to be mass media content actually gets into the media.* The process called gatekeeping involves selection of items from the universe of possible ones. Not every film idea becomes a film; not every event is covered in the news.
- *Media routines developed as a way of making the media worker's job more efficient.* The media operate under certain expectations about the nature of content from the audience and work under constraints imposed by sources.
- *The ultimate power in a media organization comes from the owner.* Although lower-level employees exert influences over media content, the owners set the direction and the ultimate policies.

- *All mass media are controlled in one way or another.* Control is exerted through media financing. Where the media are government owned, this control is direct. Where the media are primarily privately owned, control is exerted through laws, regulations, licenses, taxes, and other more indirect forms of ideological direction.

PROPOSITIONS ABOUT THE NATURE OF MEDIA CONTENT

- *Television content (both news and entertainment) contains a high level of violence that is consistent over time.* Although year-to-year and program-to-program fluctuations do occur, the overall picture is one of substantial violence. When crimes are depicted, they are more likely to be violent than nonviolent.
- *In media content, women and the aged appear less often than men and younger adults, and they are presented differently.* About two-thirds of television characters are males, and when women are presented with men, the women are generally shown as younger and in inferior roles. Women are more likely to be victims than perpetrators of violence, and they are more likely to be portrayed as mentally ill. The aged are treated stereotypically, so that age is their primary attribute.
- *Most news is about people who are already prominent.* For a nonprominent person to be covered often requires that he or she do something deviant (such as demonstrating or breaking a law).
- *Most news comes from "official" (primarily government) channels, but journalists will use other sources when they are available.* Government and business sources are most accessible to journalists, often preparing events or information specifically for journalists. Individual sources or representatives of small groups are less accessible to journalists and may not be as skilled in getting their messages out.
- *In the United States, news coverage of a state is not related to its population.* States along the Pacific and Atlantic coasts are overcovered, relative to their population, whereas Midwestern states are undercovered.
- *Among television characters, there are more people with high-status than low-status jobs.*
- *Minority characters and newscasters are generally underrepresented and portrayed stereotypically.* In the United States, white characters are shown as being more powerful. The more a minority newsmaker has acculturated to white society and the higher his or her socioeconomic level is, the more prominently he or she will be covered.
- *In general, portrayals in media reflect the power relations of the general society.*

HYPOTHESES ABOUT INFLUENCES ON MEDIA CONTENT

Individual Media Workers

- *Media workers who have a "communication" college degree produce content with different characteristics than do those with other majors.* Some media employers believe that journalism majors are preferable; others want liberal arts (especially American Studies) degrees. Such preferences are based on assumptions about the kind of educational experience that makes the best journalist.
- *People who are similar to a journalist will be covered differently from people who are dissimilar.* The demographic characteristics of the communicator may affect the content he or she produces, especially when communicating about others within the demographic group. Women write about women differently than men do. Hispanics cover the Hispanic community differently than Anglos do.
- *Media workers' personal attitudes affect the content they produce, contingent on their having the power sufficient to influence the production of content and on the lack of a strong routine covering the task.* Journalists have substantial leeway in the selection of words and visuals to include in a story, and therefore their personal attitudes may translate into selections that undermine the political legitimacy of the covered person or event. Sports announcers may select words or phrases based on their racial prejudices. Filmmakers' personal attitudes and values may influence their choice of projects and the ways in which the projects are accomplished. Publishers and media owners may make decisions against the interests of their organization or class if they have strongly held personal views.
- *Journalists' role conceptions affect content.* Whether they see their roles as interpreting what others do, disseminating information, or serving as an adversary of the powerful, these roles may determine how they define their jobs, the kinds of things they believe should be covered, and the ways in which they cover them.
- *The more unethical media workers think an action is, the less likely they are to take part in it.* Because there is no required ethical code for communicators, however, they do not always agree about what is ethical.

Links between Influences from Individuals and Those from Routines

- *The longer people work for a media organization, the more socialized they are to the policies—stated and unstated—of the organization.* Media workers learn what their organizations want by observing others, by receiving feedback from their superiors, and by observing what makes it into the finished communication product.

- *Media workers are less likely to insert their own value judgments or opinions into straight news accounts than in other types of content (such as features or entertainment).* The journalistic routine of objectivity overrules an individual's tendency to communicate his or her opinion.
- *The more media workers follow the routines of their organizations, the more likely their content is to be used.* The routines by which the mass media collect, shape, and disseminate information affect media content. For example, gatekeeping involves the selection, shaping, and repetition of information. Deadlines may prevent the communication of "truth." The inverted pyramid arrays the information in a story according to how important the journalist thinks it is. The routine of objectivity provides journalists with a set of standard procedures for covering people and events. If the routines were different, media content would be different.
- *The more media workers learn the routines associated with their jobs, the more professional they are rated by coworkers.* The communicator's job requires the handling and manipulation of a lot of information. Those who follow established procedures for dealing with the information will be positively reinforced. Communicators learn these procedures through a process of socialization to their jobs.
- *On stories or subjects without established routines, in early stages of an issue, for example, individual factors will be relatively more influential, compared with routines.* Routines provide a way for handling a story that transcends the individual media worker and that therefore also supersedes an individual's influence.

Routines of Media Work

- *Events that are congruent with media routines are more likely to be covered than discongruent events.* News that is off the beaten path (e.g., not on the journalists' beat) may go unreported. Issues and events that don't include good film/video footage may not be included in television newscasts. A press conference held just before a newspaper's deadline is more likely to be included than one just after. Events that fit an organization's definition of news are most likely to be covered.
- *Events are more likely to be covered than issues.* Journalists can more easily defend covering events than issues, which by definition are more ambiguous. Covering events is so common in journalism that covering events has itself become a routine.
- *The closer an event is to the media organization's routine definition of newsworthiness, the more likely it is to be covered.* News organizations value consistency in their coverage over time.

- *The more journalists cover an event, the more similar their coverage will be.* "Pack journalism" results in sharing of ideas and confirmation of news judgments and the observation of other journalists. Editors tend to question coverage that is different from that of other news organizations.
- *The more that journalists read (or view) each others' stories, the more similar is their subsequent coverage of an event or issue.* Journalists often read or view each others' stories, at least partially looking for confirmation that their own decisions have been correct.
- *The more powerful or successful people or groups are, the more negative news coverage of them will be.* Coverage of political candidates is more negative toward front-runners and incumbents than toward the underdog. Looking for flaws in potential winners and in the powerful has become a routine part of investigative journalism. Journalists may feel they they can be magnanimous toward losers.

Link between Routines and Organizational Influences

- *The larger and more complex a media organization is, the less influence professional routines will have on content and the more influence larger organizational forces will have.* The more layers of bureaucracy exist between reporters and top management of media organizations, the less sensitive the top managers will be to the professional concerns of these lower-level workers. As bureaucracy increases, the problems of the reporter become more abstract to top management. Instead of making most decisions based on professional considerations, top management will base decisions on economic concerns. Top management will not normally intervene against professional routines unless they threaten the larger organization's goals. As the organization's resources become more limited, routines will be followed that enable the organization to best gather content from sources and distribute it to audiences as efficiently as possible.

Organizational Influences

- *The more elite a medium is, the less similar its workers will be to the general population.* Research shows, for example, that journalists at elite news organizations are more liberal than journalists are on the average. Elite organizations tend to hire people from more elite backgrounds.
- *The extent to which the organization's need to make a profit affects media content is contingent on the overall economic health of the organization.* Media organizations that are making a satisfactory profit are more likely to permit professional influences to win over economic ones. If, however, the organization is economically at risk, the need to make a profit may win out over professional considerations.

- *Television and radio are more sensitive to the need to make a profit than are newspapers and magazines.* Virtually all television and radio income derives from advertisers, and these media compete head to head against similar products in the same market. Virtually every programming decision has economic ramifications.
- *Upper-level media management personnel whose background is on the business side of the organization are more likely to make decisions based on economics rather than on professional considerations.* Their backgrounds have sensitized them to economic concerns as primary.
- *Middle-level media management personnel are more closely attuned to the organization's goals than are lower-level personnel, who are more attuned toward their sources.* Editors may be more sensitive to the business side of the organization, thus bringing reporters and editors into constant conflict over the direction that content should take.
- *When editorial routines conflict with the organization's need to make a profit, if the editor controls both the business and editorial sides of a newspaper, the editorial side will be given a lower priority than the business side.* The business concerns may seem more concrete and immediate to editors, thus taking precedence over editorial concerns.
- *The higher an individual is in a media organization, the more likely he or she is to have connections with nonmedia organizations.* While reporters are cautioned against getting involved in community organizations, publishers often serve as board members of businesses and may serve as officers in local civic groups.
- *The personal attitudes and values of news media owners may be reflected not only in editorials and columns, but also in news and features.* Not only can owners hire and fire editors, columnists, and reporters according to their stated political beliefs, but they can also cause subtle "slants" in coverage as the employees try to anticipate what the owner wants.
- *The further the owner of a news organization lives from the organization, the less local news, editorials, and features the organization transmits.* Absentee ownership is common among companies that own more than one media organization, and absentee owners may be less likely to adopt aggressive coverage in the local community and more likely to follow policies that will aid the overall corporation.
- *Media workers from organizations owned by chains form weaker attachments to the local community than do workers for independent organizations.* The employees' loyalty may be more toward the corporation than toward the local community. Chain employees may move from organization to organization and never develop strong ties to any one community.
- *Chain organizations are more likely to endorse presidential candidates than independent organizations, and the endorsement is generally homogeneous throughout the chain.* This may be the result of a convergence toward similar views among editorial writers in the chain, rather than overt collusion to stress one political party or issue. Promotions and salary increases go to

employees who perform their jobs well, and the higher workers are in the organization, the more likely their promotions and raises are to be affected by administrators of the chain.

Links between Organizational and Extramedia Influences

- *The more sources know about and adapt to the media organization's routines, the more likely they are to get favorable coverage.* For example, sources that can deliver news releases in the form generally used and at the time preferred by the media are most likely to get coverage.
- *The more advertising a newspaper or magazine has, the more pages it will devote to editorial (i.e., nonadvertising) content.* Print media generally work on the assumption that a certain percentage of their overall pages will be advertising content and that the remainder will be editorial. If advertising pages increase, there is more room available to run stories.
- *The more connections there are between extramedia organizations and media organizations, the more influence extramedia firms will have.* Pressure can be put on media organizations through connections made at upper-level management between media and nonmedia companies.

Extramedia Influences

- *The more economic or political power a source has, the more likely he or she is to influence news reports.* Such sources generally have accessible staff members who keep regular office hours assigned specifically to get information out to the media in a quick and concise manner.
- *Although "official" sources (e.g., government officials or police) dominate nearly all news content, the percentage of official sources will be higher in stories about issues than in those about events.* Issues are more likely than events to involve the vested interests of official sources, who will seek out journalists to get their points across.
- *The more critical of media coverage an interest group is, the more likely the media are to self-censor.* Criticisms from interest groups do have an influence on media content, both through their own publicity-generated efforts and because interest groups often target advertisers for boycotts. The media may make a specific change asked for by the interest group, but they may try to anticipate the groups' complaints and influence content accordingly.
- *The slower the news day, the more likely media content is to be generated by public relations practitioners.* When no big issue or event dominates a day's news coverage, journalists are still obliged to put out a preset amount of news content. Public relations practitioners and interest groups provide media events and new information for the media to cover.

- *The more coverage the opinion-leading media give an issue or event, the more likely other media are to give subsequent coverage to the issue or event.* Journalists read each others' stories and watch each others' newscasts. Elite media organizations, such as the *New York Times,* serve as agenda setters for other media.
- *The more a media organization promotes itself within a target audience, the more its content will reflect the interests of that audience.* Some newspapers have abandoned the mass audience for deep penetration in audiences most attractive to advertisers, with content that appeals most to the preferred audience members. Television programming is often dependent upon ratings, which show not only how many people are watching, but also their characteristics. Programming with an unattractive (to advertisers) audience may be abandoned for content that attracts the preferred sort of audience.
- *Advertisers influence media content.* The more advertisers support one kind of media content, the more of that type of content the media will offer. In addition, some advertisers work directly to delete or shape the nature of media content by specifically withdrawing advertising support from objectionable content or by letting it be known that they do not want to support media that run certain types of articles. Advertisers have also created media content specifically to showcase their products.
- *The more the mass media criticize a country's government, the more the government will try to control the media.* Controls can take place through media financing, laws, regulations, court cases, licenses, taxes, manipulation of the release and availability of information, and direct communication of a government official to a (generally high-level) manager of a media organization.
- *The more sources and interest groups criticize the mass media, the more the government will try to control the media.*
- *The characteristics of the community within which a medium operates may influence its content.* The larger the market, the more the media will cover spontaneous news events and local news. The presence of a competing newspaper, however, apparently does not increase diversity in newspaper content.
- *The wider the geographic area a medium covers, the more standardized its content will be.* Messages must be broadened to appeal to people with varying interests and tastes. Such content will take few chances and make few innovations.

Ideology

- *The more deviant people or events are, the more likely they are to be included in media content and the more likely they are to be stereotyped.* The media help maintain the boundaries of social order by showing what is approved and not approved. Deviant people and events may be trivialized or shown as dangerous. This is apparently true of the U.S. media, regardless of whether they are covering people or events in the United States or in another country.

- *The more political, economic, or cultural significance one country has for another, the more the former will appear in the latter's mass media.* Such social system–level attachments between countries affect priorities in media coverage. Although the same news values may apply for domestic and foreign news coverage, measures of political, economic, and cultural significance affect what is considered important, one of the main criteria for establishing newsworthiness.
- *Journalists will not use objective routines, such as balance, when subjects are outside the area of legitimate controversy and in the areas of consensus or deviance.*
- *Elites will respond to media as a class when core ideological principles are threatened.* Actions of business, for example, will be more unified and coordinated, transcending the actions of any given company or industry, as more capitalist values come under attack.
- *The more closely media are connected to other elites, the more media content will be consistent with those elite ideological viewpoints.* Examples of elite connections include board interlocks and club memberships.
- *Violations of occupational paradigms—anomalies—must be repaired in order to preserve the paradigm.* This repair is most evident when the violation crosses important ideological boundaries.
- *On a given issue, television coverage will be more ideologically charged than the print media.*

Future Research

Although many more such hypotheses could be derived, these examples should give readers an idea of the many studies that are waiting to be mined from this rich vein of theory. In particular, many more connections could be made between these various levels, and development of interlevel links is an important topic for future research.

The hierarchy of influences model is useful for research in two important respects. First, by approaching media studies from several levels, we can better appreciate the different perspectives that are possible. Any single perspective does not present a complete picture, and any given study cannot address all of these levels at once. But an awareness of these multiple perspectives helps keep our thinking open. Many studies make observations at one level of analysis and interpret those findings at a higher level. For example, many scholars have examined individual journalists and then drawn conclusions about media organizations as a whole. Individual bias, however, does not translate automatically into media bias. Similarly, ideological analyses may yield elegant theories of media and society, but individuals still have latitude in their behavior. Their actions, although constrained, are not automatically determined by higher-level social forces.

Second, combining these multiple levels of analysis draws our attention to the connections between them. Indeed, this may be one of the most fruitful areas of future research. Occupational routines are related to larger ideological requirements. Personal values of journalists cannot be separated from their routines. Organizational structure is related to media routines, and so on. Ideological forces must work through people and practices, and finding out how that happens is important.

Until recently, in mainstream U.S. media research, the greatest theoretical and methodological precision has been found in the studies of mass communication processes and effects. We hope that the same kind of precision and systematic study can be directed at media content and the influences on it. Organizing theory and research is an important start. In addition, we hope that even studies at the lower levels of analysis will be informed by the theories of power and society developed at the higher levels. And that ideological-level studies will be conditioned by an understanding of individuals and their practices. By combining our insights and observations in this way, a more complete understanding of the mass media's role in society will be possible.

Index